The German Criminal Code
A Modern English Translation

Translated by Michael Bohlander

·HART·
PUBLISHING

OXFORD AND PORTLAND, OREGON
2008

Published in North America (US and Canada) by
Hart Publishing
c/o International Specialized Book Services
920 NE 58th Avenue, Suite 300
Portland, OR 97213-3786
USA
Tel: +1 503 287 3093 or toll-free: (1) 800 944 6190
Fax: +1 503 280 8832
E-mail: orders@isbs.com
Website: http://www.isbs.com

Hart Publishing, 16C Worcester Place, OX1 2JW
Telephone: +44 (0)1865 517530 Fax: +44 (0)1865 510710
E-mail: mail@hartpub.co.uk
Website: http://www.hartpub.co.uk

British Library Cataloguing in Publication Data
Data Available

ISBN: 978-1-84113-831-2

Typeset by Hope Services, Abingdon
Printed and bound in Great Britain by
TJ International Ltd, Padstow, Cornwall

For Christine and Laura

PREFACE

German substantive criminal law has enjoyed wide popularity in many countries of the so-called civil law tradition, most notably in the Hispanic world. In the common law countries, not surprisingly because of the systemic differences in approach, its impact has been much less, if not negligible. Much of that will also have to do with the language barrier and the complexity of German legal terminology and drafting style which may pose formidable problems even to linguistically gifted non-native speakers—as indeed they do to German lawyers. An up-to-date reliable English translation of the Criminal Code has been conspicuously missing for some time.

I thought it worthwhile to present an English translation of the *Strafgesetzbuch*, the Criminal Code, in its most recent amended form of December 2007. The Criminal Code is the centrepiece of German substantive criminal law and informs the interpretation and application of any other criminal provisions which can be found in special legislation. I have decided not to include the Criminal Code (Introduction) Act (*Einführungsgesetz zum Strafgesetzbuch*) because it contains many transitional provisions and such as are related to the interplay of Federal and member state law, etc, that are not necessary to gain an understanding of the principles. The same applies to the criminal provisions contained in other pieces of special legislation.

German law has a long-standing tradition of codification in the major fields of law and can thus inform the debate of any country looking at harmonising and consolidating its own law. Obviously, many facets of the German Code in their pure form will be unusable in other legal systems. However, the underlying principles are often very similar, if not identical, and where they differ markedly the differences in themselves can tell the reader something about his or her own system and maybe open new avenues for research as to alternatives. This should not be understood as a declaration of superiority of the German approach. It is merely an offer to profit from a tradition that belongs to those which had a major influence over history and has a rich experience of doctrinal analysis.

The translation tries to adhere as closely as possible to the textual structure of the original, but I have taken the liberty of departing from it if it was necessary to achieve better understanding and to produce a version that is still palatable to an English ear. I have striven to apply the terminology of the law of England and Wales to the closest approximation. Inevitably, German colleagues will find that I have deviated too much from the original in some places while anglophone colleagues will complain that it still does not sound much like the Queen's English. To both I offer my apologies and hope they will give me the benefit of their advice as to how to improve.

This translation is meant as a companion volume to my book, *Principles of German Criminal Law*, which will appear from Hart Publishing in 2008. Some questions which the mere reading of the Code will raise will, I hope, be answered there. The short introduction in this volume should at least give the reader some background to understand the structure and terminology better.

I have been aided in my work mainly by four factors. Since exchanging a 13-year career on the German bench for an academic career in Durham in 2004, I have had the opportunity to teach English and Welsh criminal law to undergraduate students at Durham University, which allowed (and forced) me to gain a much deeper insight into the principles than I had previously had. I take this opportunity to thank my distinguished colleague and dear friend, Professor Kaiyan Homi Kaikobad, and his wife Dhun for playing a great part in making that career change a professionally and personally rewarding experience.

Secondly, I was fortunate enough to obtain a fellowship at the International Institute of the Sociology of Law (IISJ) at Oñati in the Basque Country during my research leave in October 2007, which gave me the time and peace of mind to concentrate on the translation, apart from research on another project. I thank my friend and colleague Professor Joxerramon Bengoetxea, the IISJ's previous academic director, and the current academic director, Professor Carlos Lista, for their generous support and hospitality. An occasional and good-humoured victim of my linguistic musings was Professor Michael King of Reading University, who spent two weeks in Oñati in an office next to mine and offered very useful advice.

Thirdly, I am very grateful to the German Federal Ministry of Justice, especially to Regierungsdirektorin Renate Huttner-Thompson of the Ministry's Language Service, for providing me with an unofficial translation of the Criminal Code as it stood in September 2006. Although it needed some updating and I chose to depart from its diction to quite a large extent, it proved to be an invaluable starting point which made the task a lot easier.

Finally, and most importantly, I am deeply indebted to my colleague from Sunderland University, Christopher J Newman, senior lecturer in law, who very kindly read the entire manuscript and gave generously of his time to make sure the whole thing makes sense to an English speaker. If it does not always do so, it is through no fault of his.

As always, working on such a project meant taking (too much) time away from my family. My wife Christine and my daughter Laura have, as always, been very understanding and patient and let me go off to Spain for a month believing my protestations that I would not merely be basking in the splendid Basque autumn sun most of the time.

Michael Bohlander
Durham and Cedar Falls, Iowa, March 2008

CONTENTS

A Brief Introduction

I IDEOLOGICAL APPROACH

German criminal law is heavily doctrine-driven, much more so than is the case under the approach taken by English criminal law or, for that matter, the criminal law of many common law systems. Whilst it is true that parliamentary law-making has gained a lot of ground, especially in recent decades, the latter have traditionally relied on a judge-based development on a case-by-case basis. Because their law had to be tailored for use by lay people as fact-finders in the criminal process, be they jurors or lay magistrates, a high emphasis was put on remaining as close as possible to what judges like to call 'common sense'. The well-known English case[1] on the effects of voluntary intoxication on the mens rea of the accused, *DPP v Majewski*, is a good example of this attitude:

> A number of distinguished academic writers support this contention on the ground of logic. As I understand it, the argument runs like this. Intention, whether special or basic (or whatever fancy name you choose to give it), is still intention. If voluntary intoxication by drink or drugs can, as it admittedly can, negative the special or specific intention necessary for the commission of crimes such as murder and theft, how can you justify in strict logic the view that it cannot negative a basic intention, e g the intention to commit offences such as assault and unlawful wounding? *The answer is that in strict logic this view cannot be justified. But this is the view that has been adopted by the common law of England, which is founded on common sense and experience rather than strict logic.* There is no case in the 19th century when the courts were relaxing the harshness of the law in relation to the effect of drunkenness on criminal liability in which the courts ever went so far as to suggest that drunkenness, short of drunkenness producing insanity, could ever exculpate a man from any offence other than one which required some special or specific intent to be proved. [Emphasis added.]

Nothing could in principle be further from the truth under German law. German law has widely subscribed to the use of historical and teleological interpretation, which includes the application of public policy arguments like the one used by the court in the *Majewski* case, but such a bare-faced rejection of the appeal of logic would be an alien thought to any German judge, let alone academic. Despite the fact that the development of German criminal law, too, has increasingly come under the influence of judicial reasoning about legal principles, especially if it happens at the levels of the Bundesgerichtshof (BGH) or Bundesverfassungsgericht (BVerfG) or, as far as a lot of the procedural law is concerned, the European Court

---

[1] *DPP v Majewski* [1977] AC 443, repeated in *R v Powell and another; R v English* [1999] AC 1.

1

of Human Rights (ECtHR), there is still a discernible impact of and reliance on academic writing, mainly based on the German legal commentary culture. German academics and practitioners have over the centuries produced large and intricate commentaries on the different codified laws, and handbooks on practice and procedure. Only the latter can be equated with common law publications such as *Archbold* or *Stone's Justice Manual*. Big multi-volume commentaries on specific codes, such as, for example, the *Leipziger Kommentar zum Strafgesetzbuch*, or the *Löwe-Rosenberg* on the Criminal Procedure Code, as much as one-volume works such as the *Schönke/Schröder* or *Tröndle/Fischer* on the Criminal Code, as well as the *Meyer-Goßner* or the *Karlsruher Kommentar* on the *Strafprozeßordnung*, written by respected academics, seasoned judges and practitioners through many editions, do not just digest the development of literature and jurisprudence, but they also analyse them and criticise the arguments put forward by the writers and judges and, if they happen to disagree with them, set out their own view of how things should be done, something hardly ever found, for example, in *Archbold*. It is no rarity to find a court change its long-standing jurisprudence on a certain topic because the logic behind the arguments of renowned academic writers, often made in such commentaries, convinces the judges that their previous views were wrong.

The fact that German law is to a large extent based on the more or less strict application of logic and well-developed methods of interpretation is also a function of the German academics' attitude to the judicial process: they do not see academia as the mere handmaiden of the judges, but as their guiding light. To their minds, judicial practice should follow abstract reasoning rather than adhere to a casuistic approach that favours justice in the individual case over systemic coherence to the major and overarching legal principles across the board.[2] The German approach, to use a simplistic description, is thus deductive in nature, as opposed to the more inductive one of the common law, and it runs counter to the inclination of laymen who have been said to be 'likely to prefer warm confusion to cool consistency'.[3] I hasten to add that in some areas of German law, notably labour and employment law, large sections are almost wholly judge-made because the Government has for some reason or other not taken up the burden of providing for proper codification. Very often, Parliament will in its acts codify a long-standing and proven judicial tradition and to that extent there is, of course, a judicial influence on codified law-making, too.

The function and view of the trial and its effect on legal reasoning in the sphere of substantive law are markedly different. This begins with the nature and structure of the German criminal process, on which a few words must be said. German criminal proceedings are by their nature not a contest between parties, but an objective, judge-led inquiry into the material truth of the facts underlying a criminal charge. Equality of arms is not a principle that would apply to a similar

---

[2] This is another typical area of divergence between common and civil law systems, as has been shown by Mirjan Damaska in his seminal work *The Faces of Justice and State Authority: A Comparative Approach to the Legal Process* (Yale University Press, New Haven and London, 1986).
[3] Damaska, *ibid*, 28.

extent as it does in adversarial systems. From the German point of view, the prosecution, on the one hand, has no individual rights of fair trial; it has powers and duties, with the consequence that the prosecution cannot argue a violation of the right to equality of arms because the system is not adversarial, but the court *itself* is under a duty to find the truth. The defence on the other hand has no duties, only rights, yet it may suffer if it does not exercise them properly, as is the case under the well-known common law 'save-it-or-waive-it' principle relating to grounds of appeal, which appears to find more and more favour with German courts, too, especially in connection with § 238 (2) StPO. The defence is seen as being by definition inferior in power and facilities to the prosecution, so from a German point of view equality of arms is a principle that protects the defence, but not the prosecution. Any idea of changing the law, for example by introducing probative burdens of proof on the defence or reading down the requirements the prosecution has to prove in order to make it easier for the prosecution to bring its case, would have no equivalent in German doctrine, and indeed would be seen as constitutionally questionable. Difficulties of the prosecution to prove its case cannot lead to an abridgment of the defence's position by interpreting down the threshold of certain offence requirements.

II SOURCES OF CRIMINAL LAW AND HIERARCHY OF NORMS

German law follows, in principle, the strict application of the maxim *nullum crimen, nulla poena sine lege*. As far as the criminal liability of a person is concerned, the maxim is augmented by the adjective *scripta*, ie, the law must be a written law, and Article 103(2) of the *Grundgesetz* (Basic Law—hereinafter GG) makes it clear that criminal liability must be based on a full act of Parliament; mere secondary governmental instruments and regulations will not normally suffice, unless the act of Parliament refers to those in order to demarcate the conduct which it criminalises. Such laws are called *Blankettgesetze*, or 'blanket acts', because they themselves do not contain (all) the elements of the offence but refer to other legislation for that purpose.

Yet recent German history after the Second World War and the 1990 Unification Treaty appears to have accepted one category of law that would stand outside the requirements of Article 103(2) GG: the demands of natural justice or natural law. After the abject failure of the post-war German judiciary to address the gross abuse of the formal legal process from 1933 to 1945, this issue arose again when the courts of the unified Germany after 1990 had to deal with the murders committed by GDR border guards, and with the orders given by their superiors in the military and political chain of command. This time, everyone was bent on not repeating the mistakes made after the Third Reich. The thinking behind this approach is based on the so-called 'Radbruch formula', after the German philosopher Gustav Radbruch (1878–1949), who analysed the relationship between positive law and natural law using the example of the Nazi regime's legislation.

The formula states that formally valid positive normal law prevails over substantive concepts of justice, even if it is unjust and irrational. This primacy ends when there are breaches of principles of justice, of intolerable proportions, which are in turn defined as instances where the positive law explicitly and systematically neglects its goal of pursuing the aims of justice, and when the principle of equality is ignored on purpose. In short, the German courts held that former East German soldiers and judges were bound to interpret the socialist law in the light of the liberal spirit of fundamental concepts of human rights over the commands of the written law.

The courts in these cases used considerations of natural justice to establish the liability of the defendants by debunking positivistic rules of justification based on GDR law, whereas the much more common application of these ideas occurs in arguments which are to the benefit of the accused. This approach to the primacy of natural justice over positive law had been taken in the last century with the famous decision by the Reichsgericht in the 'Abortion Case', when the Supreme Court of the German Reich accepted in 1927 that a pregnancy could be terminated if otherwise there would be a grave danger to the mother's health or life. At the time, German law had no provision to this effect, and the Reichsgericht 'invented' the so-called '*übergesetzlicher Notstand*' (supra-legal state of necessity) from the commands of natural justice. The decision was the basis on which § 34 StGB on necessity was finally modelled. For the offence of abortion, it can also be found explicitly in § 218a(2) StGB.

Natural justice, from the German point of view, should be seen as a kind of safety-valve in a legal system tending towards a positivistic approach, as far as the usual primacy of the written law is concerned. One might compare it to the function that the principles of equity jurisprudence have had as a corrective to the stricter rules of the common law in English legal history. It is difficult to place natural justice firmly into a hierarchy of laws, as it applies in different shapes and forms at any level of the German legal system. It permeates the law as a guiding principle of interpretation. It would not be unfair to say, however, that the principle of natural justice has the force of influencing the application even of the highest-ranking legal rules at the constitutional level. Looking at it that way, one can make the statement that it represents the top tier in the hierarchy of laws.

The more tangible sources of criminal law begin with the next rung down on the ladder, the constitution and international law. These two we must mention together because at least in some cases there is an overlap or exchange of hierarchical position between them. The ground rule is that the constitution is the supreme law of the land. International law must be ratified and implemented by a domestic act of legislation and normally takes the rank of simple federal law except for generally accepted rules of international law, which under Article 25 GG rank between the *Grundgesetz* and simple federal law and do not, as a matter of principle, require domestic implementation. Yet care should be taken not to interpret Article 25 GG as meaning that criminal liability can be established on the basis of international customary law, even if it has the quality of *jus cogens*. The tension between Article 25 GG and the above-mentioned Article 103(2) GG must be resolved in favour of the latter, meaning that criminal liability always requires implementation by domestic law.

The *Grundgesetz* and international law can trade places in the hierarchy when we look at the supranational effect of European law: even the lowest category of self-executing and binding European law takes precedence over the constitution. This had, however, been disputed by the BVerfG for some time when the court at first claimed the final word on the applicability of EC legislation as long as it conflicted with German constitutional law and especially the fundamental civil rights therein, but then moved on to accepting that the European law had reached a level of protection that made such control superfluous unless the complainant showed good cause that the degree of protection on the European level had slipped below that of the *Grundgesetz*. Similar problems arise when Germany has to abide by resolutions of the UN Security Council adopted under the powers of Chapter VII of the UN Charter.

At the next level down, to which the Criminal Code belongs, we have the simple federal legislation, both parliamentary and to some extent derivative governmental instruments, as long as there is an act of Parliament authorising the government to fill in the conditions of criminal liability. Federal law, which these days contains the vast bulk of criminal law applicable in all the member states of the Federation, outranks the law of those states, even their constitutional law. At the very bottom there is the municipal law, which may in restricted cases be made the basis of minor regulatory offences, *Ordnungswidrigkeiten*, which no longer count as proper criminal offences.

Judicial case law, as should have become clear by now, can never be the basis of creating new criminal offences; in this respect the laws in Germany and in England and Wales have converged substantially after the 2006 decision by the House of Lords in *Jones*,[4] where it was held that the courts could no longer create new offences based on their traditional common law powers, and that it was for Parliament to do so.

III PRINCIPLES OF INTERPRETATION AND THE ROLE OF PRECEDENT

German criminal law, as with any area of German law, knows of and applies five methods of interpretation, which to some extent vary from the approach taken in England and Wales. They are, in their supposed order of application:

- Literal
- Grammatical
- Systematic
- Historical
- Teleological

[4] [2006] UKHL 16.

Courts will usually start by interpreting any provision literally. If that does not result in a clear picture, the expression in question will be looked at in its grammatical context. Should the exercise remain unsatisfactory, the rule will then be placed in its systematic context, ie, how does it fit together with other rules or provisions using the same wording? The next step is the question of what problem the law was meant to address in its historical development; this is akin to the English 'mischief rule'. Finally, and more or less anathema for many common lawyers of the old school, the court will ask what aim the legislator intended to achieve by making that particular rule, ie, what was the *telos* of the lawgiver, hence the name teleological. This sequence is, of course, only a sequence in theory, as German courts will regularly base their decisions on a combination of these arguments, each corroborating the others.

German courts are not bound by a doctrine of *stare decisis*, such as is found, for example, in the UK. However, for pragmatic reasons lower level courts will as a rule not deviate from the settled jurisprudence of the superior courts of their districts and the federal courts. This is done to avoid pushing the parties into an appeal the outcome of which is practically clear. Yet any judge at the lowest court is free to disregard the jurisprudence of the highest courts of the land, even that of the BVerfG, unless the latter's decision in question has the force of an act of Parliament or the appellate decision is binding because it determines an appeal in a specific case—yet in the next case, even if identical on the facts, the judge is no longer bound.

IV THE TRIPARTITE STRUCTURE OF OFFENCES—AN OVERVIEW

In this overview of basic concepts, we need to take a brief look at the tripartite structure of German criminal law. The StGB is divided into a General Part (*Allgemeiner Teil*) applicable to all offences, and a Special Part (*Besonderer Teil*), containing the individual offences. Further offences can be found in special legislation, but as a rule the General Part applies to these too. Each offence, based on this two-fold division, is subject to three stages of examination, hence the name 'tripartite structure' (*dreistufiger Verbrechensaufbau*):

- *Tatbestand* = Offence description or (loosely translated) actus reus (*objektiver Tatbestand*) plus mens rea (*subjektiver Tatbestand*);
- *Rechtswidrigkeit* = the general element of unlawfulness and the absence of justificatory defences;
- *Schuld* = the general element of blameworthiness or guilt and the absence of excusatory defences.

The *objektiver Tatbestand* contains the objective elements of offences, similar to the actus reus as understood in the common law. The element of unlawfulness is not a general element of the actus reus, but a separate and distinct category; its absence therefore, unlike under English law in some cases, does not negate the *objektiver Tatbestand*. In connection with offences requiring intention, the *objektiver Tatbestand* is made out if and when the elements listed in it have been fulfilled. With offences based on negligence the general elements of the *objektiver Tatbestand* are augmented by the requirement of a violation of a duty of care and the foreseeability of the result. Negligence is only a basis of liability if the law expressly provides for it: § 15 StGB. Simple negligence, unlike in English law, can be sufficient, unless the law requires a higher degree of negligence.

The *subjektiver Tatbestand* only refers to forms of intent. Negligence in its subjective form is commonly seen as a matter for the third tier, *Schuld*, or guilt. An honest mistake of fact eliminates intent. The *subjektiver Tatbestand* does not normally encompass such issues as intoxication or insanity; these belong to the general element of *Schuld*.

The general element of unlawfulness, *Rechtswidrigkeit*, is in the normal course of events made out if the *Tatbestand* has been infringed (*Tatbestandsmäßigkeit indiziert Rechtswidrigkeit*), unless a justificatory defence eliminates it. Potential justificatory defences are self-defence, necessity, superior orders, citizen's arrest, etc.

The law assumes *Schuld* with young adult and adult offenders, but requires the court to establish the individual maturity of juveniles. The law requires the court to establish the individual maturity of young adults in order to decide whether juvenile law is to be applied. Potential excusatory defences include insanity, diminished responsibility, duress, excessive self-defence, provocation and crimes of passion and unavoidable mistake of law.

Finally, the law recognises categories outside the tripartite structure, such as *Strafausschließungsgründe*, ie, reasons that eliminate the need for punishment (eg, withdrawal from attempts) and *objektive Bedingungen der Strafbarkeit*, ie, factors that must be present before liability is triggered, but that do not form part of the tripartite structure and are thus not subject to the mens rea requirements. In both cases, mistakes are usually irrelevant.

V *VERBRECHEN* AND *VERGEHEN*

An important distinction is the one between *Verbrechen* (equivalent to the old UK category of felonies) and *Vergehen* (akin to misdemeanours). The definition is provided by § 12 StGB, which states that a *Verbrechen* is any offence with a minimum sentence of one year's imprisonment, whereas a *Vergehen* is one punishable by fine or with a minimum sentence below one year's imprisonment. Note that the reference to minimum sentences is an abstract one, referring to the sentencing frames set by the provisions on the individual offences, and does not relate to the sentence in the case at hand.

§ 12(3) StGB furthermore clarifies that the effects of any extenuating or aggravating circumstances arising from the General Part or specific sentencing provisions based on such circumstances are irrelevant for the purposes of the classification. For example, murder under § 212 StGB with its minimum sentence of five years is a *Verbrechen*, murder under mitigating circumstances (mainly provocation) according to the old[5] § 213 StGB was punishable with imprisonment from six months to five years; despite this it remained a *Verbrechen*, as it was a mere sentencing qualification to § 212 StGB. There is a third category, the lowest one, which is called *Ordnungswidrigkeiten* and which arose out of the previous French classification of the *contraventions*; however, these are no longer considered criminal offences proper and are regulated by their own code, the *Ordnungswidrigkeitengesetz* or OWiG, which only refers to the StGB inasmuch as the OWiG does not make specific provision for general principles.

The most important consequences of the dichotomy between *Verbrechen* and *Vergehen* in the substantive criminal law lie in the treatment of attempts and of attempts at participation. § 23 StGB provides that attempted *Verbrechen* always trigger criminal liability, whereas the same can be said for *Vergehen* only if the law expressly provides for this consequence. A good example in this context of how important it is to recognise the proper substance of, and relationship between, offences is § 216 StGB (*Tötung auf Verlangen*), the offence of mercy killing or killing at the request of the victim: the sentencing frame is six months to five years and one might be tempted to say that it is a mere privileged qualification of § 212 StGB, and as such its attempt is always punishable. However, § 216(2) StGB explicitly provides for attempt liability, which is an indicator that § 216 StGB is a wholly separate and not a derivative offence. § 30 StGB allows for punishment only in cases of incitement (ie, in the meaning of an attempted but fruitless act of abetting) or conspiracy[6] if the offence that is the object of that attempted participation or conspiracy is a *Verbrechen*.

VI A BRIEF OVERVIEW OF THE DEVELOPMENT OF THE CRIMINAL CODE[7]

The Criminal Code of the German Reich in its original form of 1871 was to a large extent based on the 1851 Prussian Criminal Code, but has since been amended numerous times.

The first major change after the Second World War was brought about by the first and second Criminal Law (Reform) Acts of 1969 and 1975, which introduced an entirely new General Part and reformed the law of sanctions and sentencing in an unprecedented manner. They did away with the offences of adultery and

---

[5] The minimum sentence is now one year.

[6] This is a loose utilisation of the common law concept, as the substance of the offence differs in common and civil law systems. However, *conspiracy* as a general term neatly catches the actual facts and actions of the offenders. As long as one bears that in mind, there is little harm in using the word in the German context.

[7] For more information on the development, including further reading, see Schönke-Schröder/Eser, *Strafgesetzbuch, Kommentar*, 27th edn, 2006, Einführung.

homosexuality. The highly controversial fifth Criminal Law (Reform) Act of 1974 saw a complete reformulation of the law of abortion. A first attempt at incorporating the piecemeal reforms was made by the Criminal Code (Introduction) Act of 1974, which also took the step of de-criminalising the previous offence category of *Übertretungen* mentioned above and made them into *Ordnungswidrigkeiten*. The sixth Criminal Law (Reform) Act of 1998 amended the law of the Special Part; it was promulgated on the same date as the Tackling of Sexual and Dangerous Offences Act of 1998. After this last major reform in 1998, it was re-published as a coherent whole in 1998, yet there have been more reforms since then.

Another major aspect was the German re-unification of 1990, which made it necessary to provide for transitional regulations as to how the law in force until that date in the former GDR and now the five new East German member states of the Federation was to be adapted to the West German standard. This was done in the annex of the Treaty of Unification and in an amendment of the Criminal Code (Introduction) Act.

Recent reforms include the Code of International Criminal Law of 2002 and, in the law of sanctions and sentencing, the law of 2004 on the subsequent imposition of incapacitation orders after a previous conviction. As opposed to the attempts at a grand reform early in the second half of the last century, criminal law reforms these days are mostly based on policy issues of the day and are often rushed through without proper consultation. Generally, the tendency is for more drastic and punitive laws. In this respect, German criminal law policy resembles that of the UK to a large extent.

List of translations

Transportation of Dangerous Goods Act	Gesetz über die Beförderung gefährlicher Güter
Treaty on the European Economic Area	Abkommen über den Europäischen Wirtschaftsraum
Water Resources Act	Wasserhaushaltsgesetz
Weapons Act	Waffengesetz
Weapons of War (Control) Act	Kriegswaffenkontrollgesetz
Work at Home Act	Heimarbeitsgesetz

Translations of German Public Authorities as used in the Code

(Member) State/s	Land/Länder
District Court	Landgericht
Federal Constitutional Court	Bundesverfassungsgericht
Federal Council	Bundesrat
Federal Government	Bundesregierung
Federal Ministry of Justice	Bundesministerium der Justiz
Federal Parliament	Bundestag
Federation	Bund
President of the Federation	Bundespräsident
Public Employment Agency	Agentur für Arbeit

A note on citation and style

I have kept to the German way of citation of laws. To keep the text as short and uncluttered as possible I have used the German symbol for 'section', which is '§'. After that, the subdivisions are 'subsection' ('(1)', or '(2) to (7)'), 'sentence' ('1st sentence'), 'number' ('No 1', or 'Nos 2 to 5') and letters ('(a)'), 'alternatives', etc. This is not necessarily an exclusive hierarchical sequence as, depending on the length of individual provisions, numbers could have several sentences, etc.

Thus, for example, the following citation

'§ 211(2) 3rd alt'

would read:

'Section 211, subsection (2), third alternative'

and would denote killing a person out of greed.

The double '§§' means 'sections' and has only been used here, other than in the German practice, to denote an uninterrupted sequence of sections, such as '§§ 176 to 177'. Otherwise, the '§' has been used for each provision cited. Sometimes the Code itself uses enumerations of the individual sections of an uninterrupted sequence of provisions, eg, 'sections 5, 6, 7, 8, 9, 10' rather than merely stating 'sections 5 to 10'. Where the original does that, the translation does it, too, and uses the '§' for each of them. This applies also to cases where two provisions are linked by 'and'.

Sometimes, individual provisions are mentioned 'in conjunction with' another, which means it is necessary to read both provisions together to obtain the full meaning. The fact that the Criminal Code is meant to be a monolithic fundamental codification has led to the technique of manifold cross-references, either to other provisions of the Code or even to laws outside the Code. This takes some getting used to. Often these references take the form of '§§ 56a–56d shall apply mutatis mutandis', which means that the cited provisions apply by analogy.

THE GERMAN CRIMINAL CODE

As amended on 31 December 2007[1]

Table of contents

GENERAL PART

---

[1] Bundesgesetzblatt I (2007), 3209.
[2] The old English division into felonies and misdemeanours is used for want of a better translation that captures the essence of the distinction.

---

[3] This English term is used for crispness of expression; the concept is not entirely congruent with the German law.

[4] See above n 3.

[5] See above n 3.

[6] The German law is not identical to the English concept of conspiracy, but the word is used as its closest equivalent.

FIFTH TITLE
IMMUNITY FOR STATEMENTS AND REPORTS MADE IN PARLIAMENT

CHAPTER THREE
SANCTIONS

FIRST TITLE
PENALTIES

—Imprisonment—

—Fine—

—*Confiscatory expropriation order*—

—Ancillary penalty—

—Ancillary measures—

SECOND TITLE
SENTENCING

[7] This provision was declared unconstitutional and void by the BVerfG by judgment of 20 March 2002: see further at § 43a below.

[8] This is in its effect similar to imprisonment for public protection under the Criminal Justice Act 2003. However, because it is not a penalty but a measure, I have chosen to use a neutral title.

SPECIAL PART

CHAPTER EIGHT
COUNTERFEITING OF MONEY AND OFFICIAL STAMPS

CHAPTER NINE
FALSE TESTIMONY AND PERJURY

CHAPTER SIXTEEN
OFFENCES AGAINST LIFE

CHAPTER SEVENTEEN
OFFENCES AGAINST THE PERSON

CHAPTER EIGHTEEN
OFFENCES AGAINST PERSONAL FREEDOM

CHAPTER NINETEEN
THEFT AND UNLAWFUL APPROPRIATION

CHAPTER TWENTY
ROBBERY AND BLACKMAIL

CHAPTER TWENTY-FOUR
OFFENCES IN THE STATE OF INSOLVENCY

CHAPTER TWENTY-FIVE
CRIMINAL SELF-SEEKING

CHAPTER TWENTY-SIX
RESTRICTIVE PRACTICES OFFENCES

CHAPTER TWENTY-SEVEN
CRIMINAL DAMAGE

CHAPTER TWENTY-EIGHT
OFFENCES CAUSING A COMMON DANGER

CHAPTER TWENTY-NINE
OFFENCES AGAINST THE ENVIRONMENT

CHAPTER THIRTY
OFFENCES COMMITTED IN PUBLIC OFFICE

GENERAL PART

CHAPTER ONE
THE CRIMINAL LAW

FIRST TITLE
APPLICATION, JURISDICTION RATIONE LOCI ET TEMPORIS

§ 1 No punishment without law

An act may only be punished if criminal liability had been established by law before the act was committed.

§ 2 Jurisdiction ratione temporis; lex mitior

(1) The penalty and any ancillary measures shall be determined by the law which is in force at the time of the act.
(2) If the penalty is amended during the commission of the act, the law in force at the time the act is completed shall be applied.
(3) If the law in force at the time of the completion of the act is amended before judgment, the most lenient law shall be applied.
(4) A law intended to be in force only for a determinate time shall be continued to be applied to acts committed while it was in force even after it ceases to be in force, unless otherwise provided by law.
(5) Subsections (1) to (4) shall apply mutatis mutandis to confiscation, deprivation and destruction.
(6) Unless otherwise provided by law, measures of rehabilitation and incapacitation shall be determined according to the law in force at the time of the decision.

§ 3 Offences committed on the territory of the Federal Republic of Germany

German criminal law shall apply to acts committed on German territory.

§ 4 Offences committed on German ships and aircraft

German criminal law shall apply, regardless of the law applicable in the locality where the act was committed, to acts committed on a ship or an aircraft entitled to fly the federal flag or the national insignia of the Federal Republic of Germany.

§ 5 Offences committed abroad against domestic legal interests

German criminal law shall apply, regardless of the law applicable in the locality where the act was committed, to the following acts committed abroad:

1. preparation of a war of aggression (§ 80);
2. high treason against the Federation (§§ 81 to 83);
3. endangering the democratic state under the rule of law

    (a) in cases under § 89 and § 90a(1), and § 90b, if the offender is German[1] and has his main livelihood in the territory of the Federal Republic of Germany[2]; and
    (b) in cases under § 90 and § 90a(2);

4. treason and endangering external national security (§§ 94 to 100a);
5. offences against the national defence:

    (a) in cases under § 109 and §§ 109e to 109g; and
    (b) in cases under § 109a, § 109d and § 109h, if the offender is German and has his main livelihood in the territory of the Federal Republic of Germany

6. Causing the danger of political persecution (§ 234a, §241a) if the act is directed against a German who has his domicile or usual residence in Germany[3];
6a. abduction of minors in cases under § 235(2) No 2, if the act is directed against a person who has his domicile or usual residence in Germany;
7. violation of business or trade secrets of a business physically located within the territory of the Federal Republic of Germany, or of an enterprise, which has its seat there, or of an enterprise with its seat abroad and which is dependent on an enterprise with its seat within the territory of the Federal Republic of Germany and which forms a group with the latter;
8. offences against sexual self-determination:

    (a) in cases under § 174(1) and (3), if the offender and the victim are German at the time of the offence and have their main livelihood in Germany; and
    (b) in cases under §§ 176 to 176b and § 182, if the offender is German;

---

[1] The German text uses the word 'Deutscher', which translates literally as 'German'. In the vast majority of cases this will mean somebody holding German citizenship. However, the law also encompasses refugees of German ethnicity who had found sanctuary on the territory of the former German Reich, as well as their spouses and descendants.

[2] The German text uses the awkward expression 'räumlicher Geltungsbereich dieses Gesetzes', which is now in effect the territory of the Federal Republic of Germany. The phrase had been deemed necessary to distinguish between West Germany and the GDR, a distinction which has become obsolete after German re-unification. The term has therefore been substituted by 'the territory of the Federal Republic of Germany' or just 'Federal Republic of Gemany' for reasons of style.

[3] Note that the courts traditionally included the former GDR for the purposes of *this* number.

9. abortion (§ 218), if the offender at the time of the offence is German and has his main livelihood in the territory of the Federal Republic of Germany;
10. false testimony, perjury and false sworn affidavits (§§ 153 to 156) in proceedings pending before a court or another German authority within the territory of the Federal Republic of Germany that has the authority to administer oaths or affirmations in lieu of oath;
11. offences against the environment under § 324, § 326, § 330 and § 330a committed within Germany's exclusive economic zone, to the extent that international conventions on the protection of the sea allow for their prosecution as criminal offences;
11a. offences under § 328(2) Nos 3 and 4, (4) and (5), also in conjunction with § 330, if the offender is German at the time of the offence;
12. offences committed by a German public official or a person entrusted with special public service functions during their official stay or in connection with their official duties;
13. acts committed by a foreigner as a public official or as a person entrusted with special public service functions;
14. acts committed against public officials, persons entrusted with special public service functions, or soldiers in the Armed Forces during the discharge of their duties or in connection with their duties;
14a. bribing delegates (§ 108e) if the offender is German at the time of the offence or the offence was committed vis-à-vis a German;
15. trafficking in human organs (§ 18 of the Transplantation Act), if the offender is German at the time of the offence.

§ 6 Offences committed abroad against internationally protected legal interests

German criminal law shall further apply, regardless of the law of the locality where they are committed, to the following offences committed abroad:

1. *(repealed)*;
2. offences involving nuclear energy, explosives and radiation under § 307 and § 308(1) to (4), § 309(2) and § 310;
3. attacks on air and maritime traffic (§ 316c);
4. human trafficking for the purpose of sexual exploitation, for the purpose of work exploitation and assisting human trafficking (§§ 232 to 233a);
5. unlawful drug dealing;
6. distribution of pornography under § 184a and § 184b(1) to (3), also in conjunction with § 184c, 1st sentence;
7. counterfeiting money and securities (§ 146, § 151 and § 152), credit cards etc and blank eurocheque forms (§ 152b(1) to (4)) as well as the relevant preparatory acts (§§ 149, 151, 152 and 152b(5));
8. subsidy fraud (§ 264);

9. offences which on the basis of an international agreement binding on the Federal Republic of Germany must be prosecuted even though committed abroad.

§ 7 Offences committed abroad—other cases

(1) German criminal law shall apply to offences committed abroad against a German, if the act is a criminal offence at the locality of its commission or if that locality is not subject to any criminal jurisdiction.
(2) German criminal law shall apply to other offences committed abroad if the act is a criminal offence at the locality of its commission or if that locality is not subject to any criminal law jurisdiction, and if the offender:

1. was German at the time of the offence or became German after the commission; or
2. was a foreigner at the time of the offence, is discovered in Germany and, although the Extradition Act would permit extradition for such an offence, is not extradited because a request for extradition within a reasonable period of time is not made, is rejected, or the extradition is not feasible.

§ 8 Time of the offence

An offence is deemed to have been committed at the time when the principal or the secondary participants acted, or, in the case of an omission, should have acted. The time when the result occurs is irrelevant.

§ 9 Place of the offence

(1) An offence is deemed to have been committed in every place where the offender acted or, in the case of an omission, should have acted, or in which the result if it is an element of the offence occurs or should have occurred according to the intention of the offender.
(2) Acts of secondary participation are committed not only in the place where the offence was committed, but also in every place where the secondary participant acted or, in the case of an omission, should have acted or where, according to his intention, the offence should have been committed. If the secondary participant to an offence committed abroad acted within the territory of the Federal Republic of Germany, German criminal law shall apply to the secondary participation even though the act is not a criminal offence according to the law of the locality of its commission.

§ 10 Special provisions for juveniles and young adults

This law shall apply to offences committed by juveniles and young adults unless the Juvenile Courts Act provides otherwise.

SECOND TITLE
TERMINOLOGY

§ 11 Definitions

(1) For the purposes of this law

1. 'relative' means any member of the following category of persons:

(a) relations by blood or marriage in direct line, the spouse, the same sex partner, the fiancé(e)—also within the meaning of the Same Sex Partnership Act—, siblings, the spouses or same sex partners of siblings, siblings of spouses or same sex partners, even if the marriage or same sex partnership upon which the relationship was based no longer exists, or when the relationship by blood or marriage has ceased to exist;

(b) foster parents and foster children;

2. 'public official' means any of the following if under German law

(a) they are civil servants or judges;

(b) otherwise carry out public official functions; or

(c) have otherwise been appointed to serve with a public authority or other agency or have been commissioned to perform public administrative services regardless of the organisational form chosen to fulfil such duties;

3. 'judge' means any person who under German law is either a professional or a lay judge;

4. 'persons entrusted with special public service functions' means any person who, without being a public official, is employed by, or is acting for

(a) a public authority or other agency, which performs public administrative services; or

(b) an association or other union, business or enterprise, which carries out public administrative services for a public authority or other agency,

and who is formally required by law to fulfil their duties with due diligence;

5. 'unlawful act' exclusively means an act that fulfils all the elements of a criminal provision;

6. 'Unternehmen (undertaking)'[4] of an offence means both attempt and completion;

7. 'public authority' also means a court;

---

[4] This word cannot be translated into a correct English legal term. It covers the idea of engaging in an act, preparing it, endeavouring to bring about a result. However, the legal definition in § 11 extends it to mean attempts and completion of offences. It is mainly relevant for those specific types of offence that extend liability far into the inchoate stage and use the term in their actus reus.

8. 'measure' means the measures of rehabilitation and incapacitation, confiscation, deprivation and destruction;

9. 'consideration' means any material benefit given in exchange for someone's acts.

(2)   An act is also deemed intentional for the purposes of this law, if it fulfils the statutory elements of an offence, which requires intent in relation to the offender's conduct but lets negligence suffice as to a specific result caused thereby.

(3)   Audiovisual media, data storage media, illustrations and other depictions shall be equivalent to written material in the provisions which refer to this subsection.

§ 12 Felonies and misdemeanours

(1)   Felonies are unlawful acts punishable by a minimum sentence of one year's imprisonment.

(2)   Misdemeanours are unlawful acts punishable by a lesser minimum term of imprisonment or by fine.

(3)   Aggravations or mitigations provided for under the provisions of the General Part, or under especially serious or less serious cases in the Special Part, shall be irrelevant to this classification.

CHAPTER TWO
THE OFFENCE

FIRST TITLE
FOUNDATIONS OF CRIMINAL LIABILITY

§ 13 Omissions

(1)   Whosoever fails to avert a result which is an element of a criminal provision shall only be liable under this law if he is responsible under law to ensure that the result does not occur, and if the omission is equivalent to the realisation of the statutory elements of the offence through a positive act.

(2)   The sentence may be mitigated pursuant to § 49(1).

§ 14 Acting for another

(1)   If a person acts:

1. in his capacity as an organ authorised to represent a legal entity or as a member of such an organ;

2.   as a partner authorised to represent a partnership with independent legal capacity; or
3.   as a statutory representative of another,

any law according to which special personal attributes, relationships or circumstances (special personal characteristics) form the basis of criminal liability, shall apply to the representative, if these characteristics do not exist in his person but in the entity, partnership or person represented.

(2) If a person, whether by the owner of a business or somebody delegated by him, has been

1.   commissioned to manage the business, in whole or in part; or
2.   expressly commissioned to perform autonomous duties which are incumbent on the owner of the business,

and the person acts on the basis of this commission, any law, according to which special personal characteristics give rise to criminal liability shall apply to the person commissioned, if these characteristics do not exist in his but in the person of the owner of the business. Within the meaning of the first sentence an enterprise shall be the equivalent of a business. If a person acts on the basis of a similar commission for an agency performing public administrative services, the first sentence shall apply mutatis mutandis.

(3) Subsections (1) and (2) above shall apply even if the act of commission intended to create the power of representation or the agency is void.

§ 15 Intent and negligence

Unless the law expressly provides for criminal liability based on negligence, only intentional conduct shall attract criminal liability.

§ 16 Mistake of fact

(1) Whosoever at the time of the commission of the offence is unaware of a fact which is a statutory element of the offence shall be deemed to lack intention. Any liability for negligence remains unaffected.
(2) Whosoever at the time of commission of the offence mistakenly assumes the existence of facts which would satisfy the elements of a more lenient provision, may only be punished for the intentional commission of the offence under the more lenient provision.

§ 17 Mistake of law

If at the time of the commission of the offence the offender lacks the awareness that he is acting unlawfully, he shall be deemed to have acted without guilt if the mistake was unavoidable. If the mistake was avoidable, the sentence may be mitigated pursuant to § 49(1).

§ 18 Aggravated sentence based on special consequences of the offence

If the law imposes a more serious sentence based on an extended result of an offence, any principal or secondary participant is liable to the increased sentence only if they acted at least negligently with respect to that result.

§ 19 Lack of criminal capacity of children

Persons who have not attained the age of fourteen at the time of the commission of the offence shall be deemed to act without guilt.

§ 20 Insanity

Any person who at the time of the commission of the offence is incapable of appreciating the unlawfulness of their actions or of acting in accordance with any such appreciation due to a pathological mental disorder, a profound consciousness disorder, debility or any other serious mental abnormality, shall be deemed to act without guilt.

§ 21 Diminished responsibility

If the capacity of the offender to appreciate the unlawfulness of his actions or to act in accordance with any such appreciation is substantially diminished at the time of the commission of the offence due to one of the reasons indicated in § 20, the sentence may be mitigated pursuant to § 49(1).

SECOND TITLE
ATTEMPT

§ 22 Definition

A person attempts to commit an offence if he takes steps which will immediately lead to the completion of the offence as envisaged by him.

§ 23 Liability for attempt

(1) Any attempt to commit a felony entails criminal liability; this applies to attempted misdemeanours only if expressly so provided by law.
(2) An attempt may be punished more leniently than the completed offence (§ 49(1)).
(3) If the offender due to gross ignorance fails to realise that the attempt could under no circumstances have led to the completion of the offence due to the nature of its object or the means by which it was to be committed, the court may order a discharge, or mitigate the sentence as it sees fit (§ 49(2)).

§ 24 Withdrawal

(1) A person who of his own volition gives up the further execution of the offence or prevents its completion shall not be liable for the attempt. If the offence is not completed regardless of his actions, that person shall not be liable if he has made a voluntary and earnest effort to prevent the completion of the offence.

(2) If more than one person participate in the offence, the person who voluntarily prevents its completion shall not be liable for the attempt. His voluntary and earnest effort to prevent the completion of the offence shall suffice for exemption from liability, if the offence is not completed regardless of his actions or is committed independently of his earlier contribution to the offence.

THIRD TITLE
PRINCIPALS AND SECONDARY PARTICIPANTS

§ 25 Principals

(1) Any person who commits the offence himself or through another shall be liable as a principal.

(2) If more than one person commit the offence jointly, each shall be liable as a principal (joint principals).

§ 26 Abetting

Any person who intentionally induces another to intentionally commit an unlawful act (abettor) shall be liable to be sentenced as if he were a principal.

§ 27 Aiding

(1) Any person who intentionally assists another in the intentional commission of an unlawful act shall be convicted and sentenced as an aider.

(2) The sentence for the aider shall be based on the penalty for a principal. It shall be mitigated pursuant to § 49(1).

§ 28 Special personal characteristics

(1) If special personal characteristics (§ 14(1)) that establish the principal's liability are absent in the person of the secondary participant (abettor or aider) their sentence shall be mitigated pursuant to § 49(1).

(2) If the law provides that special personal characteristics aggravate, mitigate or exclude punishment this shall apply only to the accomplices (principals or secondary participants) in whose person they are present.

§ 29 Separate criminal liability of the accomplice

Each accomplice shall be liable according to the measure of his own guilt and irrespective of the guilt of the others.

§ 30 Conspiracy

(1) A person who attempts to induce another to commit a felony or abet another to commit a felony shall be liable according to the provisions governing attempted felonies. The sentence shall be mitigated pursuant to § 49(1). § 23(3) shall apply mutatis mutandis.

(2) A person who declares his willingness or who accepts the offer of another or who agrees with another to commit or abet the commission of a felony shall be liable under the same terms.

§ 31 Withdrawal from conspiracy

(1) A person shall not be liable under § 30 if he voluntarily

1. gives up the attempt to induce another to commit a felony and averts any existing danger that the other may commit the offence;
2. after having declared his willingness to commit a felony, gives up his plan; or
3. after having agreed to commit a felony or accepted the offer of another to commit a felony prevents the commission of the offence.

(2) If the offence is not completed regardless of his actions or if it is committed independently of his previous conduct, his voluntary and earnest effort to prevent the completion of the offence shall suffice for exemption from liability.

FOURTH TITLE
SELF-DEFENCE, NECESSITY AND DURESS

§ 32 Self-defence

(1) A person who commits an act in self-defence does not act unlawfully.
(2) Self-defence means any defensive action that is necessary to avert an imminent unlawful attack on oneself or another.

§ 33 Excessive self-defence

A person who exceeds the limits of self-defence out of confusion, fear or terror shall not be held criminally liable.

§ 34 Necessity

A person who, faced with an imminent danger to life, limb, freedom, honour, property or another legal interest which cannot otherwise be averted, commits an act to avert the danger from himself or another, does not act unlawfully, if, upon weighing the conflicting interests, in particular the affected legal interests and the degree of the danger facing them, the protected interest substantially outweighs the one interfered with. This shall apply only if and to the extent that the act committed is an adequate means to avert the danger.

§ 35 Duress

(1) A person who, faced with an imminent danger to life, limb or freedom which cannot otherwise be averted, commits an unlawful act to avert the danger from himself, a relative or person close to him, acts without guilt. This shall not apply if and to the extent that the offender could be expected under the circumstances to accept the danger, in particular, because he himself had caused the danger, or was under a special legal obligation to do so; the sentence may be mitigated pursuant to § 49(1) unless the offender was required to accept the danger because of a special legal obligation to do so.

(2) If at the time of the commission of the act a person mistakenly assumes that circumstances exist which would excuse him under subsection (1) above, he will only be liable if the mistake was avoidable. The sentence shall be mitigated pursuant to § 49(1).

FIFTH TITLE
IMMUNITY FOR STATEMENTS AND REPORTS MADE IN PARLIAMENT

§ 36 Parliamentary statements

Delegates of the Federal Parliament, the Federal Assembly or of a legislative body of a member state shall at all times be immune from external liability because of a vote they cast or a statement they made within one of those bodies or one of their committees. This shall not apply to intentional defamations.

§ 37 Parliamentary reports

Truthful reports about the public sessions of the bodies indicated in § 36 or their committees shall not give rise to any liability.

CHAPTER THREE
SANCTIONS

FIRST TITLE
PENALTIES

—Imprisonment—

§ 38 Term of imprisonment

(1)   Imprisonment shall be for a fixed term unless the law provides for life imprisonment.
(2)   The maximum term of fixed-term imprisonment shall be fifteen years, the minimum term one month.

§ 39 Determination of fixed-term imprisonment

Imprisonment for less than a year shall be determined in full weeks and months, imprisonment for a longer period in full months and years.

—Fine—

§ 40 Day fine units

(1)   A fine shall be imposed in daily units. The minimum fine shall consist of five and, unless the law provides otherwise, the maximum shall consist of three hundred and sixty full daily units.
(2)   The court shall determine the amount of the daily unit taking into consideration the personal and financial circumstances of the offender. In doing so, it shall typically base its calculation on the actual average one-day net income of the offender or the average income he could achieve in one day. A daily unit shall not be set at less than one and not at more than five thousand euros.
(3)   The income of the offender, his assets and other relevant assessment factors may be estimated when setting the amount of a daily unit.
(4)   The number and amount of the daily units shall be indicated in the decision.

§ 41 Fines in addition to imprisonment

If the offender through the commission of the offence enriched or tried to enrich himself, a fine which otherwise would not have been provided for or only in the alternative may be imposed in addition to imprisonment if this appears appropriate taking into consideration the personal and financial circumstances of the offender. This does not apply if the court imposes an order pursuant to § 43a.

§ 42 Allowing time for payment; instalments

If a convicted offender, due to his personal or financial circumstances, cannot be expected to pay the full fine immediately, the court shall allow a certain time for payment or allow payment in specified instalments. The court may also order that the privilege of paying the fine in fixed instalments will be revoked if the convicted offender fails to pay an instalment in time. The court shall also allow for such conditions of payment if without them the restitution by the offender of any damage caused by the offence were to be substantially impaired; the court may require the offender to present proof of restitution.

§ 43 Imprisonment for default of payment

If the fine cannot be recovered, it shall be replaced by imprisonment. One daily unit shall correspond to one day of imprisonment. The minimum term of imprisonment for default of payment shall be one day.

—Confiscatory expropriation order[5]—

§ 43a Confiscatory expropriation order

(1) If the law refers to this provision the court may, in addition to imprisonment for life or for a fixed term of more than two years, order payment of a sum of money the amount of which shall be limited by the value of the offender's assets (confiscatory expropriation order). Material benefits which have been confiscated shall not be taken into account when assessing the value of the assets. The value of the assets may be estimated.

(2) § 42 shall apply mutatis mutandis.

(3) The court shall indicate a term of imprisonment which shall be substituted if the amount cannot be recovered (default imprisonment). The maximum term of default imprisonment shall be two years, its minimum one month.

—Ancillary penalty—

§ 44 Temporary driving ban

(1) If a person has been sentenced to imprisonment or to a fine for an offence committed in connection with the driving of a motor-vehicle or in violation of the duties of a driver of a motor-vehicle, the court may impose a ban prohibiting him from driving any class of motor-vehicle or a specific class on public roads for a period of from one to three months. A driving ban shall typically be imposed in cases of a conviction under § 315c(1) No 1(a), (3) or § 316 unless a disqualification order has been made under § 69.

---

[5] This provision was declared unconstitutional and void by the BVerfG in 2002: judgment of 20 March 2002, Docket No 2 BvR 794/95, as a violation of the principle of specifity and fair labelling under Article 103(2) GG. It has not yet been deleted from the text of the Code.

(2)   The driving ban shall take effect upon the judgment having become final. National and international driving licences issued by a German public authority shall be kept in official safekeeping for its duration. This shall also apply if the driving licence was issued by a public authority of a member state of the European Union or another signatory state of the Treaty on the European Economic Area if the holder is ordinarily resident in Germany. The driving ban shall be endorsed on any other foreign driving licences.

(3)   If a driving licence is to be kept in official safekeeping or the driving ban to be endorsed on a foreign driving licence, the duration of the ban shall be calculated from the day that those conditions have been complied with. Any period during which the offender was kept in detention in an institution pursuant to an order of a public authority shall not count towards the duration.

—Ancillary measures—

§ 45 Loss of ability to hold public office, to vote and be elected in public elections

(1)   A person who has been sentenced for a felony to a term of imprisonment of not less than one year shall, for a period of five years, lose the ability to hold public office and be elected in public elections.

(2)   The court may deprive a convicted person of the ability indicated in subsection (1) above for a period of from two to five years if the law expressly so provides.

(3)   At the same time that the loss of ability to hold public office takes effect, the convicted person shall lose any corresponding legal positions and rights he may at that time hold.

(4)   At the same time the loss of the ability to be elected in public elections takes effect, the convicted person shall lose any corresponding legal positions and rights he may hold unless the law provides otherwise.

(5)   The court may deprive the convicted person of the right to take part in elections or to vote in public affairs for a period of from two to five years if the law expressly so provides.

§ 45a Entry into effect and calculation of duration

(1)   The loss of the ability, legal positions and rights shall take effect upon the judgment having become final.

(2)   The duration of the loss of ability or of a right shall be calculated from the day the term of imprisonment has been served, barred by the statute of limitations or remitted. If a custodial measure of rehabilitation and incapacitation had been ordered in addition to imprisonment, the duration shall begin on the day that measure has been served.

(3)   If the sentence or the measure had been suspended or conditional early release granted under a period of probation, or an executive pardon granted,

any operational probationary period shall be included in the calculation of the duration if, after its expiration, the sentence or the remainder thereof has been remitted, or when the measure has been completed.

§ 45b Reinstatement

(1) The court may reinstate abilities lost pursuant to § 45(1) and (2), and rights lost pursuant to § 45(5), if

    1. the loss has been in effect for half of its duration; and

    2. it can be expected that the convicted person will commit no further intentional offences.

(2) Any period during which the offender was kept in detention in an institution pursuant to an order of a public authority shall not count towards the duration.

SECOND TITLE
SENTENCING

§ 46 Principles of sentencing

(1) The guilt of the offender is the basis for sentencing. The effects which the sentence can be expected to have on the offender's future life in society shall be taken into account.

(2) When sentencing the court shall weigh the circumstances in favour of and against the offender. Consideration shall in particular be given to

    the motives and aims of the offender;

    the attitude reflected in the offence and the degree of force of will involved in its commission;

    the degree of the violation of the offender's duties;

    the modus operandi and the consequences caused by the offence to the extent that the offender is to blame for them;

    the offender's prior history, his personal and financial circumstances;

    his conduct after the offence, particularly his efforts to make restitution for the harm caused as well as the offender's efforts at reconciliation with the victim.

(3) Circumstances which are already statutory elements of the offence must not be considered.

§ 46a Reconciliation; restitution

If the offender

1. in an effort to achieve reconciliation with the victim, has made full restitution or the major part thereof for his offence, or has earnestly tried to make restitution; or
2. in a case in which making restitution for the harm caused required substantial personal services or personal sacrifice on his part, has made full compensation or the major part thereof to the victim,

the court may mitigate the sentence pursuant to § 49(1) or, unless the sentence to be imposed on the offender is imprisonment of more than one year or a fine of more than three hundred and sixty daily units, may order a discharge.

§ 47 Short terms of imprisonment as the exception

(1) The court shall not impose a term of imprisonment of less than six months unless special circumstances exist, either in the offence or the person of the offender, that strictly require the imposition of imprisonment either for the purpose of reform of the offender or for reasons of general deterrence.
(2) If the law does not provide for a fine and a term of imprisonment of six months or more is not to be imposed, the court shall impose a fine unless the imposition of a sentence of imprisonment is strictly required pursuant to subsection (1) above. If the law provides for an increased minimum term of imprisonment, the minimum fine in cases covered by the 1st sentence of this subsection shall be determined by the minimum term of imprisonment; thirty daily units shall correspond to one month's imprisonment.

§ 48 *(repealed)*

§ 49 Special mitigating circumstances established by law

(1) If the law requires or allows for mitigation under this provision, the following shall apply:

1. Imprisonment of not less than three years shall be substituted for imprisonment for life.
2. In cases of imprisonment for a fixed term, no more than three quarters of the statutory maximum term may be imposed. In case of a fine the same shall apply to the maximum number of daily units.
3. Any increased minimum statutory term of imprisonment shall be reduced as follows:

    a minimum term of ten or five years, to two years;

    a minimum term of three or two years, to six months;

    a minimum term of one year, to three months;

    in all other cases to the statutory minimum.

(2) If the court may in its discretion mitigate the sentence pursuant to a law which refers to this provision, it may reduce the sentence to the statutory minimum or impose a fine instead of imprisonment.

§ 50 Multiple mitigating circumstances

A circumstance which alone or together with other circumstances justifies the assumption of a mitigated offence under the provisions of the special part and which is also a special statutory mitigating circumstance for the purposes of § 49, may only be considered once.

§ 51 Effect of time spent in custody

(1) If a convicted person had been remanded in custody or otherwise been kept in detention because of an offence which is or was the object of the proceedings, any time spent in such custody or detention shall be credited towards a fixed term of imprisonment or a fine. The court may order for such time not to be credited in whole or in part if in light of the conduct of the convicted person after the offence this would be inappropriate.

(2) If in a later proceeding another sentence is substituted for a previously imposed sentence after that sentence had become final, time served under or credited towards the earlier sentence shall be credited against the new sentence.

(3) If a convicted person has already been sentenced abroad for the same offence, the foreign sentence, to the extent it has been served, shall be credited towards the new sentence. Subsection (1) above shall apply mutatis mutandis to any other detention suffered abroad.

(4) For the purpose of crediting a fine against time in detention, or vice versa, one day of detention shall correspond to one daily unit. If a foreign sentence or time in detention is to be credited, the court shall determine the rate as it sees fit.

(5) For the purpose of crediting a period of provisional disqualification from driving (§ 111a of the Code of Criminal Procedure) against a driving ban under § 44, subsection (1) above shall apply mutatis mutandis. For this purpose, the provisional deprivation of a driving licence or its seizure (§ 94 of the Code of Criminal Procedure) shall be equivalent to a provisional disqualification.

THIRD TITLE
SENTENCING FOR MULTIPLE OFFENCES

§ 52 One act violating multiple laws or the same law more than once

(1) If the same act violates more than one law or the same law more than once, only one sentence shall be imposed.

(2)   If more than one law has been violated the sentence shall be determined according to the law that provides for the most severe sentence. The sentence may not be more lenient than the other applicable laws permit.

(3)   The court may impose an additional fine to any term of imprisonment under the provisions of § 41.

(4)   If one of the applicable laws allows for the imposition of a confiscatory expropriation order the court may impose it in addition to imprisonment for life or a fixed term of more than two years. In addition, ancillary penalties and measures (§ 11(1) No 8) must or may be imposed if one of the applicable laws so requires or allows.

§ 53 Multiple offences committed by multiple acts

(1)   If a person has committed more than one offence, all of which are to be adjudicated at the same time, and incurred more than one sentence of imprisonment or more than one fine, an aggregate sentence shall be imposed.

(2)   If a term of imprisonment concurs with a fine, an aggregate sentence shall be imposed. The court may impose a separate fine; if fines are to be imposed for more than one offence, an aggregate fine shall to that extent be imposed.

(3)   If the offender, pursuant to a law according to which § 43a is applicable or under the terms of § 52(4), has as one of the individual sentences incurred imprisonment for life or a fixed term of more than two years, the court may impose a confiscatory expropriation order in addition to the aggregate sentence formed pursuant to subsections (1) or (2) above; if in such cases a confiscatory deprivation order is to be imposed for more than one offence, an aggregate expropriation order shall to that extent be imposed. § 43a(3) shall apply mutatis mutandis.

(4)   § 52(3) and (4) 2nd sentence shall apply mutatis mutandis.

§ 54 Fixing of aggregate sentence

(1)   If one of the sentences for the individual offences is imprisonment for life, an aggregate sentence of imprisonment for life shall be imposed. In all other cases the aggregate sentence shall be fixed by increasing the most severe individual sentence incurred and, in the case of different kinds of penalties, by increasing the sentence that is most severe in nature. The person of the offender and the individual offences shall be considered in their totality.

(2)   The aggregate sentence shall be less than the sum of the individual sentences. It shall not, in the case of imprisonment for a fixed term, exceed fifteen years, in the case of a confiscatory expropriation order, the value of the offender's assets, and in the case of a fine, seven hundred and twenty daily units; § 43a(1) 3rd sentence shall apply mutatis mutandis.

(3)   If an aggregate sentence is to be fixed based on a term of imprisonment and a fine, one daily unit shall correspond to one day's imprisonment for the purpose of calculating the sum of the individual sentences.

§ 55 Subsequent fixing of aggregate sentence

(1) §§ 53 and 54 shall also apply to a convicted person who has had a sentence imposed upon him by a final judgment which has neither been enforced, barred by the statute of limitations nor remitted, when that person is convicted of another offence which he committed before the previous conviction. That previous conviction shall be the judgment in those proceedings in which the factual findings underlying the new conviction could last have been examined.

(2) Confiscatory expropriation orders, ancillary penalties and measures (§ 11(1) No 8) imposed in the previous sentence shall be upheld to the extent they have not been rendered moot by the new judgment. This applies also when the amount of the expropriation order imposed in the previous sentence exceeds the value of the offender's assets at the time of the new sentence.

FOURTH TITLE
SUSPENDED SENTENCES OF IMPRISONMENT

§ 56 Power of court to suspend sentence

(1) If a person is sentenced to a term of imprisonment not exceeding one year the court shall suspend the enforcement of the sentence for a probationary period if there are reasons to believe that the sentence will serve as s sufficient warning to the convicted person and that he will commit no further offences without having to serve the sentence. The court shall particularly take into account the character of the convicted person, his previous history, the circumstances of his offence, his conduct after the offence, his circumstances and the effects to be expected from the suspension.

(2) The court may, under the conditions of subsection (1) above suspend the enforcement of a term of imprisonment not exceeding two years for a probationary period, if after a comprehensive evaluation of the offence and character of the convicted person special circumstances can be found to exist. In making its decision, the court shall particularly take into account any efforts by the convicted person to make restitution for the harm caused by the offence.

(3) The enforcement of a sentence of imprisonment exceeding six months shall not be suspended when reasons of general deterrence so require.

(4) The suspension must not be limited to a part of the sentence. It shall not be excluded by any crediting of time served in custody on remand or any other form of detention.

§ 56a Operational period

(1) The court shall determine the operational probationary period. This must not exceed five years nor be less than two years.

(2)   The operational period shall commence when the decision to suspend the sentence becomes final. It may subsequently be reduced to the minimum or prolonged to the maximum before its expiration.

§ 56b Conditions

(1)   The court may impose conditions on the convicted person directed at repairing the harm caused. No unreasonable demands shall be made from the convicted person.

(2)   The court may order the convicted person

    1.   to make restitution to the best of his ability for the harm caused by the offence;

    2.   to pay a sum of money to a charitable organisation if this appears appropriate in light of the offence and the character of the offender;

    3.   to perform community service; or

    4.   to pay a sum of money to the public treasury.

The court shall not impose a condition pursuant to the 1st sentence of this subsection Nos 2 to 4 unless the fulfilment of the condition does not impair the restitution for the harm caused.

(3)   If the convicted person offers to perform appropriate services for the purpose of repairing the harm caused, the court shall typically preliminarily refrain from imposing conditions if it is to be expected that the offer will be fulfilled.

§ 56c Directions

(1)   The court shall impose directions for the duration of the operational period, if the convicted person requires such assistance to abstain from committing offences. No unreasonable demands should be imposed on the convicted person's lifestyle.

(2)   The court may, in particular, direct the convicted person

    1.   to follow instructions which relate to his residence, education, work or leisure, or to the ordering of his financial affairs;

    2.   to report at certain times to the court or another authority;

    3.   not to make or maintain contact with the victim, or certain persons or persons from a certain group who may induce him to commit further offences, nor to employ, train or harbour them;

    4.   not to possess, carry or entrust to another for safekeeping, particular objects which could induce him to commit further offences; or

    5.   to meet maintenance obligations.

(3)   A direction

    1.   to undergo medical treatment of an invasive nature or treatment for addiction; or

2. to reside in a suitable home or institution

may only be given with the consent of the convicted person.

(4) If the convicted person gives assurances relating to his future conduct, the court shall typically refrain provisionally from issuing directions if it is to be expected that the assurances will be fulfilled.

§ 56d Supervision order

(1) The court shall place the convicted person under the supervision and guidance of a probation officer for all or part of the operational period if this appears necessary to prevent him from committing offences.
(2) The court shall typically issue an order pursuant to subsection (1) above if it suspends a sentence of imprisonment of more than nine months and the convicted person is less than twenty-seven years of age.
(3) The probation officer shall offer assistance and care to the convicted person. In cooperation with the court he shall supervise the fulfilment of any conditions and directions as well as of any offers and assurances. He shall report on the way the convicted person is conducting himself, at intervals determined by the court. He shall inform the court as to serious or persistent violations of the conditions, directions, offers or assurances.
(4) The probation officer shall be appointed by the court. It may give him instructions concerning his functions under subsection (3) above.
(5) The functions of the probation officer shall be exercised on a full-time official or honorary basis.

§ 56e Subsequent decisions

The court may also make, modify or vacate decisions pursuant to §§ 56b to 56d at a later date.

§ 56f Order for suspended sentence to take effect

(1) The court shall order the suspended sentence to take effect if the convicted person:

1. commits an offence during the operational period showing that the expectation on which the suspension was based, has been disappointed;
2. grossly or persistently violates directions or persistently evades the supervision and guidance of the probation officer, thereby causing reason for fear that he will re-offend; or
3. grossly or persistently violates conditions.

No 1 of the 1st sentence of this subsection shall apply mutatis mutandis if the offence was committed in the interim period between the decision suspending the sentence and its becoming final; it shall also apply in cases of the subsequent fixing of aggregate sentences if the offence was committed in the period between the decision on the suspension of a judgment included in the aggregate sentence and the date when the aggregate sentence became final.

(2) The court shall not order the suspended sentence to take effect if it is of the opinion that it would suffice

1. to impose further conditions or directions, in particular to place the convicted person under the supervision of a probation officer; or

2. to prolong the operational period or period of supervision.

In cases pursuant to No 2 above the operational period must not be prolonged for more than one-half of the originally imposed period.

(3) The convicted person shall not be compensated for services rendered in fulfilment of conditions, offers, directions or assurances. If a suspended sentence is put into effect the court may credit services which the convicted person has rendered in fulfilment of conditions under § 56b(2) 1st sentence Nos 2 to 4, or related offers under § 56b(3) towards the sentence.

§ 56g Remission of sentence

(1) Unless the court orders the suspended sentence to take effect, it shall remit the sentence after expiration of the operational period. § 56f(3) 1st sentence shall apply.

(2) The court may revoke the remission if the convicted person has been sentenced to imprisonment of not less than six months within the Federal Republic of Germany for an intentional offence committed during the operational period. The revocation may only be declared within one year after the expiration of the operational period and six months after the new judgment has become final. § 56f (1) 2nd sentence and (3) shall apply mutatis mutandis.

§ 57 Conditional early release—fixed-term imprisonment

(1) The court shall grant conditional early release from a fixed-term sentence of imprisonment under an operational period of probation, if

1. two thirds of the imposed sentence, but not less than two months, have been served; and

2. the release is appropriate considering public security interests; and

3. the convicted person consents.

The decision shall particularly consider the personality of the convicted person, his previous history, the circumstances of his offence, the importance of the legal interest endangered should he re-offend, the conduct of the convicted person while serving his sentence, his circumstances and the effects an early release are to be expected to have on him.

(2) After one half of a fixed-term sentence of imprisonment, but not less than six months, have been served, the court may grant conditional early release, if

1. the convicted person is serving his first sentence of imprisonment, the term not exceeding two years; or
2. a comprehensive evaluation of the offence, the personality of the convicted person and his development while in custody warrant the acceptance of special circumstances,

and the remaining requirements of subsection (1) above have been fulfilled.

(3) §§ 56a to 56g shall apply mutatis mutandis; the operational period, even if subsequently reduced, must not be less than the remainder of the sentence. If the convicted person has served at least one year of his sentence before conditional early release is granted the court shall typically place him under the supervision and guidance of a probation officer for all or a part of the operational period.

(4) To the extent a sentence of imprisonment has been reduced through credit for time served it shall be deemed as having been served within the meaning of subsections (1) to (3) above.

(5) § 56f and § 56g shall apply mutatis mutandis. The court shall also revoke the early release if the convicted person, in the period between his conviction and the decision about the early release, has committed an offence which could for factual reasons not be taken into account by the court when deciding on the early release and which would have led to a denial of early release, had it been known at that time; the conviction shall be the judgment in those proceedings in which the underlying factual findings could last have been examined.

(6) The court may deny early release from a fixed-term sentence of imprisonment, if the convicted person makes insufficient or false statements concerning the whereabouts of objects which are subject to confiscation or are not subject thereto only because the offence has given rise to a claim by the victim under § 73(1) 2nd sentence.

(7) The court may fix a term not exceeding six months before the expiry of which an application by the convicted person for early release shall be inadmissible.

§ 57a Conditional early release—life imprisonment

(1) The court shall grant conditional early release from a sentence of imprisonment for life under an operational period of probation, if

1. fifteen years of the sentence have been served;
2. the particular seriousness of the convicted person's guilt does not require its continued enforcement; and
3. the requirements of § 57(1) 1st sentence Nos 1 and 3 are met.

§ 57(1) 2nd sentence and (6) shall apply mutatis mutandis.

(2) Any detention suffered by the convicted person as a result of the offence shall qualify as a sentence within the meaning of subsection (1) 1st sentence No 1 above.

(3) The operational period shall be five years. § 56a(2) 1st sentence, §§ 56b to 56g and § 57(3) 2nd sentence and (5) 2nd sentence shall apply mutatis mutandis.

(4) The court may fix terms not exceeding two years, before the expiration of which an application by the convicted person for early release shall be inadmissible.

§ 57b Conditional early release—life imprisonment as aggregate sentence

If imprisonment for life has been imposed as an aggregate sentence the individual offences shall be comprehensively evaluated in determining the particular seriousness of the guilt (§ 57a(1) 1st sentence No 2).

§ 58 Aggregate sentence and suspension of sentence

(1) If a person has committed more than one offence the length of the aggregate sentence shall be dispositive for a suspension under § 56.

(2) If in cases under § 55(1) the previous sentence had been suspended or early release from it granted and if the aggregate sentence has also been suspended, the minimum of the new operational period shall be reduced by any operational period already expired, but not to less than one year. If the aggregate sentence is not suspended § 56f(3) shall apply mutatis mutandis.

FIFTH TITLE
WARNING COMBINED WITH DEFERMENT OF SENTENCE; DISCHARGE

§ 59 Conditions for warning and deferment

(1) If a person has incurred a fine of not more than one hundred and eighty daily units, the court may warn him at the time of conviction, indicate the sentence and defer its imposition if

  1. it can be expected that the offender will commit no further offences without the immediate imposition of the sentence;
  2. a comprehensive evaluation of the offence and the personality of the offender warrant the existence of special circumstances which obviate the imposition of a sentence; and
  3. reasons of general deterrence do not demand the imposition of a sentence.

§ 56(1) 2nd sentence shall apply mutatis mutandis.

(2) Ancillary orders for confiscation, deprivation or destruction may be imposed in addition to a warning. A warning with deferment shall not be considered alongside measures of rehabilitation and incapacitation.

§ 59a Operational period, conditions and directions

(1) The court shall determine the length of the operational period. It may not exceed two years nor be less than one year.
(2) The court may direct the convicted person

   1. to make efforts at reconciliation with the victim or otherwise make restitution for the harm caused by the offence;
   2. to meet his maintenance obligations;
   3. to pay a sum of money to a charitable organisation or the public treasury;
   4. to undergo outpatient medical treatment or outpatient treatment for addiction; or
   5. to participate in road traffic training.

   No unreasonable demands should be imposed on the convicted person's lifestyle; the conditions and directions under the 1st sentence of this subsection Nos 3 to 5 must not be disproportionate to the significance of the offence committed by the convicted person. § 56c(3) and (4) and § 56e shall apply mutatis mutandis.

§ 59b Order for deferred sentence to take effect

(1) § 56f shall apply mutatis mutandis to the order for the deferred sentence to take effect.
(2) If the deferred sentence is not brought into effect the court shall, upon expiry of the operational period, declare that no further action will be taken.

§ 59c Warning and deferment in cases of aggregate sentences

(1) If a person has committed more than one offence §§ 53 to 55 shall apply mutatis mutandis to the calculation of the sentence to be deferred.
(2) If the convicted person is subsequently sentenced to a fine or term of imprisonment for an offence committed before the warning was given, the provisions for fixing an aggregate sentence (§§ 53 to 55, § 58) shall apply, the deferred sentence shall, for the purposes of § 55, be equal to an immediate sentence.

§ 60 Discharge

The court may order a discharge if the consequences of the offence suffered by the offender are so serious that an imposition of penalties would be clearly inappropriate. This shall not apply if the offender has incurred a sentence of imprisonment of more than one year for the offence.

SIXTH TITLE
MEASURES OF REHABILITATION AND INCAPACITATION

§ 61 Overview

The measures of rehabilitation and incapacitation are

1. mental hospital orders;
2. custodial addiction treatment orders;
3. detention for the purpose of incapacitation;
4. supervision orders;
5. disqualification from driving;
6. disqualification from exercising a profession.

§ 62 Principle of proportionality

A measure of rehabilitation and incapacitation must not be ordered if its use is disproportionate to the seriousness of the offence committed by or expected to be committed by the convicted person and to the degree of danger he poses to society.

—Custodial measures—

§ 63 Mental hospital order

If a person has committed an unlawful act in a state of insanity (§ 20) or diminished responsibility (§ 21) the court shall make a mental hospital order if a comprehensive evaluation of the offender and the act leads to the conclusion that as a result of his condition, future serious unlawful acts can be expected of him and that he therefore presents a danger to the general public.

§ 64 Custodial addiction treatment order

If a person has an addiction to alcohol or other drugs and is convicted of an unlawful act committed while he was intoxicated or as a result of his addiction, or is not convicted only because he has been found to be insane or insanity cannot be excluded on the evidence, the court shall make a custodial addiction treatment order if there is a danger that he will commit future serious unlawful acts as a consequence of his addiction.

Such order shall not be made unless ab initio there is a sufficiently certain prospect of success that the person can be healed by way of custodial addiction treatment or that a relapse into addictive behaviour and the commission of serious unlawful acts caused by that addiction can be prevented for a substantial period of time.

§ 65 (repealed)

§ 66 Detention for the purpose of incapacitation

(1) If a person has been sentenced for an intentional offence to a term of imprisonment of not less than two years, the court shall make an incapacitation order in addition to the term of imprisonment if

　　1. the convicted person has already been sentenced twice, each time to a term of imprisonment of not less than one year for intentional offences which he committed prior to the offence now at trial;
　　2. as a result of one or more of these prior offences he has served a term of imprisonment or detention under a measure of rehabilitation and incapacitation for a total term of not less than two years; and
　　3. a comprehensive evaluation of the convicted person and his offences reveals that, due to his propensity to commit serious offences, particularly of a kind resulting in serious emotional trauma or physical injury to the victim or serious economic damage, he poses a danger to the general public.

(2) If a person has committed three intentional offences for each of which he incurred a sentence of imprisonment of not less than one year and has been sentenced to a term of imprisonment of not less than three years for one or more of these offences, the court may, under the conditions indicated in subsection (1) No 3 above, make an incapacitation order in addition to the sentence of imprisonment notwithstanding that there was no prior detention (subsection (1) Nos 1 and 2 above).

(3) If a person is sentenced to a term of imprisonment of at least two years for a felony or an offence under §§ 174 to 174c, § 176, § 179(1) to (4), § 180, § 182, § 224, § 225(1) or (2), or § 323a as long as the act committed while intoxicated is a felony or one of the aforementioned offences, the court may make an incapacitation order in addition to the sentence if the offender had already been sentenced to imprisonment of at least three years for one or more of those offences committed prior to the new offence, and if the requirements indicated in subsection (1) Nos 2 and 3 above are fulfilled. If a person has committed two of the offences listed in the 1st sentence of this subsection for each of which he has incurred a sentence of imprisonment of not less than two years and if he is sentenced for one or more of these offences to a term of imprisonment of not less than three years, the court may, under the conditions indicated in subsection (1) No 3 above, make an incapacitation order in addition to the sentence even in the absence of a prior sentence of imprisonment or detention (subsection (1) Nos 1 and 2). Subsections (1) and (2) above shall remain unaffected.

(4) Within the meaning of subsection (1) No 1 above an aggregate sentence shall be deemed a single sentence. If time spent in custody on remand or other detention is credited against any term of imprisonment it shall be deemed as

time served for the purposes of subsection (1) No 2 above. A previous offence shall not be considered if a period of more than five years has passed between its commission and the subsequent offence. Any term during which the convicted person was kept in detention by order of a public authority shall not be included in that period. An offence adjudicated abroad shall be equivalent to an offence adjudicated in the Federal Republic of Germany as long as it would be an intentional offence under German criminal law, or, in cases under subsection (3) above, it would be one of the offences listed in subsection (3) 1st sentence above.

§ 66a Deferred incapacitation order

(1) If on conviction for one of the offences listed in § 66(3) 1st sentence it cannot be established with sufficient certainty whether the convicted person presents a danger to the general public within the meaning of § 66(1) No 3, the court may make a deferred incapacitation order if the remaining conditions of § 66(3) are fulfilled.

(2) The court shall decide on making an incapacitation order no later than six months before the date when the convicted person becomes eligible for early conditional release under § 57(1) No 1, § 57a(1) 1st sentence No 1, also in conjunction with § 454b(3) of the Code of Criminal Procedure. It shall make the order if a comprehensive evaluation of the person, his offences and his development in custody indicate that he is likely to commit serious offences resulting in serious emotional trauma or physical injury to the victims.

(3) Any decision regarding early conditional release must not be made before the decision under subsection (2) 1st sentence above has become final. This does not apply in cases where the conditions of § 57(2) No 2 are clearly not met.

§ 66b Subsequent incapacitation order

(1) If prior to the end of a term of imprisonment imposed on conviction for a felony against life and limb, personal freedom or sexual self-determination, or a felony pursuant to § 250 and § 251, also in conjunction with § 252 or § 255, or for one of the misdemeanours in § 66(3) 1st sentence, evidence comes to light which indicates that the convicted person presents a significant danger to the general public, the court may subsequently make an incapacitation order if a comprehensive evaluation of the convicted person, his offences and his development in custody indicate a high likelihood of his committing serious offences resulting in seriously emotional trauma or physical injury to the victim and if the remaining conditions in § 66 are fulfilled. If making the order at the time of conviction was impossible under law, the court shall, for the purpose of the 1st sentence of this subsection, also take into account any facts that were already evident at that time.

(2) If evidence of facts of the kind listed in subsection (1) above comes to light after a sentence of imprisonment of a term of not less than five years has been imposed for one or more felonies against life or limb, personal freedom, sexual self-determination or pursuant to § 250 and § 251, also in conjunction with § 252 or § 255, the court may subsequently make an incapacitation order if a comprehensive evaluation of the convicted person, his offence or offences and his development in custody indicate a high likelihood that he will commit serious offences resulting in serious emotional trauma or physical injury to the victims.

(3) If pursuant to § 67d(6) a mental hospital order has been declared moot because the condition causing insanity or diminished responsibility on which the order was based did not exist at the time of that declaration, the court may subsequently make an incapacitation order

1. if the mental hospital order pursuant to § 63 was made based upon more than one of the offences set forth in § 66(3) 1st sentence or if the person had either previously been sentenced to a term of imprisonment of not less than three years or had a mental hospital order made against him because of one or more such offences having been committed by him prior to the offence leading to the mental hospital order pursuant to § 63, and

2. if a comprehensive evaluation of the person, his offences and his development during detention under the measure indicate a high likelihood of his committing serious offences resulting in serious emotional trauma or physical injury to the victims.

§ 67 Sequence of enforcement

(1) If custodial orders for measures under § 63 and § 64 are made in addition to a sentence of imprisonment, the measures shall be served before the sentence of imprisonment.

(2) The court shall order that all or part of the sentence be served before the measure, if the purpose of the measure will thereby be better facilitated. When making an order for custodial addiction treatment in addition to a term of imprisonment of not less than three years the court shall order that a part of the sentence shall be served before the measure. That part of the sentence is to be calculated in a manner that enables a decision under subsection (5) 1st sentence below to be made after the part of the sentence and the measure have been served. The court shall determine that the sentence shall be served before the measure if the convicted person is obliged to leave and may be deported from the Federal Republic of Germany and if there is reason to believe that his residence within Germany will be terminated during the sentence or immediately after the sentence will have been served.

(3) The court may subsequently make, modify or vacate an order pursuant to subsection (2) 1st or 2nd sentences above, if deemed appropriate based on the circumstances of the convicted person.

(4)   If the measure is served in whole or in part before the sentence, any time spent serving the measure shall be credited against the sentence up to a maximum of two thirds of the term of imprisonment.

(5)   If the measure is served before the sentence or a remainder of the sentence the court may grant early conditional release under § 57(1) 1st and 2nd sentences if half of the sentence has been served. If early release is not granted the measure shall continue; the court may order that the sentence be served instead if deemed appropriate based on the circumstances of the convicted person.

§ 67a Transfer to another measure

(1)   If a mental hospital order or a custodial addiction treatment order have been made the court may subsequently transfer the convicted person to serve the other of those measures if this would improve the chances of re-socialisation of the convicted person.

(2)   Under the condition of subsection (1) above the court may subsequently transfer a person subject to an incapacitation order to one of the measures listed in subsection (1). This applies also if the person is still serving a sentence of imprisonment and the conditions of § 20 or § 21 are met by that person.

(3)   The court may modify or vacate a decision under subsections (1) and (2) above, if there is reason to believe that this would improve the chances of resocialisation of the person. The court may further vacate a decision under subsection (2), if there is reason to believe that serving the measures named in subsection (1) will not lead to the desired result.

(4)   The length of the terms for serving a measure and the periods of review shall be the same that apply for an order made in a judgment. In the case of subsection (2) above the court shall review for the first time after one year, and in the case of the 2nd sentence, before the measure is implemented, within regular intervals of no more than two years, whether the conditions for a decision under subsection (3) 2nd sentence above are met.

§ 67b Immediate order for suspended measure

(1)   If the court makes a mental hospital order or a custodial addiction treatment order it shall suspend the measure for an operational probationary period if special circumstances justify the expectation that the purpose of the measure may be achieved in this manner. A suspension shall not be ordered if the person is to serve a sentence of imprisonment imposed at the same time as the measure and which has not been suspended.

(2)   The order for suspension shall automatically lead to the person being subjected to supervision.

§ 67c Deferred start date of detention

(1) If a sentence of imprisonment is served prior to a custodial measure ordered at the same time, the court shall review, before the sentence has been served, whether the purpose of the measure still requires its enforcement. If it does not, the court shall suspend the measure for an operational probationary period; the order for suspension shall automatically lead to the person being subject to supervision.

(2) If the custodial measure has not commenced within a period of three years of its order becoming final, and unless a case of subsection (1) above or § 67b exists, the measure must not be enforced unless the court so orders. Time spent by the convicted person in detention by order of a public authority shall not be credited to the period. The court shall order its enforcement if the purpose of the measure still so requires. If the purpose of the measure has not been achieved, yet special circumstances justify the expectation that it may be achieved by a suspension order, the court shall suspend the measure for an operational probationary period; the order for suspension shall automatically lead to the person being subjected to supervision. If the purpose of the measure has been achieved, the court shall declare it terminated.

§ 67d Duration of detention

(1) Detention under a custodial addiction treatment order may not exceed a period of two years. This term shall run from the commencement of the detention. If a custodial measure is enforced before a sentence of imprisonment imposed at the same time, the maximum period shall be extended by the length of the term of imprisonment to the extent the time spent in the measure is credited towards the sentence.

(2) If no maximum period has been provided or the period has not yet expired, the court shall suspend the measure for an operational probationary period if it can be expected that the person subject to the measure will not commit any more unlawful acts if released. The order for suspension shall automatically lead to the person being subjected to supervision.

(3) If ten years of an incapacitation order have been served, the court shall declare the measure terminated and order the release if there is no danger that the person under placement will, due to his propensity, commit serious offences resulting in serious emotional trauma or physical injury to the victims. The order for release shall automatically lead to the person being subject to supervision.

(4) If the maximum period has expired the person shall be released. The measure shall thereby be terminated. The release shall automatically lead to the person being subject to supervision.

(5) The court shall declare the custodial addiction treatment order terminated if the conditions of § 64 no longer exist. The release shall automatically lead to the person being subject to supervision.

(6) If, after the enforcement of a mental hospital order has begun, the court finds that the conditions for the measure no longer exist or that the continued enforcement of the measure would be disproportionate, the court shall declare it terminated. The release shall automatically lead to the person being subjected to supervision. The court shall waive supervision if it can be expected that the person will not commit any further offences without it.

§ 67e Review

(1) The court may review at any time whether the further enforcement of the custodial measure should be suspended or the measure be declared terminated. It must perform the review within specified periods.

(2) The specified periods shall be

> six months for a custodial addiction treatment order;
> one year for a mental hospital order;
> two years for incapacitation orders.

(3) The court may reduce the period. It may also set dates within the statutory limits for review before the expiration of which an application for review shall be inadmissible.

(4) The period shall run from the commencement of the detention. If the court denies suspension or termination the period shall commence anew with that decision.

§ 67f Multiple orders

If the court makes a custodial addiction treatment order any previous such order shall be deemed to be terminated.

§ 67g Revocation of suspended measure

(1) The court shall revoke the suspension of a custodial measure if the convicted person

1. commits an unlawful act during the period of supervision;
2. grossly and persistently violates directions under § 68b; or
3. persistently evades the supervision and guidance of the probation officer or the supervision authority

and there is reason to believe that the purpose of the measure requires his detention. The 1st sentence above shall apply mutatis mutandis if the reason for revocation arose between the decision on suspension and the start of the supervision (§ 68c(4)).

(2) The court shall also revoke the suspension of a measure pursuant to § 63 and § 64 if there is evidence during the operational period of the supervision that unlawful acts are to be expected from the convicted person as a result of his condition and the purpose of the measure requires his detention.

(3) The court shall further revoke the suspension if evidence, which has come to its attention during the period of the supervision and which would have led to the suspension being denied, shows that the purpose of the measure requires the detention of the convicted person.

(4) The period of detention before and after the revocation must not in its totality exceed the maximum statutory period for the measure.

(5) If the court does not revoke the suspension of the measure the measure shall be deemed terminated at the conclusion of the operational period of supervision.

(6) Services which the convicted person has rendered in fulfilment of directions shall not be reimbursed.

§ 67h Limited order for measure taking effect; crisis intervention

(1) During the period of supervision the court may make an order that the suspended measure under § 63 or § 64 take effect for a duration of not more than three months if there has been an acute deterioration of the state of the released person or a relapse into his addictive behaviour and if the measure is necessary in order to avoid a revocation under § 67g. Under the conditions of the 1st sentence above it may order the renewal of the measure or extend its duration; the maximum duration of the measure must not exceed a total of six months. § 67g shall apply mutatis mutandis.

(2) The court shall vacate the measure before the expiry of the period set pursuant to subsection (1) above if its purpose has been achieved.

—Supervision—

§ 68 Conditions of supervision

(1) If a person has incurred a fixed-term sentence of imprisonment of not less than six months for an offence in relation to which the law specifically provides for the availability of a supervision order, the court may make such an order in addition to the sentence if there is a danger that the person will commit further offences.

(2) The statutory provisions providing for supervision (§ 67b, § 67c, 67d(2) to (6) and § 68f) remain unaffected.

§ 68a Supervising authority, probation support, forensic ambulance service

(1) The convicted person shall be assigned to a supervising authority; the court shall appoint a probation officer to support him for the period of supervision.

(2) The probation officer and supervising authority shall act together to assist and offer care to the convicted person.

(3) The supervising authority shall supervise the conduct of the convicted person and the fulfilment of the directions in cooperation with the court and with the support of the probation officer.

(4) If there is disagreement between the supervising authority and the probation officer as to questions which affect assistance and care for the convicted person the court shall resolve the matter.

(5) The court may give instructions to the supervising authority and the probation officer concerning their functions.

(6) Before filing a request to prosecute under § 145a 2nd sentence the supervising authority shall hear the probation officer; subsection (4) above does not apply.

(7) If a direction pursuant to § 68b(2) 2nd and 3rd sentences has been ordered, the forensic ambulance service shall work together with the parties mentioned in subsection (2) above. Subsections (3) and (6) above on the position of the probation officer above shall apply mutatis mutandis to the forensic ambulance service.

(8) The parties mentioned in subsection (1) above and the staff of the forensic ambulance service mentioned in § 203(1) Nos 1, 2 and 5 shall disclose third party secrets to each other which have come to their attention in the course of their activities within the relationship mentioned in § 203 or otherwise, to the extent that this is necessary to support the convicted person in avoiding the commission of future offences. Moreover, the staff of the forensic ambulance service mentioned in § 203(1) Nos 1, 2 and 5 shall disclose such secrets to the supervising authority and the court, if in their opinion

1. this is necessary for the purpose of ensuring that the convicted person adheres to a direction under § 68b(1) 1st sentence No 11 to present himself at certain intervals, or that he participates, within the remit of a direction under § 68b(2) 2nd and 3rd sentences, in treatment,

2. the conduct of the convicted person gives reason to believe that measures under § 67g, § 67h or § 68c(2) or (3) are necessary, or

3. if this is necessary to avert a serious and present danger to life and limb, personal freedom or the sexual self-determination of third parties.

In cases under the 1st sentence and the 2nd sentence Nos 2 and 3 of this subsection, information within the meaning of § 203(1) disclosed by staff of the forensic ambulance service may only be used for the purposes mentioned therein.

§ 68b Directions

(1) The court may, for the duration of the supervision or for a shorter period, direct the convicted person

1. not to leave his place of domicile or his residence or a specified area without the permission of the supervising authority;

2. not to frequent specified places which may induce him to commit further offences;

3. not to make or maintain contact with the victim, or certain persons or persons from a certain group who may induce him to commit further offences, nor to employ, train or harbour them;
4. not to engage in particular activities which in certain circumstances may be exploited for criminal purposes;
5. not to possess, carry or entrust to another for safekeeping particular objects which could induce him to commit further offences;
6. not to possess or drive motor-vehicles or particular types of motor-vehicles or other vehicles, which in certain circumstances may be misused by him for criminal purposes;
7. to report at particular times to the supervising authority, to another public authority or to the probation officer;
8. to report promptly every change of residence or employment to the supervising authority;
9. to report in the case of unemployment to the Public Employment Agency or to another authorised employment agency;
10. not to consume alcohol or other drugs, if based on certain information there is reason to believe that their consumption will contribute to the commission of future offences, and to undergo alcohol and drug tests of a non-invasive nature; or
11. to present himself at certain times or at certain intervals to a doctor, a psychotherapist or the forensic ambulance service.

The court shall indicate the prohibited or required conduct as precisely as possible in its directions.

(2) The court may, for the duration of the supervision or for a shorter period, give directions to the convicted person, particularly in relation to education, employment, leisure, ordering of financial affairs, or the fulfilment of maintenance obligations. The court may direct the convicted person to undergo psychiatric, psycho—or sociotherapy (therapy direction). § 56c(3) shall apply mutatis mutandis, also for the direction to undergo invasive alcohol or drug tests.

(3) No unreasonable demands may be made in the directions on the lifestyle of the convicted person.

(4) If by the commencement of a supervision period an already existing state of supervision is deemed terminated pursuant to § 68e(1) 1st sentence No 3, the court shall include the directions issued under the previous supervision in its own order.

(5) To the extent that the supervision of a convicted person in the cases of subsection (1) No 11 above or his treatment under subsection(2) above is not carried out by a forensic ambulance service §68a(8) shall apply mutatis mutandis.

§ 68c Duration

(1) The period of supervision shall last no less than two and no more than five years. The court may reduce the maximum duration.

(2) The court may make an indeterminate supervision order exceeding the maximum in subsection (1) 1st sentence above if the convicted person

    1.   does not consent to a direction under § 56c(3) No 1; or

    2.   does not comply with a direction to undergo medical treatment or addiction treatment or a therapy direction

and if a danger to the general public through the commission of further serious offences is to be expected. If the convicted person subsequently consents, the court shall fix the further duration of the supervision. § 68e(3) shall apply.

(3) The court may make an indeterminate supervision order exceeding the maximum in subsection (1) 1st sentence above if

    1.   in the case of a suspended mental hospital order under § 67d(2) there is reason to believe that the convicted person is otherwise about to lapse into a state under § 20 or § 21 resulting in a danger to the general public by the commission of further serious unlawful acts, or

    2.   the convicted person has, for an offence listed under § 181b, been sentenced to a single or aggregate term of imprisonment of not less than two years or a mental hospital order or a custodial addiction treatment order and if the violation of directions under § 68b(1) or (2) or other facts give reason to believe that there may be a danger to the general public by the commission of further serious unlawful acts.

(4) In the case of § 68b(1) supervision shall commence when the order becomes final; in the cases of § 67b(2), § 67c(1) 2nd sentence and (2) 4th sentence and of § 67d(2) 2nd sentence it shall commence when the suspension order becomes final or at a later date as specified by the court. Any time during which the person was a fugitive, was hiding, or was kept in detention by order of a public authority shall not be credited against its duration.

§ 68d Subsequent decisions

The court may subsequently make, modify or vacate decisions pursuant to § 68a(1) and (5), § 68b, § 68c(1) 2nd sentence, (2) and (3).

§ 68e Termination or stay of supervision

(1) Unless the supervision order is indeterminate, the supervision ends

    1.   with the commencement of a custodial measure,

    2.   with the commencement of a sentence of imprisonment, in addition to which a custodial measure has been ordered,

    3.   with the commencement of a new supervision.

In all other cases the supervision shall be stayed for the time a person serves a sentence of imprisonment or a custodial measure. If a new supervision is added to an already existing indeterminate supervision, the court shall order the cessation of the new measure if it is not necessary in view of the existing one.

(2) The court shall terminate the supervision if there is reason to believe that the person will not commit any further offences without it. The termination must not be ordered before the expiry of the statutory minimum period. The court may set periods of not more than six months before the expiry of which an application for termination of supervision is inadmissible.

(3) In the case of indeterminate supervision, the court shall

1. in the case of § 68c(2) 1st sentence no later than after expiry of the maximum period under § 68c(1) 1st sentence,
2. in the case of § 68c(3) before the expiry of two years,

review whether a decision under subsection (2) 1st sentence above is appropriate. If the court denies the termination of supervision, it shall review the case before the expiry of a further two years.

§ 68f Supervision after serving full sentence

(1) If a single or aggregate sentence of imprisonment of not less than two years has been imposed for intentional offences, or not less than one year for an offence listed in § 181b, has been fully served, supervision shall commence upon the release of the convicted person. This shall not apply if a custodial measure of rehabilitation and incapacitation is enforced immediately afterwards.

(2) The court may waive supervision if there is reason to believe that the convicted person will not commit further offences without supervision.

§ 68g Supervision coinciding with suspended sentence, conditional early release or suspended professional disqualification order

(1) If a suspended sentence, conditional early release or a suspension of the professional disqualification has been ordered and if the convicted person is at the same time under supervision for the same or another offence, only § 68a and § 68b shall apply in relation to supervision and directions. Supervision shall not cease before the expiry of any operational period.

(2) If the suspended sentence, conditional early release and the supervision have been ordered on the basis of the same offence, the court may determine that the supervision shall be stayed until the expiry of any operational period. In this case the operational period shall not be credited towards the period of supervision.

(3) If after the expiry of the operational period the sentence or the remainder thereof is remitted or the professional disqualification declared terminated,

supervision ordered because of the same offence shall cease at the same time, unless the supervision is indeterminate (§ 68c(2) 1st sentence or (3)).

—Disqualification from driving—

§ 69 Disqualification order

(1) If a person has been convicted of an unlawful act he committed in connection with the driving of a motor-vehicle or in violation of the duties of the driver of a motor-vehicle, or has not been convicted merely because he was proven to have acted in a state of insanity or his having so acted could not be excluded, the court shall make a driving disqualification order if the act shows that he is unfit to drive a motor-vehicle. A further examination pursuant to § 62 shall not be required.

(2) If the unlawful act under subsection (1) above is one of the following misdemeanours:

    1. endangering road traffic (§ 315c);
    2. driving while under the influence of alcohol or drugs (§ 316);
    3. leaving the scene of an accident without cause (§ 142) although the offender knows or should have known that a person was killed, seriously injured or significant damage to the property of another was caused in the accident; or
    4. committing offences in a senselessly drunken state (§ 323a), if the offence committed is one of the offences in Nos 1 to 3

the person shall typically be deemed unfit to drive motor-vehicles.

(3) The driving licence shall cease when the judgment becomes final. A driving licence issued by a German public authority shall be subject to a deprivation order in the judgment.

§ 69a Order for period before new licence may be issued

(1) If the court makes a disqualification order it shall at the same time order that no new driving licence shall be issued for a period from six months to five years (ban). The court may order a permanent ban if there is reason to believe that the statutory maximum period will not suffice to avert the danger posed by the offender. If the offender has no driving licence only a ban shall be imposed.

(2) The court may exempt particular types of motor-vehicles from the ban if special circumstances justify the assumption that the purpose of the measure will not be put at risk.

(3) The minimum ban shall be for a period of one year if during the last three years before the offence a ban had been ordered against the offender.

(4) If the offender's driving licence had been provisionally seized because of the offence (§ 111a of the Code of Criminal Procedure), the minimum ban shall

be reduced by the time during which the provisional deprivation was in effect. In no case shall the ban be less than three months.

(5) The ban shall commence when the judgment becomes final. The time of a provisional deprivation ordered because of the offence shall be credited towards the period of the ban to the extent it has run following the date of the judgment in those proceedings in which the factual findings underlying the measure could last have been examined was pronounced.

(6) For the purposes of subsections (4) and (5) above the provisional seizure of a driving licence or its seizure (§ 94 of the Code of Criminal Procedure) shall be equivalent to a provisional disqualification.

(7) If there is reason to believe that the offender is no longer unfit to drive motor-vehicles the court may terminate the ban. This termination may not be ordered unless the ban has been in effect for three months, or a year in cases pursuant to subsection (3) above; subsection (5) 2nd sentence and subsection (6) above shall apply mutatis mutandis.

§ 69b Effect of disqualification in case of foreign licence

(1) If the offender is allowed to drive motor-vehicles in Germany on the basis of a licence granted abroad, without a driving licence having been issued by a German public authority, the disqualification order shall have the effect of a loss of the right to make use of the licence in Germany. The right to drive motor-vehicles in Germany ceases when the decision becomes final. For the duration of the ban neither a German licence may be issued nor the right to make use of the foreign licence be reinstated.

(2) If the foreign driving licence was issued by a public authority of a member state of the European Union or another signatory state of the Treaty on the European Economic Area and the holder has his domicile in Germany the driving licence shall be ordered confiscated in the judgment and sent back to the issuing authority. In all other cases the loss of the right to drive and the ban shall be endorsed on the foreign driving licences.

—Disqualification from exercising a profession—

§ 70 Order for professional disqualification

(1) If a person has been convicted of an unlawful act he committed in abuse of his profession or trade or in gross violation of the attendant duties, or has not been convicted merely because he was proven to have acted in a state of insanity or his having so acted could not be excluded the court may make an order disqualifying him from engaging in that profession, branch of profession, trade or branch of trade, for a period from one year to five years, if a comprehensive evaluation of the offender and the offence shows that by further engagement in the profession, branch of profession, trade or branch of trade there is a danger that he will commit serious unlawful acts of the kind

indicated above. The disqualification order may be made in permanence if there is reason to believe that the statutory maximum period will not suffice to avert the danger posed by the offender.

(2) If the offender had been provisionally disqualified from engaging in a profession, branch of profession, trade or branch of trade (§ 132a of the Code of Criminal Procedure), the minimum term of disqualification shall be reduced by the time during which the provisional disqualification was in effect. In no case may it be less than three months.

(3) For the duration of the disqualification the offender must neither engage in the profession, branch of profession, trade or branch of trade on behalf of another nor have a person who is subject to his instructions engage in it on his behalf.

(4) The disqualification shall commence when the judgment becomes final. Any period of a provisional disqualification imposed because of the act shall be credited to the disqualification period to the extent it has run following the date of the judgment in those proceedings in which the factual findings underlying the measure could last have been examined was pronounced. Any period during which the offender was kept in detention by order of a public authority shall not be so credited.

§ 70a Order suspending professional disqualification

(1) If, after a disqualification order has been made, there is reason to believe that there is no longer a danger that the offender will commit serious unlawful acts of the kind mentioned in § 70(1) the court may suspend the order for a probationary operational period.

(2) The order must not be made before the expiry of one year. Any time of a provisional disqualification shall be credited to the period of disqualification under § 70(4) 2nd sentence. Any period during which the offender was kept in detention by order of a public authority shall not be so credited.

(3) If the disqualification order is suspended, § 56a and §§ 56c to 56e shall apply mutatis mutandis. The operational period shall be extended by any time during which a sentence of imprisonment or a custodial measure, which was imposed on or ordered against the convicted person because of the offence, was served.

§ 70b Revocation of order

(1) The court shall revoke the suspension of the disqualification order if the convicted person

   1. commits an unlawful act in abuse of his profession or trade or of the attendant duties during the operational period;
   2. grossly or persistently violates a direction; or

3. persistently evades the supervision and guidance of the probation officer

and there is reason to believe that the purpose of the disqualification requires its enforcement.

(2) The court shall further revoke the suspension if evidence, which has come to its attention during the period of the supervision and which would have led to the suspension being denied, shows that the purpose of the measure requires the enforcement of the disqualification.

(3) Any period of the suspension shall not be credited to the period of disqualification.

(4) Services which the convicted person has rendered in fulfilment of directions and assurances shall not be reimbursed.

(5) After the operational period has expired the court shall declare the disqualification terminated.

—Common provisions—

§ 71 Independent orders

(1) The court may make an independent mental hospital order or a custodial addiction treatment order if criminal proceedings are impracticable because the offender is insane or unfit to plead.

(2) The same shall apply to driving and professional disqualification orders.

§ 72 Orders for joint measures

(1) If the conditions for more than one measure are fulfilled but the intended purpose can be achieved through individual orders from among their number, only those individual measures shall be ordered. Priority among a number of suitable measures shall be given to those which pose the least burden on the offender.

(2) In all other cases, measures shall be ordered concurrently unless the law provides otherwise.

(3) If more than one custodial measure is imposed the court shall determine the sequence of their enforcement. Before any measure has been fully served the court shall order the enforcement of the next if its purpose still requires detention. § 67c(2) 4th and 5th sentences shall apply mutatis mutandis.

SEVENTH TITLE
CONFISCATION AND DEPRIVATION ORDERS

§ 73 Conditions of confiscation

(1) If an unlawful act has been committed and the principal or a secondary participant has acquired proceeds from it or obtained anything in order to

commit it, the court shall order the confiscation of what was obtained. This shall not apply to the extent that the act has given rise to a claim of the victim the satisfaction of which would deprive the principal or secondary participant of the value of what has been obtained.

(2)   The order of confiscation shall extend to benefits derived from what was obtained. It may also extend to objects which the principal or secondary participant has acquired by way of sale of the acquired object, as a replacement for its destruction, damage to or forcible loss of it or on the basis of a surrogate right.

(3)   If the principal or secondary participant acted for another and that person acquired anything thereby, the order of confiscation under subsections (1) and (2) above shall be made against him.

(4)   The confiscation of an object shall also be ordered if it is owned or subject to a right by a third party, who furnished it to support the act or with knowledge of the circumstances of the act.

§ 73a Confiscation of monetary value

To the extent that the confiscation of a particular object is impossible due to the nature of what was obtained or for some other reason or because confiscation of a surrogate object pursuant to § 73(2) 2nd sentence has not been ordered, the court shall order the confiscation of a sum of money which corresponds to the value of what was obtained. The court shall also make such an order in addition to the confiscation of an object to the extent that its value falls short of the value of what was originally obtained.

§ 73b Assessment of value

The scope of what was obtained and its value as well as the amount of the victim's claim the satisfaction of which would deprive the principal or secondary participant of that which was obtained may be estimated.

§ 73c Hardship

(1)   Confiscation shall not be ordered to the extent it would constitute an undue hardship for the person affected. The order may be waived to the extent the value of what was obtained is no longer part of the affected person's assets at the time of the order or if what was obtained is only of minor value.

(2)   As to conditions of payment § 42 shall apply mutatis mutandis.

§ 73d Extended confiscation

(1)   If an unlawful act has been committed pursuant to a law which refers to this provision, the court shall also order the confiscation of objects of the principal or secondary participant if the circumstances justify the assumption that these objects were acquired as a result of unlawful acts, or for the purpose of

committing them. The 1st sentence shall also apply if the principal or secondary participant does not own or have a right to the object merely because he acquired the object as a result of an unlawful act or for the purpose of committing it. § 73(2) shall apply mutatis mutandis.

(2) If the confiscation of a particular object has, after the act, become impossible in whole or in part § 73a and § 73b shall apply mutatis mutandis.

(3) If after an order of confiscation pursuant to subsection (1) above, due to another unlawful act which the principal or secondary participant committed before that order, a decision must again be taken as to the confiscation of objects of the principal or secondary participant, the court in doing so shall take into account the previous order.

(4) § 73c shall apply mutatis mutandis.

§ 73e Effect of confiscation

(1) If the confiscation of an object is ordered title to the property or the right confiscated shall pass to the state once the order becomes final if the person affected by the order has a right to it at the time. The rights of third parties in the object remain unaffected.

(2) Prior to its becoming final the order shall have the effect of a prohibition to sell within the meaning of § 136 of the Civil Code; the prohibition shall also cover dispositions other than sales.

§ 74 Conditions of deprivation

(1) If an intentional offence has been committed objects generated by or used or intended for use in its commission or preparation, the court may make a deprivation order.

(2) A deprivation order shall not be admissible unless

1. the principal or secondary participant owns or has a right to the objects at the time of the decision; or
2. the objects, due to their nature and the circumstances, pose a danger to the general public or if there is reason to believe that they will be used for the commission of unlawful acts.

(3) Under the provisions of subsection (2) No 2 above the deprivation of objects shall also be admissible if the offender acted without guilt.

(4) If deprivation is prescribed or permitted by a special provision apart from subsection (1) above, subsections (2) and (3) above shall apply mutatis mutandis.

§ 74a Extended conditions of deprivation

If the law refers to this provision, objects may be subject to a deprivation order as an exception to § 74(2) No 1 if at the time of the decision the person who owns or has a right to them

    1.   at least with gross negligence contributed to the property or the right being the object of or being used for the act or its preparation; or

    2.   acquired the objects dishonestly with knowledge of the circumstances that would have allowed their deprivation.

§ 74b Principle of proportionality

(1)   If deprivation is not otherwise prescribed it may not be ordered in cases under § 74(2) No 1 and § 74a if it is disproportionate to the significance of the act committed and the blameworthiness of the principal or secondary participant or of the third party in cases of § 74a.

(2)   In cases under § 74 and § 74a the court shall defer the deprivation order and impose a less incisive measure if the purpose of a deprivation order can also be attained thus. Particular consideration shall be given to instructions

    1.   to destroy the objects;

    2.   to remove particular fittings or distinguishing marks from or otherwise modify the objects; or

    3.   to dispose of the objects in a specified manner.

If the instructions are carried out the deferment order shall be rescinded; otherwise the court shall subsequently order the deprivation.

(3)   If deprivation is not otherwise proscribed it may be limited to a part of the objects.

§ 74c Deprivation of monetary value

(1)   If the principal or secondary participant has used, particularly disposing of it or consuming it, the object which he owned or had a right to at the time of the offence and which could have been subject to deprivation, or if he has otherwise obstructed the deprivation of the object, the court may order the deprivation from the principal or secondary participant, of a sum of money no greater than the amount equivalent to the value of the object.

(2)   The court may also make such an order in addition to the deprivation of an object or in place thereof, if the principal or secondary participant has, prior to the decision on the deprivation, encumbered it with the right of a third party, the extinguishment of which cannot be ordered without compensation or could not be ordered in the case of deprivation (§ 74e(2) and § 74f); if the court makes the order in addition to the deprivation, then the amount of the surrogate value shall be assessed according to the value of the encumbrance.

(3)   The value of the object and the encumbrance may be estimated.

(4)   As to conditions of payment § 42 shall apply mutatis mutandis.

§ 74d Deprivation and destruction of publication media

(1) Written materials (§ 11(3)) of a content every intentional dissemination of which with knowledge of the content would fulfil the elements of a criminal provision, shall be subject to a deprivation order if at least one copy was disseminated through an unlawful act or was intended for such dissemination. At the same time the equipment used for or intended for the production of the written material, such as plates, frames, type, blocks, negatives or stencils, shall be destroyed.

(2) The deprivation shall extend only to those copies which are in the possession of the persons involved in their dissemination or preparation or which have been publicly displayed or, if they were sent for dissemination, have not yet been distributed to the recipient.

(3) Subsection (1) above shall apply mutatis mutandis to written materials (§ 11(3)) of a content the intentional dissemination of which with knowledge of the content would fulfil the elements of a criminal provision only under additional circumstances. Deprivation and destruction shall not be ordered unless

    1. the copies and the objects indicated in subsection (1) 2nd sentence above are in the possession of the principal or secondary participant or another on whose behalf the principal or secondary participant acted, or are intended by these people for dissemination; and

    2. the measures are required to prevent any unlawful dissemination by these persons.

(4) Dissemination within the meaning of subsections (1) to (3) above shall also mean providing access to written material (§ 11(3)) or at least one copy of it to the public by putting it on display, putting up posters, performances or other means.

(5) § 74b(2) and (3) shall apply mutatis mutandis.

§ 74e Effect of deprivation

(1) If the deprivation of an object is ordered, title to the property or the right ordered deprived shall pass to the state once the order becomes final.

(2) The rights of third parties in the object remain unaffected. The court shall order the cessation of these rights if it bases the deprivation on the fact that the conditions of § 74(2) No 2 are met. It may also order the cessation of the rights of a third party if no compensation is due to him pursuant to § 74f(2) Nos 1 or 2.

(3) § 73e(2) shall apply mutatis mutandis to the order of deprivation and the order deferring deprivation before they have become final.

§ 74f Compensation

(1) If a third party had title to the property or to the right ordered deprived at the time the decision on deprivation or destruction became final or if the object was encumbered by a right of a third party which was extinguished or prejudiced by the decision, the third party shall be adequately compensated in money from the public treasury, taking into consideration the fair market value.

(2) Compensation shall not be granted if

1. the third party at least with gross negligence contributed to the property or the right being the object of or being used for the act or its preparation,
2. the third party acquired the objects or the right dishonestly with knowledge of the circumstances that would have allowed their deprivation, or
3. it would be lawful under the circumstances which justified the deprivation or destruction, to deprive the third party permanently of the object and without compensation on the basis of provisions outside the criminal law.

(3) In cases under subsection (2) above the court may grant compensation to the extent that it would constitute an undue hardship to deny it.

§ 75 Special provision for organs and representatives

If a person commits an act

1. in his capacity as an organ authorised to represent a legal entity or as a member of such an organ;
2. in his capacity as a director or member of board of directors of an association lacking independent legal capacity;
3. as a partner authorised to represent a partnership with independent legal capacity; or
4. as an authorised representative with full power of attorney or in a management position as general agent or authorised representative, with a commercial power of attorney, of a legal entity or association listed in Nos 2 or 3 above; or
5. as another person acting in a responsible capacity for the management of the business or enterprise of a legal entity or association listed in Nos 2 or 3 above, including the supervision of the management of the business, or other exercise of controlling powers in a senior management position,

which in relation to him and under the other conditions of §§ 74 to 74c and § 74f would allow the deprivation of an object or its surrogate value or justify the denial of compensation, his act shall be attributed and these provisions applied to the person or entity represented. § 14(3) shall apply mutatis mutandis.

—Common provisions—

§ 76 Subsequent orders for confiscation or deprivation of monetary value

If an order for confiscation or deprivation of an object is not enforceable or inadequate because after making it one of the conditions indicated in § 73a, § 73d(2), or § 74c has arisen or come to its attention, the court may subsequently order the confiscation or deprivation of the monetary value.

§ 76a Independent orders

(1) If for reasons of fact no person can be prosecuted or convicted of the offence, confiscation or deprivation of the object or the monetary value or destruction must or may be independently ordered if the conditions under which the measure is prescribed or available otherwise are met.

(2) Subsection (1) above shall, under the provisions of § 74(2) No 2, (3) and § 74d, apply if

   1. prosecution of the offence is barred by the statute of limitations; or
   2. for other reasons of law no person may be prosecuted and the law does not provide otherwise.

   Deprivation or destruction must not be ordered in the absence of a request or authorisation to prosecute or a request by a foreign state.

(3) Subsection (1) above shall apply if the court orders a discharge or if the proceedings are terminated pursuant to a provision allowing this in the discretion of either the public prosecution service or the court or with their mutual agreement.

CHAPTER FOUR
REQUEST TO PROSECUTE; AUTHORISATION TO PROSECUTE; REQUEST TO PROSECUTE BY A FOREIGN STATE

§ 77 Locus standi for request

(1) If an offence may only be prosecuted upon a request to prosecute, the victim may file the request unless the law provides otherwise.

(2) If the victim dies, his right to file a request passes, if so provided by law, to his spouse, same sex partner and children. If the victim leaves neither a spouse, same sex partner nor children or if they have died before the expiry of the time limit for filing the request, the right to file the request passes to his parents and, if they have died before the expiry of the time limit for filing the request, to his siblings and grandchildren. If a relative has participated in the

offence or his quality as a relative of the victim has ceased, he is excluded from the list of those to whom the right to file the request may pass. The right to file the request does not pass if a prosecution were to contravene the professed will of the victim.

(3) If the person entitled to file a request lacks legal capacity or has only limited legal capacity, his statutory representative for his personal affairs and the person responsible for the care of the person are entitled to file a request.

(4) If more than one person is entitled to file a request, each may file a request independently.

§ 77a Request by a superior

(1) If the offence has been committed by or against a public official, persons entrusted with special public service functions, or a soldier in the Armed Forces and may be prosecuted upon request by his superior in the public service, the superior under whom the person concerned served at the time of the act is entitled to file the request.

(2) In the case of professional judges the person exercising disciplinary supervision over the judge shall be entitled to file the request in place of the superior in the public service. In the case of soldiers the superior in the public service shall be the disciplinary superior officer.

(3) In the case of a public official or a person entrusted with special public service functions who does not or did not have a superior in the public service, the public authority for which he acted may file the request. If the public official or the entrusted person is the head of this public authority, the state supervisory authority is entitled to file the request.

(4) In the case of members of the Federal Government or members of a state government, the Federal Government and state government, as the case may be, shall be entitled to file the request.

§ 77b Time limit

(1) An offence which may only be prosecuted upon request shall not be prosecuted if the person entitled to file the request fails to do so before the expiry of a three-month period. If the end of the period falls on a Sunday, a general holiday or a Saturday, then the period shall end with the expiry of the next working day.

(2) The period shall commence upon the expiry of the day on which the entitled person acquired knowledge of the offence and the identity of the offender. If the prosecution of the offence is also dependent on a decision as to the nullity or dissolution of a marriage, the period shall not begin before the expiry of the day on which the entitled person acquires knowledge that the decision is final. For a request by the statutory representative or the person responsible for the care of the person, their own knowledge is dispositive.

(3) If more than one person is entitled to file a request or more than one person participated in the offence the period shall run separately for and against each person.

(4) If as a result of the death of the victim the right to file a request has passed to relatives the period shall end no sooner than three months and no later than six months after the death of the victim.

(5) The course of the period shall be stayed if an application has been received by a settlement board to conduct a reconciliation attempt pursuant to § 380 of the Code of Criminal Procedure until the certificate pursuant to § 380(1) 3rd sentence of the Code of Criminal Procedure has been issued.

§ 77c Offences committed mutually

If in the case of offences committed mutually which may only be prosecuted upon request one entitled person has filed a request for the prosecution of the other, the other person's right to file a request ceases if he does not exercise it before the completion of his last word in the trial proceedings at first instance. He may file a request notwithstanding that for him the period for filing it may have expired.

§ 77d Withdrawal of request

(1) The request may be withdrawn. The withdrawal must be declared before the final conclusion of the proceedings. A withdrawn request cannot be filed afresh.

(2) If the victim, or, in the case of his death, the person entitled, dies after he has filed the request, the spouse, the same sex partner, children, parents, siblings or grandchildren of the victim party may withdraw the request in the order of precedence indicated in § 77(2). Several relatives of equal precedence may only exercise the right jointly. A relative who participated in the offence may not withdraw the complaint.

§ 77e Authorisation; request by a foreign state

If the offence may only be prosecuted upon authorisation or upon a request to prosecute by a foreign state, § 77 and § 77d shall apply mutatis mutandis.

CHAPTER FIVE
LIMITATION PERIOD

FIRST TITLE
LIMITATION ON PROSECUTION

§ 78 Limitation period

(1)   The imposition of punishment and measures (§ 11(1) No 8) shall be excluded on expiry of the limitation period. § 76a(2) 1st sentence No 1 remains unaffected.

(2)   Felonies under § 211 (murder under specific aggravating circumstances) are not subject to the statute of limitations.

(3)   To the extent that prosecution is subject to the statute of limitations, the limitation period shall be

1.   thirty years in the case of offences punishable by imprisonment for life;
2.   twenty years in the case of offences punishable by a maximum term of imprisonment of more than ten years;
3.   ten years in the case of offences punishable by a maximum term of imprisonment of more than five years but no more than ten years;
4.   five years in the case of offences punishable by a maximum term of imprisonment of more than one year but no more than five years;
5.   three years in the case of other offences.

(4)   The period shall conform to the penalty provided for in the law defining the elements of the offence, irrespective of aggravating or mitigating circumstances provided for in the provisions of the General Part or of aggravated or privileged offences in the Special Part .

§ 78a Commencement

The limitation period shall commence to run as soon as the offence is completed. If a result constituting an element of the offence occurs later, the limitation period shall commence to run from that time.

§ 78b Stay of limitation

(1)   The limitation period shall be stayed

1.   until the victim of offences under §§ 174 to 174c and §§ 176 to 179 has reached the age of eighteen;
2.   as long as the prosecution may, according to the law, not be commenced or continued; this shall not apply if the act may not be prosecuted only because of the absence of a request or authorisation to prosecute or a request to prosecute by a foreign state.

(2) If a prosecution is not feasible because the offender is a member of the Federal Parliament or a legislative body of a state, the stay of the limitation period shall only commence upon expiry of the day on which

1. the public prosecutor or a public authority or a police officer acquires knowledge of the offence and the identity of the offender; or
2. a criminal complaint or a request to prosecute is filed against the offender (§ 158 of the Code of Criminal Procedure).

(3) If a judgment has been delivered in the proceedings at first instance before the expiry of the limitation period, the limitation period shall not expire before the time the proceedings have been finally concluded.

(4) If the Special Part provides for a sentence of imprisonment of more than five years in aggravated cases and if the trial proceedings have been instituted in the District Court, the statute of limitations shall be stayed in cases under § 78(3) No 4 from the admission of the indictment by the trial court, but no longer than for five years; subsection (3) above remains unaffected.

(5) If the offender resides in a country abroad and if the competent authority makes a formal request for extradition to that state, the limitation period is stayed from the time the request is served on the foreign state,

1. until the surrender of the offender to the German authorities,
2. until the offender otherwise leaves the territory of the foreign state,
3. until the denial of the request by the foreign state is served on the German authorities or
4. until the withdrawal of the request.

If the date of the service of the request upon the foreign state cannot be ascertained, the request shall be deemed to have been served one month after having been sent to the foreign state unless the requesting authority acquires knowledge of the fact that the request was in fact not served on the foreign state or only later. The 1st sentence of this subsection shall not apply to requests for surrender for which, in the requested state, a limitation period similar to § 83c of the Law on International Assistance in Criminal Matters exists, either based on the Framework Decision of the Council of 13 June 2002 on the European Arrest Warrant and the surrender agreements between the member states (OJ L 190, 18.7.2002, p 1), or based on an international treaty.

§ 78c Interruption

(1) The limitation period shall be interrupted by

1. the first interrogation of the accused, notice that investigations have been initiated against him, or the order for such an interrogation or notice thereof;
2. any judicial interrogation of the accused or the order for that purpose;

3. any commissioning of an expert by the judge or public prosecutor if the accused has previously been interrogated or has been given notice of the initiation of investigations;
4. any judicial seizure or search warrant and judicial decisions upholding them;
5. an arrest warrant, a provisional detention order, an order to be brought before a judge for interrogation and judicial decisions upholding them;
6. the preferment of a public indictment;
7. the admission of the indictment by the trial court;
8. any setting of a trial date;
9. a summary judgment order or another decision equivalent to a judgment;
10. the provisional judicial dismissal of the proceedings due to the absence of the indicted accused as well as any order of the judge or public prosecutor issued after such a dismissal of the proceedings or in proceedings in absentia in order to ascertain the whereabouts of the indicted accused or to secure evidence;
11. the provisional judicial dismissal of the proceedings due to the unfitness to plead of the indicted and any order of the judge or public prosecutor issued after such a dismissal of the proceedings for the purposes of reviewing the fitness of the indicted accused to plead; or
12. any judicial request to undertake an investigative act abroad.

In separate proceedings for measures of rehabilitation and incapacitation and in an independent proceeding for deprivation or confiscation, the limitation period shall be interrupted by acts in these proceedings corresponding to those in the 1st sentence of this subsection.

(2) The limitation period shall be interrupted by a written order or decision at the time at which the order or decision is signed. If the document is not immediately processed after signing the time it is actually submitted for processing shall be dispositive.

(3) After each interruption the limitation period shall commence to run anew. The prosecution shall be barred by limitation once twice the statutory limitation period has elapsed since the time indicated in § 78a, or three years if the limitation period is shorter than three years. § 78b shall remain unaffected.

(4) The interruption shall have effect only for the person in relation to whom the interrupting act is done.

(5) If a law which applies at the time the offence is completed is amended before a decision and the limitation period is thereby shortened, acts leading to an interruption which have been undertaken before the entry into force of the new law shall retain their effect, notwithstanding that at the time of the interruption the prosecution would have been barred by the statute of limitations under the amended law.

SECOND TITLE
LIMITATION ON ENFORCEMENT

§ 79 Limitation period

(1) Any imposed penalty or measure (§ 11(1) No 8) which has become final may no longer be enforced after the expiry of the limitation period.

(2) The enforcement of sentences of imprisonment for life is not subject to a statute of limitations.

(3) The limitation period shall be

   1. twenty-five years for a term of imprisonment of more than ten years;
   2. twenty years for a term of imprisonment of more than five years but not more than ten years;
   3. ten years for a term of imprisonment of more than one year but not more than five years;
   4. five years for a term of imprisonment of not more than one year and fines of more than thirty daily units;
   5. three years for fines of not more than thirty daily units.

(4) The enforcement of an incapacitation order and of an indeterminate supervision order (§ 68c(2) 1st sentence or (3)) shall not be subject to a statute of limitations. The limitation period shall be

   1. five years in all other cases of supervision orders and the first custodial addiction treatment order,
   2. ten years for all other measures.

(5) If a sentence of imprisonment and a fine are imposed at the same time, or if in addition to a sentence a custodial measure, confiscation, deprivation or destruction are ordered, the enforcement of the sentence or the measure shall not be barred by the statute of limitations before the enforcement of the others. A simultaneous incapacitation order shall not prevent the course of the limitation period for the enforcement of penalties or other measures.

(6) The limitation period shall commence when the decision becomes final.

§ 79a Stay of limitation

The limitation period shall be stayed

   1. as long as the enforcement may for reasons of law not commence or continue;
   2. as long as the convicted person is granted

      (a) a deferment or interruption of the enforcement;
      (b) suspension of sentence by judicial decision or by act of pardon; or
      (c) terms of payment in the case of a fine, confiscation or deprivation,

3.   as long as the convicted person is detained in an institution by order of a public authority in Germany or abroad.

§ 79b Prolongation

The court may, upon application of the enforcing authority, once prolong the period of limitation before its expiry by one half of the statutory limitation period if the convicted person resides in a territory from which his extradition or surrender cannot be achieved.

SPECIAL PART

CHAPTER ONE
CRIMES AGAINST THE PEACE OF NATIONS; HIGH TREASON; ENDANGERING THE DEMOCRATIC STATE UNDER THE RULE OF LAW

FIRST TITLE
CRIMES AGAINST THE PEACE OF NATIONS

§ 80 Preparation of a war of aggression

Whosoever prepares a war of aggression (Article 26(1) of the Basic Law) in which the Federal Republic of Germany is meant to participate and creates a danger of war for the Federal Republic of Germany, shall be liable to imprisonment for life or for not less than ten years.

§ 80a Incitement to a war of aggression

Whosoever publicly incites to a war of aggression (§ 80) in a meeting or through the dissemination of written materials (§ 11(3)) within the Federal Republic of Germany shall be liable to imprisonment from three months to five years.

SECOND TITLE
HIGH TREASON

§ 81 High treason against the Federation

(1) Whosoever undertakes, by force or through threat of force,

    1. to undermine the continued existence of the Federal Republic of Germany; or

    2. to change the constitutional order based on the Basic Law of the Federal Republic of Germany,

shall be liable to imprisonment for life or for not less than ten years.

(2) In less serious cases the penalty shall be imprisonment from one to ten years.

§ 82 High treason against a member state

(1) Whosoever undertakes, by force or through threat of force,

1. to incorporate the territory of one member state in whole or in part into another member state of the Federal Republic of Germany or to separate a part of a member state from it; or
2. to change the constitutional order based on the constitution of a member state

shall be liable to imprisonment from one to ten years.

(2) In less serious cases the penalty shall be imprisonment from six months to five years.

§ 83 Preparation of an enterprise directed at high treason

(1) Whosoever prepares a specific enterprise directed at high treason against the Federal Government shall be liable to imprisonment from one to ten years, in less serious cases to imprisonment from one to five years.
(2) Whosoever prepares a specific enterprise directed at high treason against a member state shall be liable to imprisonment from three months to five years.

§ 83a Preventing completion of offence

(1) In cases under § 81 and § 82 the court in its discretion may mitigate the sentence (§ 49(2)) or order a discharge if the offender voluntarily gives up the further commission of the offence and averts or substantially lessens any danger known to him that others will continue with the commission or if he voluntarily prevents the completion of the offence.
(2) In cases under § 83 the court may proceed according to subsection (1) above if the offender voluntarily gives up his plan and averts or substantially lessens a danger known and caused by him that others will further prepare or continue with the commission or if he voluntarily prevents the completion of the offence.
(3) If the danger is averted or substantially lessened or the completion of the offence is prevented regardless of the contribution of the offender his voluntary and earnest effort to avert or lessen the danger or to prevent the completion of the offence shall suffice.

THIRD TITLE
ENDANGERING THE DEMOCRATIC STATE UNDER THE RULE OF LAW

§ 84 Continuation of a political party declared unconstitutional

(1) Whosoever within the Federal Republic of Germany as a ringleader or hinterman,[6] maintains the organisational existence of

---

[6] The word 'hinterman' as such does not exist in English, but there is no one-word translation for the German 'Hintermann' and the concept embodied by it. A Hintermann (literally translated: 'the man behind') is a person who is pulling the strings from behind the scenes, a 'puppet master' of

1. a political party which has been declared unconstitutional by the Federal Constitutional Court; or
2. a political party, which the Federal Constitutional Court has determined to be a surrogate organisation for a banned party,

shall be liable to imprisonment from three months to five years. The attempt shall be punishable.

(2) Whosoever is an active member in a party indicated in subsection (1) above or whosoever supports its organisational existence shall be liable to imprisonment of not more than five years or a fine.

(3) Whosoever contravenes a decision on the merits of the Federal Constitutional Court issued in a proceeding pursuant to Article 21(2) of the Basic Law or in a proceeding pursuant to § 33(2) of the Law on Political Parties or an enforceable measure imposed in execution of a decision on the merits issued in such proceedings, shall be liable to imprisonment of not more than five years or a fine. A proceeding pursuant to Article 18 of the Basic Law shall be the equivalent of the proceedings indicated in the 1st sentence of this subsection.

(4) In cases under subsection (1) 2nd sentence and subsections (2) and (3) 1st sentence above the court in its discretion may mitigate the sentence (§ 49(2)) or order a discharge in the case of accomplices whose guilt is minor and whose participation is of a minor nature.

(5) In cases under subsections (1) and (3) 1st sentence above the court in its discretion may mitigate the sentence (§ 49(2)) or order a discharge if the offender makes a voluntarily and earnest effort to prevent the continued existence of the party; if he achieves this goal or if it is achieved regardless of his efforts the offender shall not be held liable.

§ 85 Violation of a ban on forming an association

(1) Whosoever, within the Federal Republic of Germany as a ringleader or hinterman, maintains the organisational existence of

1. a political party or organisation which has been finally determined in a proceeding pursuant to § 33(3) of the Law on Political Parties to be a surrogate organisation of a banned party; or
2. an organisation, which has been banned by final decision because it is directed against the constitutional order or against the idea of the comity of nations or which has been held by final decision to be a surrogate organisation of such a banned organisation,

shall be liable to imprisonment of not more than five years or a fine. The attempt shall be punishable.

---

sorts. The prefix 'hinter-', however, is well known in English from borrowed German words such as 'hinterland'. I have therefore decided to coin this new word in the hope that the reader will easily connect to its connotations.

(2)   Whosoever is an active member in a party or organisation indicated in sub-section (1) above or whosoever supports its organisational existence shall be liable to imprisonment of not more than three years or a fine.

(3)   § 84(4) and (5) shall apply mutatis mutandis.

§ 86 Dissemination of propaganda material of unconstitutional organisations

(1)   Whosoever within Germany disseminates or produces, stocks, imports or exports or makes publicly accessible through data storage media for dissemination within Germany or abroad, propaganda material

  1.   of a political party which has been declared unconstitutional by the Federal Constitutional Court or a political party or organisation which has been held by final decision to be a surrogate organisation of such a party;
  2.   of an organisation which has been banned by final decision because it is directed against the constitutional order or against the idea of the comity of nations or which has been held by final decision to be a surrogate organisation of such a banned organisation;
  3.   of a government, organisation or institution outside the Federal Republic of Germany active in pursuing the objectives of one of the parties or organisations indicated in Nos 1 and 2 above; or
  4.   propaganda materials the contents of which are intended to further the aims of a former National Socialist organisation,

shall be liable to imprisonment of not more than three years or a fine.

(2)   Propaganda materials within the meaning of subsection (1) above shall only be written materials (§ 11(3)) the content of which is directed against the free, democratic constitutional order or the idea of the comity of nations.

(3)   Subsection (1) above shall not apply if the propaganda materials or the act is meant to serve civil education, to avert unconstitutional movements, to promote art or science, research or teaching, the reporting about current or historical events or similar purposes.

(4)   If the guilt is of a minor nature, the court may order a discharge under this provision.

§ 86a Using symbols of unconstitutional organisations

(1)   Whosoever

  1.   domestically distributes or publicly uses, in a meeting or in written materials (§ 11(3)) disseminated by him, symbols of one of the parties or organisations indicated in § 86(1) Nos 1, 2 and 4; or
  2.   produces, stocks, imports or exports objects which depict or contain such symbols for distribution or use in Germany or abroad in a manner indicated in No 1,

shall be liable to imprisonment of not more than three years or a fine.

(2) Symbols within the meaning of subsection (1) above shall be in particular flags, insignia, uniforms and their parts, slogans and forms of greeting. Symbols which are so similar as to be mistaken for those named in the 1st sentence shall be equivalent to them.

(3) § 86(3) and (4) shall apply mutatis mutandis.

§ 87 Acting as a secret agent with the aim of sabotage

(1) Whosoever carries out the instructions of a government, organisation or institution outside the Federal Republic of Germany, in preparation of acts of sabotage which are to be committed in Germany, by

1. maintaining readiness to commit such acts upon the instructions of one of the indicated bodies;
2. gathering information about objects of sabotage;
3. producing, procuring for oneself or another, storing, supplying to another or importing means of sabotage into Germany;
4. establishing, maintaining or inspecting depots for the storage of means of sabotage or bases for sabotage activity;
5. accepting or giving training to others in how to commit acts of sabotage; or
6. establishing or maintaining the link between one of the agents of sabotage (Nos 1 to 5 above) and one of the indicated bodies,

and thereby intentionally or knowingly supports efforts against the continued existence or security of the Federal Republic of Germany or against its constitutional principles, shall be liable to imprisonment of not more than five years or a fine.

(2) Acts of sabotage within the meaning of subsection (1) above shall be

1. acts which fulfil the elements of any of the following offences: § 109e, § 305, §§ 306 to 306c, §§ 307 to 309, § 313, § 315, § 315b, § 316b, § 316(1) No 2, § 317 or § 318; and
2. other acts which obstruct or disturb the operation of an enterprise vital for the national defence, the protection of the civilian population from the dangers of war, or the national economy by destroying, damaging, removing, altering or rendering unusable anything of use to the operation or depriving the operation of its energy supply.

(3) The court may order a discharge pursuant to these provisions if the offender gives up his conduct and discloses his knowledge to a government authority in time for the acts of sabotage, the planning of which he is aware of, to be prevented.

§ 88 Sabotage against the constitution

(1) Whosoever as ringleader or hinterman of a group or individually without acting with or for such a group intentionally causes, by acts of interference within the Federal Republic of Germany

1.   enterprises or facilities which provide public mail services or public transportation;
2.   telecommunications facilities, which serve public functions;
3.   enterprises or facilities which provide the public with water, light, heat or power or are otherwise vital for the supply of the population;
4.   government agencies, facilities, installations or objects which entirely or predominantly serve public safety or order,

to cease to function, in whole or in part, or to be deprived of their assigned functions and thereby intentionally supports efforts against the continued existence or security of the Federal Republic of Germany or against its constitutional principles, shall be liable to imprisonment of not more than five years or a fine.

(2)   The attempt shall be punishable.

§ 89 Exerting anti-constitutional influence on the Armed Forces and public security forces

(1)   Whosoever systematically exerts influence on members of the Armed Forces or of a public security force in order to undermine their readiness to protect the security of the Federal Republic of Germany or the constitutional order and thereby intentionally supports efforts against the continued existence or security of the Federal Republic of Germany or against its constitutional principles, shall be liable to imprisonment of not more than five years or a fine.

(2)   The attempt shall be punishable.

(3)   § 86(4) shall apply mutatis mutandis.

§ 90 Defamation of the President of the Federation

(1)   Whosoever publicly defames the President of the Federation, in a meeting or through the dissemination of written material (§ 11(3)) shall be liable to imprisonment from three months to five years.

(2)   In less serious cases the court in its discretion may mitigate the sentence (§ 49(2)) unless the conditions of § 188 are met.

(3)   The penalty shall be imprisonment from six months to five years if the act constitutes an intentional defamation (§ 187) or if the offender by the act intentionally supports efforts against the continued existence of the Federal Republic of Germany or against its constitutional principles.

(4)   The offence may only be prosecuted upon the authorisation of the President of the Federation.

§ 90a Defamation of the state and its symbols

(1)   Whosoever publicly, in a meeting or through the dissemination of written materials (§11(3))

1. insults or maliciously expresses contempt of the Federal Republic of Germany or one of its states or its constitutional order; or
2. insults the colours, flag, coat of arms or the anthem of the Federal Republic of Germany or one of its states

shall be liable to imprisonment of not more than three years or a fine.

(2) Whosoever removes, destroys, damages, renders unusable or defaces, or otherwise insults by mischief a publicly displayed flag of the Federal Republic of Germany or one of its states or a national emblem installed by a public authority of the Federal Republic of Germany or one of its states shall incur the same liability. The attempt shall be punishable.

(3) The penalty shall be imprisonment of not more than five years or a fine if the offender by the act intentionally supports efforts against the continued existence of the Federal Republic of Germany or against its constitutional principles.

§ 90b Anti-constitutional defamation of constitutional organs

(1) Whosoever publicly, in a meeting or through the dissemination of written materials (§ 11(3)) defames a constitutional organ, the government or the constitutional court of the Federation or of a state or one of their members in this capacity in a manner detrimental to the respect for the state and thereby intentionally supports efforts against the continued existence of the Federal Republic of Germany or against its constitutional principles, shall be liable to imprisonment from three months to five years.

(2) The offence may only be prosecuted upon the authorisation of the constitutional organ or member affected.

§ 91 Jurisdiction ratione loci

§ 84, § 85 and § 87 shall only apply to offences committed in the course of conduct engaged in within the Federal Republic of Germany.

FOURTH TITLE
COMMON PROVISIONS

§ 92 Definition of terms

(1) Within the meaning of this law, a person undermines the continued existence of the Federal Republic of Germany if he causes the end of its freedom from foreign domination, the abolition of its national unity, or the secession of one of its constituent territories.

(2) Constitutional principles, within the meaning of this law, shall be

1. the right of the people to exercise state power in elections and ballots and through particular organs of legislative, executive and judicial power and to elect Parliament in general, direct, free, equal and secret elections;
2. the subjection of legislation to the constitutional order and the subjection of the executive and judicial power to law and justice;
3. the right to form and exercise a parliamentary opposition;
4. the possibility of dissolving the government and its responsibility to Parliament;
5. the independence of the courts; and
6. the exclusion of any government by force and arbitrary rule.

(3)   Within the meaning of this law

1. efforts against the continued existence of the Federal Republic of Germany shall mean efforts by supporters who actually work toward undermining the continued existence of the Federal Republic of Germany (subsection (1) above);
2. efforts against the security of the Federal Republic of Germany shall mean efforts by supporters who actually work toward undermining the external or internal security of the Federal Republic of Germany;
3. efforts against constitutional principles shall mean efforts by supporters who actually work toward abolishing, suspending the application of or undermining a constitutional principle (subsection (2) above).

§ 92a Ancillary measures

In addition to a sentence of imprisonment of at least six months for an offence under this chapter, the court may order the offender's professional disqualification and the loss of the ability to hold public office, to vote and be elected in public elections (§ 45(2) and (5)).

§ 92b Deprivation

If an offence under this chapter has been committed

1. objects generated by the offence or used or intended for use in its commission or preparation; and
2. objects mentioned in the offences under § 80a, § 86, § 86a, §§ 90 to 90b

may be subject to a deprivation order. § 74a shall apply.

CHAPTER TWO
TREASON AND ENDANGERING EXTERNAL NATIONAL SECURITY

§ 93 Definition of state secret

(1) State secrets are facts, objects or knowledge which are only accessible to a limited category of persons and must be kept secret from foreign powers in order to avert a danger of serious prejudice to the external security of the Federal Republic of Germany.

(2) Facts which constitute violations of the independent, democratic constitutional order or of international arms control agreements, kept secret from the treaty partners of the Federal Republic of Germany, are not state secrets.

§ 94 Treason

(1) Whosoever

　　1. communicates a state secret to a foreign power or one of its intermediaries; or

　　2. otherwise allows a state secret to come to the attention of an unauthorised person or to become known to the public in order to prejudice the Federal Republic of Germany or benefit a foreign power

and thereby creates a danger of serious prejudice to the external security of the Federal Republic of Germany, shall be liable to imprisonment of not less than one year.

(2) In especially serious cases the penalty shall be imprisonment for life or of not less than five years. An especially serious case will typically occur if the offender

　　1. abuses a position of responsibility which especially obliges him to safeguard state secrets; or

　　2. through the offence creates the danger of an especially serious prejudice to the external security of the Federal Republic of Germany.

§ 95 Disclosure of state secrets with intent to cause damage

(1) Whosoever allows a state secret which has been kept secret by an official authority or at its behest to come to the attention of an unauthorised person or become known to the public, and thereby creates the danger of serious prejudice to the external security of the Federal Republic of Germany, shall be liable to imprisonment from six months to five years unless the offence is punishable under § 94.

(2) The attempt shall be punishable.

(3) In especially serious cases the penalty shall be imprisonment from one to ten years. § 94(2) shall apply.

§ 96 Treasonous espionage; spying on state secrets

(1)   Whosoever obtains a state secret in order to disclose it (§ 94) shall be liable to imprisonment from one to ten years.

(2)   Whosoever obtains a state secret which has been kept secret by an official agency or at its behest in order to disclose it (§ 95) shall be liable to imprisonment from six months to five years. The attempt shall be punishable.

§ 97 Disclosure of state secrets and negligently causing danger

(1)   Whosoever allows a state secret which has been kept secret by an official agency or at its behest to come to the attention of an unauthorised person or become known to the public, and thereby negligently causes the danger of serious prejudice to the external security of the Federal Republic of Germany, shall be liable to imprisonment of not more than five years or a fine.

(2)   Whosoever by gross negligence allows a state secret which has been kept secret by an official agency or at its behest and which was accessible to him by reason of his public office, government position or assignment given by an official authority, to come to the attention of an unauthorised person, and thereby negligently causes the danger of serious prejudice to the external security of the Federal Republic of Germany, shall be liable to imprisonment of not more than three years or a fine.

(3)   The offence may only be prosecuted upon the authorisation of the Federal Government.

§ 97a Disclosure of illegal secrets

Whosoever communicates a secret, which is not a state secret because of one of the violations indicated in § 93(2), to a foreign power or one of its intermediaries and thereby creates the danger of serious prejudice to the external security of the Federal Republic of Germany, shall be punished as if he had committed treason (§ 94). § 96(1), in conjunction with § 94(1) No 1 shall apply mutatis mutandis to secrets of the kind indicated in the 1st sentence above.

§ 97b Disclosure based on mistaken assumption that secret is illegal

(1)   If the offender in cases under §§ 94 to 97 mistakenly assumes that a state secret is a secret of the kind indicated in § 97a he shall be punished pursuant to the those provisions if

1.   he could have avoided the mistake;
2.   he did not act with the intention of preventing the alleged violation; or
3.   the act is, under the circumstances, not an appropriate means to accomplish that purpose.

The act is typically not an appropriate means if the offender did not previously seek a remedy from a member of the Federal Parliament.

(2) If the state secret was confided or made accessible to the offender in his capacity as a public official or soldier in the Armed Forces he shall also incur liability if he did not previously seek a remedy from a superior in government service, or in the case of a soldier from a superior disciplinary officer. This shall apply mutatis mutandis to persons entrusted with special public service functions and to persons under a duty within the meaning of § 353b(2).

§ 98 Treasonous activity as an agent

(1) Whosoever

    1. engages in activity for a foreign power which is directed towards the acquisition or communication of state secrets; or

    2. declares to a foreign power or one of its intermediaries his willingness to engage in such activity,

shall be liable to imprisonment of not more than five years or a fine unless the offence is punishable pursuant to § 94 or § 96(1). In especially serious cases the penalty shall be imprisonment from one to ten years; § 94(2) 2nd sentence No 1 shall apply mutatis mutandis.

(2) The court in its discretion may mitigate the sentence (§ 49(2)) or order a discharge under these provisions if the offender voluntarily gives up his activity and discloses his knowledge to a government authority. If the offender in cases under subsection (2) 1st sentence above has been forced into the activity by the foreign power or its intermediaries, he shall not be liable under this provision if he voluntarily gives up his activity and discloses his knowledge to a government authority without unnecessary delay.

§ 99 Working as an agent for an intelligence service

(1) Whosoever

    1. engages in intelligence activity for the intelligence service of a foreign power against the Federal Republic of Germany which is directed toward communication or supply of facts, objects or knowledge; or

    2. declares to the intelligence service of a foreign power or one of its intermediaries his willingness to engage in such activity,

shall be liable to imprisonment of not more than five years or a fine unless the offence is punishable under § 94, § 96(1), § 97a, or § 97b in conjunction with § 94 or § 96(1).

(2) In especially serious cases the penalty shall be imprisonment from one to ten years. An especially serious case typically occurs if the offender communicates or supplies facts, objects or knowledge which have been kept secret by an official agency or at its behest, and he

    1. abuses a position of responsibility which especially mandates him to safeguard such secrets; or

2.   through the offence creates the danger of serious prejudice to the Federal Republic of Germany.

(3)   § 98(2) shall apply mutatis mutandis.

§ 100 Engaging in relations that endanger peace

(1)   Whosoever as a German, who has his residence in the Federal Republic of Germany, and with the intent of starting a war or armed attack against the Federal Republic of Germany, establishes or maintains relationships with a government, organisation or institution outside the Federal Republic of Germany or one of its intermediaries, shall be liable to imprisonment of not less than one year.

(2)   In especially serious cases the penalty shall be imprisonment for life or not less than five years. An especially serious case typically occurs if the offender through the offence creates a serious danger to the continued existence of the Federal Republic of Germany.

(3)   In less serious cases the penalty shall be imprisonment from one to five years.

§ 100a Treasonous forgery

(1)   Whosoever intentionally and knowingly allows falsified or altered objects, reports concerning them or untrue assertions of a factual nature to come to the attention of another or to become known to the public, which, if they were genuine or true, would be of significance for the external security of the Federal Republic of Germany or her relationships with a foreign power, in order to deceive a foreign power into believing them to be genuine objects or facts, and thereby causes the danger of serious prejudice to the external security of the Federal Republic of Germany or her relationship to a foreign power, shall be liable to imprisonment from six months to five years.

(2)   Whosoever produces such objects through falsification or alteration or procures them, in order to allow them in the manner indicated in subsection (1) above to come to the attention of another or to become known to the public in order to deceive a foreign power and thereby causes the danger of serious prejudice to the external security of the Federal Republic of Germany or her relationship to a foreign power, shall incur the same penalty.

(3)   The attempt shall be punishable.

(4)   In especially serious cases the penalty shall be imprisonment of not less than one year. An especially serious case typically occurs if the offender creates an especially serious prejudice to the external security of the Federal Republic of Germany or to her relations with a foreign power.

§ 101 Ancillary measures

In addition to a sentence of imprisonment of at least six months for an intentional offence under this chapter, the court may order the loss of the ability to hold public office, to vote and be elected in public elections (§ 45(2) and (5)).

§ 101a Deprivation

If an offence under this chapter has been committed

1. objects generated by the offence or used or intended for use in its commission or preparation; and
2. objects, which are state secrets, and objects of the kind indicated in offences under § 100a

may be subject to a deprivation order. § 74a shall apply. Objects of the kind indicated in the 1st sentence No 2 above shall be subject to a deprivation order even if the conditions of § 74(2) are not met if this is necessary in order to avert the danger of a serious prejudice to the external security of the Federal Republic of Germany; this shall also apply if the offender acted without guilt.

CHAPTER THREE
OFFENCES AGAINST FOREIGN STATES

§ 102 Attacks against organs and representatives of foreign states

(1) Whosoever commits an attack against the life or limb of a foreign head of state, a member of a foreign government or the head of a foreign diplomatic mission who is accredited in the Federal territory while the victim is in Germany in his official capacity, shall be liable to imprisonment of not more than five years or a fine, in especially serious cases to imprisonment of not less than one year.
(2) In addition to a sentence of imprisonment of at least six months, the court may order the loss of the ability to hold public office, to vote and be elected in public elections (§ 45(2) and (5)).

§ 103 Defamation of organs and representatives of foreign states

(1) Whosoever insults a foreign head of state, or, with respect to his position, a member of a foreign government who is in Germany in his official capacity, or a head of a foreign diplomatic mission who is accredited in the Federal territory shall be liable to imprisonment of not more than three years or a fine, in case of a slanderous insult to imprisonment from three months to five years.
(2) If the offence was committed publicly, in a meeting or through the dissemination of written materials (§ 11(3)) § 200 shall apply. An application for publication of the conviction may also be filed by the prosecution service.

§ 104 Violation of flags and state symbols of foreign states

(1) Whosoever removes, destroys, damages, renders unrecognisable or insults by mischief a flag of a foreign state, which is displayed according to legal

provisions or recognised custom, or a state symbol of such a state which has been publicly installed by a recognised mission of such state, shall be liable to imprisonment of not more than two years or a fine.

(2)   The attempt shall be punishable.

§ 104a Conditions for prosecution

Offences under this chapter shall only be prosecuted if the Federal Republic of Germany maintains diplomatic relations with the other state, reciprocity is guaranteed and was also guaranteed at the time of the offence, a request to prosecute by the foreign government exists, and the Federal Government authorises the prosecution.

CHAPTER FOUR
OFFENCES AGAINST CONSTITUTIONAL ORGANS AND IN THE CONTEXT OF ELECTIONS AND BALLOTS

§ 105 Blackmailing constitutional organs

(1)   Whosoever, by force or threat of force, unlawfully coerces

    1.   a legislative body of the Federation or a member state or one of its committees;

    2.   the Federal Assembly or one of its committees; or

    3.   the government or the constitutional court of the Federation or of a member state

not to exercise their functions or to exercise them in a particular manner shall be liable to imprisonment from one to ten years.

(2)   In less serious cases the penalty shall be imprisonment from six months to five years.

§ 106 Blackmailing the President of the Federation and members of constitutional organs

(1)   Whosoever, by force or threat of serious harm, unlawfully coerces

    1.   the President of the Federation; or

    2.   a member

       (a) of a legislative body of the Federation or a member state;

       (b) of the Federal Assembly; or

       (c) of the government or the constitutional court of the Federation or a member state

not to exercise their functions or to exercise them in a particular manner, shall be liable to imprisonment from three months to five years.

(2) The attempt shall be punishable.

(3) In especially serious cases the penalty shall be imprisonment from one to ten years.

§ 106a (repealed)

§ 106b Disrupting the work of a legislative body

(1) Whosoever violates regulations issued either generally or in a particular case by a legislative body of the Federation or a member state or its President relating to security and order in the building of the legislative body or the surrounding grounds and thereby hinders or disrupts the activity of the legislative body, shall be liable to imprisonment of not more than one year or a fine.

(2) Subsection (1) above shall neither apply, in the case of regulations of a legislative body of the Federation or its President to members of the Federal Parliament, members of the Federal Council and the Federal Government and their agents, nor in the case of regulations of a legislative body of a member state or its President, to the members of the legislative bodies of this member state, the members of the government of the member state and its agents.

§ 107 Disruption of election process

(1) Whosoever, by force or threat of force, prevents or disturbs an election or the determination of its results, shall be liable to imprisonment of not more than five years or a fine, in especially serious cases to imprisonment of not less than one year.

(2) The attempt shall be punishable.

§ 107a Falsification of election results

(1) Whosoever votes without being entitled thereto or otherwise causes an incorrect election result or falsifies the result, shall be liable to imprisonment of not more than five years or a fine.

(2) Whosoever incorrectly announces an election result or causes it to be incorrectly announced shall incur the same liability.

(3) The attempt shall be punishable.

§ 107b Falsification of election documents

(1) Whosoever

1. secures his registration in the electoral rolls (election register) by means of false statements;

2. registers another as a voter, whom he knows to have no right to be registered;

3.   prevents the registration of an eligible voter though he knows of his eligibility to vote;
4.   permits himself to be nominated as a candidate in an election, although he is ineligible,

shall be liable to imprisonment of not more than six months or a fine of not more than one hundred and eighty daily units unless the offence is subject to a more severe penalty under other provisions.

(2)   The issuance of election papers for direct elections in the social security system shall be equivalent to registration in the voter rolls as a voter.

§ 107c Violation of secrecy of elections

Whosoever contravenes a provision which serves to protect the secrecy of elections with the intention of obtaining for himself or another knowledge as to how a person voted, shall be liable to imprisonment of not more than two years or a fine.

§ 108 Blackmailing voters

(1)   Whosoever unlawfully, by force, threat of serious harm, abuse of a professional or economic relationship of dependence or other economic pressure, coerces another into, or prevents him from, voting or exercising his right to vote in a particular manner, shall be liable to imprisonment of not more than five years or a fine, in especially serious cases to imprisonment from one to ten years.

(2)   The attempt shall be punishable.

§ 108a Deceiving voters

(1)   Whosoever through deception causes another to be mistaken as to the content of his declaration upon casting his vote or to vote against his will or invalidly, shall be liable to imprisonment of not more than two years or a fine.

(2)   The attempt shall be punishable.

§ 108b Bribing voters

(1)   Whosoever offers, promises or furnishes to another gifts or other benefits for not voting or for voting in a particular manner, shall be liable to imprisonment of not more than five years or a fine.

(2)   Whosoever requests, is promised or accepts gifts or other benefits in exchange for not voting or voting in a particular manner, shall incur the same penalty.

§ 108c Ancillary measures

In addition to a sentence of imprisonment of at least six months for an offence pursuant to § 107, § 107a, § 108 or § 108b the court may order the loss of the ability to hold public office, to vote and be elected in public elections (§ 45(2) and (5)).

§ 108d Jurisdiction

§§ 107 to 108c shall apply to elections to the parliaments, election of members of the European Parliament, other popular elections and ballots in the Federation, the member states, municipalities and municipal associations, as well as direct elections in the social security system. The signing of nomination papers or the signing of a popular referendum shall be equivalent to an election or ballot.

§ 108e Bribing delegates

(1) Whosoever undertakes to buy or sell a vote for an election or ballot in the European Parliament or in a parliament of the Federation, the member states, municipalities or municipal associations, shall be liable to imprisonment of not more than five years or a fine.
(2) In addition to a sentence of imprisonment of at least six months for an offence pursuant to subsection (1) above the court may order the loss of the ability to hold public office, to vote and be elected in public elections (§ 45(2) and (5)).

CHAPTER FIVE
OFFENCES AGAINST THE NATIONAL DEFENCE

§ 109 Avoiding draft by mutilation

(1) Whosoever through mutilation or by other means, renders himself or another person with that person's consent, or causes himself or another person to be rendered unfit for military service, shall be liable to imprisonment from three months to five years.
(2) If the offender causes the unfitness only for a certain period of time or for a certain type of duty, the penalty shall be imprisonment of not more than five years or a fine.
(3) The attempt shall be punishable.

§ 109a Avoiding draft by deception

(1) Whosoever by deception evades or causes another to evade military service permanently or for a certain period of time, in its entirety or for a certain type of duty, shall be liable to imprisonment of not more than five years or a fine.
(2) The attempt shall be punishable.

§ 109b and § 109c (repealed)

§ 109d Disruptive propaganda against the Armed Forces

(1)   Whosoever, intentionally and knowingly and for the purpose of dissemination, makes false or grossly distorted assertions of fact, the dissemination of which is capable of disrupting the function of the Armed Forces, or disseminates such assertions with knowledge of their falseness in order to obstruct the Armed Forces in the fulfilment of their duty of national defence, shall be liable to imprisonment of not more than five years or a fine.

(2)   The attempt shall be punishable.

§ 109e Sabotage against means of defence

(1)   Whosoever unlawfully destroys, damages, alters, renders unusable or removes military resources or an installation or facility used entirely or predominantly for the national defence or the protection of the civilian population from the dangers of war, and thereby endangers the security of the Federal Republic of Germany, the fighting strength of its troops, or human life, shall be liable to imprisonment from three months to five years.

(2)   Anyone who knowingly and in a defective manner produces or supplies such an object or the raw materials required for its production and thereby knowingly causes the danger indicated in subsection (1) above, shall incur the same penalty.

(3)   The attempt shall be punishable.

(4)   In especially serious cases the penalty shall be imprisonment from one to ten years.

(5)   Whosoever causes the danger in the cases under subsection (1) above negligently, or in cases under subsection (2) above not knowingly but intentionally or negligently, shall be liable to imprisonment of not more than five years or a fine unless the offence is subject to a more severe penalty under other provisions.

§ 109f Intelligence activity endangering national security

(1)   Whosoever, on behalf of a government agency, a party or another organisation outside the Federal Republic of Germany or for a banned organisation or one of its intermediaries

1.   collects information about national defence matters;
2.   operates an intelligence service dedicated to national defence matters;
3.   recruits for or supports one of these activities,

and thereby aids efforts which are directed against the security of the Federal Republic of Germany or the fighting strength of its troops, shall be liable to imprisonment of not more than five years or a fine unless the offence is subject to a more severe penalty under other provisions. Activities meant to inform the public within the framework of normal press or radio reporting shall remain unaffected.

(2)   The attempt shall be punishable.

§ 109g Taking or drawing pictures etc endangering national security

(1)   Whosoever makes an illustration or description of military resources, a military installation or facility, or a military operation or allows another to obtain such an illustration or description, and thereby knowingly endangers the security of the Federal Republic of Germany or the fighting strength of its troops, shall be liable to imprisonment of not more than five years or a fine.

(2)   Whosoever takes an aerial photograph of a territory or object within the Federal Republic of Germany or allows another to obtain such a photograph or an illustration produced therefrom, and thereby knowingly endangers the security of the Federal Republic of Germany or the fighting strength of its troops, shall be liable to imprisonment of not more than two years or a fine unless the offence is subject to punishment in subsection (1) above.

(3)   The attempt shall be punishable.

(4)   Whosoever in cases under subsection (1) above allows another to obtain the illustration or description and thereby not knowingly, but intentionally or recklessly causes the danger, shall be liable to imprisonment of not more than two years or a fine. There shall be no liability if the offender acted under the permission of a competent government agency.

§ 109h Recruiting for foreign armed forces

(1)   Whosoever on behalf of a foreign power recruits a German for military service in a military or paramilitary organisation or introduces him to their recruiters or to the military service of such an organisation, shall be liable to imprisonment from three months to five years.

(2)   The attempt shall be punishable.

§ 109i Ancillary measures

In addition to a sentence of imprisonment of not less than one year for an offence pursuant to § 109e and § 109f the court may order the loss of the ability to hold public office, to vote and be elected in public elections (§ 45(2) and (5)).

§ 109k Deprivation

If an offence under §§ 109d to 109g has been committed

1.   objects, which were generated by the offence or used or intended for use in its commission or preparation; and

2.   illustrations, descriptions and photographs relating to an offence under § 109g

may be subject to a deprivation order. § 74a shall apply. Objects of the type indicated in the 1st sentence No 2 shall be subject to a deprivation order even if the conditions of § 74(2) are not met, if so required by national defence interests; this shall also apply if the offender acted without guilt.

CHAPTER SIX
RESISTANCE AGAINST STATE AUTHORITY

§ 110 (repealed)

§ 111　Public incitement to crime

(1)　Whosoever publicly, in a meeting or through the dissemination of written materials (§ 11(3)) incites the commission of an unlawful act, shall be held liable as an abettor (§ 26).

(2)　If the incitement is unsuccessful the penalty shall be imprisonment of not more than five years or a fine. The penalty must not be more severe than if the incitement had been successful (subsection (1) above); § 49(1) No 2 shall apply.

§ 112 (repealed)

§ 113　Resisting enforcement officers

(1)　Whosoever, by force or threat of force, offers resistance to or attacks a public official or soldier of the Armed Forces charged with the enforcement of laws, ordinances, judgments, judicial decisions or orders acting in the execution of such official duty shall be liable to imprisonment of not more than two years or a fine.

(2)　In especially serious cases the penalty shall be imprisonment from six months to five years. An especially serious case typically occurs if

1.　the principal or another accomplice carries a weapon for the purpose of using it during the commission of the offence; or
2.　the offender through violence places the person assaulted in danger of death or serious injury.

(3)　The offence shall not be punishable under this provision if the official act is unlawful. This shall also apply if the offender mistakenly assumes that the official act is lawful.

(4)　If the offender during the commission of the offence mistakenly assumes that the official act is unlawful and if he could have avoided the mistake the court may mitigate the sentence in its discretion (§ 49(2)) or order a discharge under this provision if the offender's guilt is of a minor nature. If the offender could not have avoided the mistake and under the circumstances known to him he could not have been expected to use legal remedies to defend himself against the presumed unlawful official act, the offence shall not be punishable under this provision; if the use of remedies could have been expected the court may mitigate the sentence in its discretion (§ 49(2)) or order a discharge under this provision.

§ 114 Resisting persons equal to enforcement officers

(1) Acts of enforcement by persons vested with the powers and duties of police officers or who are investigators of the public prosecution service without being public officials, shall be equivalent to the official act of a public official within the meaning of § 113.

(2) § 113 shall apply mutatis mutandis to persons who are called upon to assist in the execution of the official act.

§§ 115 to 119 (repealed)

§ 120 Facilitating escape of prisoners

(1) Whosoever frees a prisoner, or encourages him to or supports him in the escape, shall be liable to imprisonment of not more than three years or a fine.

(2) If the offender is under a duty as a public official or a person entrusted with special public service functions to prevent the escape of the prisoner the penalty shall be imprisonment of not more than five years or a fine.

(3) The attempt shall be punishable.

(4) A person otherwise in detention in an institution upon order of a public authority shall be equivalent to a prisoner within the meaning of subsections (1) and (2) above.

§ 121 Mutiny by prisoners

(1) Prisoners who gang up and with joint forces

　　1.　coerce (§ 240) or attack an official of an institution, another public official or a person charged with their supervision, care or investigation;

　　2.　escape under use of force; or

　　3.　by use of force aid one of their number or another prisoner to escape,

shall be liable to imprisonment from three months to five years.

(2) The attempt shall be punishable.

(3) In especially serious cases the penalty for mutiny shall be imprisonment from six months to ten years. An especially serious case typically occurs if the principal or another accomplice

　　1.　carries a firearm;

　　2.　carries another weapon for the purpose of using it during commission of the offence; or

　　3.　through violence places another in danger of death or serious injury.

(4)   A person subject to an incapacitation order shall be equivalent to a prisoner within the meaning of subsections (1) to (3) above.

§ 122 (repealed)

CHAPTER SEVEN
OFFENCES AGAINST PUBLIC ORDER

§ 123 Burglary

(1)   Whosoever unlawfully enters into the dwelling, business premises or other enclosed property of another, or into closed premises designated for public service or transportation, or whosoever remains therein without authorisation and does not leave when requested to do so by the authorised person, shall be liable to imprisonment of not more than one year or a fine.

(2)   The offence may only be prosecuted upon request.

§ 124 Aggravated burglary

If a crowd of people publicly gangs up with the intent to join forces to commit acts of violence against persons or objects and unlawfully intrudes into the dwelling, business premises, or other enclosed property of another, or into closed premises designated for public service, anyone taking part in these acts shall be liable to imprisonment of not more than two years or a fine.

§ 125 Rioting

(1)   Whosoever as a principal or secondary participant participates in

  1.   acts of violence against persons or objects; or
  2.   threats to persons to commit acts of violence,

  which are committed by a crowd of people who have joined forces in a manner which endangers public safety, or whosoever encourages a crowd of people to commit such acts, shall be liable to imprisonment of not more than three years or a fine unless the act is subject to a more severe penalty under other provisions.

(2)   To the extent that the offences indicated in subsection (1) Nos 1 and 2 above are punishable under § 113, § 113(3) and (4) shall apply mutatis mutandis.

§ 125a Aggravated cases of rioting

(1)   In especially serious cases of § 125(1) the penalty shall be imprisonment from six months to ten years. An especially serious case typically occurs if the offender

1. carries a firearm;
2. carries another weapon for the purpose of using it during the commission of the offence;
3. through violence places another in danger of death or serious injury or
4. commits plunder or causes significant damage to the property of another.

§ 126 Breach of the public peace by threatening to commit offences

(1) Whosoever, in a manner capable of disturbing the public peace, threatens to commit

1. an offence of rioting indicated in § 125a 2nd sentence Nos 1 to 4;
2. murder under specific aggravating circumstances (§ 211), murder (§ 212) or genocide (§ 6 of the Code of International Criminal Law) or a crime against humanity (§ 7 of the Code of International Criminal Law) or a war crime (§ 8, § 9, § 10, §11 or § 12 of the Code of International Criminal Law);
3. grievous bodily harm (§ 226);
4. an offence against personal freedom under § 232(3), (4), or (5), § 233(3), each to the extent it involves a felony, § 234, § 234a, § 239a or § 239b;
5. robbery or blackmail with force or threats to life and limb (§§ 249 to 251 or § 255);
6. a felony endangering the public under §§ 306 to 306c or § 307(1) to (3), § 308(1) to (3), § 309(1) to (4), § 313, § 314 or § 315(3), § 315b(3), § 316a(1) or (3), § 316c(1) or (3) or § 318(3) or (4); or
7. a misdemeanour endangering the public under § 309(6), § 311(1), § 316b(1), § 317(1) or § 318(1),

shall be liable to imprisonment of not more than three years or a fine.
(2) Whosoever intentionally and knowingly and in a manner capable of disturbing the public peace pretends that the commission of one of the unlawful acts named in subsection (1) above is imminent, shall incur the same penalty.

§ 127 Forming armed groups

Whosoever unlawfully forms or commands a group in possession of weapons or other dangerous instruments or joins such a group, provides it with weapons or money or otherwise supports it, shall be liable to imprisonment of not more than two years or a fine.

§ 128 (repealed)

§ 129 Forming criminal organisations

(1) Whosoever forms an organisation the aims or activities of which are directed at the commission of offences or whosoever participates in such an organisation

as a member, recruits members or supporters for it or supports it, shall be liable to imprisonment of not more than five years or a fine.

(2) Subsection (1) above shall not apply

   1. if the organisation is a political party which the Federal Constitutional Court has not declared to be unconstitutional;
   2. if the commission of offences is of merely minor significance for the objectives or activities or
   3. to the extent that the objectives or activities of the organisation relate to offences under §§ 84 to 87.

(3) The attempt to form an organisation as indicated in subsection (1) above shall be punishable.

(4) If the offender is one of the ringleaders or hintermen or the case is otherwise especially serious the penalty shall be imprisonment from six months to five years; the penalty shall be imprisonment from six months to ten years if the aim or the activity of the criminal organisation is directed at the commission of an offence set out in § 100c (2) No 1 (a), (c), (d), (e), and (g) with the exception of offences pursuant to § 239a or § 239b, (h) to (m) Nos 2 to 5 and 7 of the Code of Criminal Procedure.

(5) The court may order a discharge under subsections (1) and (3) above in the case of accomplices whose guilt is of a minor nature or whose contribution is of minor significance.

(6) The court may in its discretion mitigate the sentence (§ 49(2)) or order a discharge under these provisions if the offender

   1. voluntarily and earnestly makes efforts to prevent the continued existence of the organisation or the commission of an offence consistent with its aims; or
   2. voluntarily discloses his knowledge to a government authority in time so that offences the planning of which he is aware of may be prevented;

   if the offender succeeds in preventing the continued existence of the organisation or if this is achieved without his efforts he shall not incur criminal liability.

§ 129a Forming terrorist organisations

(1) Whosoever forms an organisation whose aims or activities are directed at the commission of

   1. murder under specific aggravating circumstances (§ 211), murder (§ 212) or genocide (§ 6 of the Code of International Criminal Law) or a crime against humanity (§ 7 of the Code of International Criminal Law) or a war crime (§ 8, § 9, § 10, §11 or § 12 of the Code of International Criminal Law); or
   2. crimes against personal liberty under § 239a or § 239b,

3.   *(repealed)*

or whosoever participates in such a group as a member shall be liable to imprisonment from one to ten years.

(2)   The same penalty shall be incurred by any person who forms an organisation whose aims or activities are directed at

1.   causing serious physical or mental harm to another person, namely within the ambit of § 226,
2.   committing offences under § 303b, § 305, § 305a or offences endangering the general public under §§ 306 to 306c or § 307(1) to (3), § 308(1) to (4), § 309(1) to (5), § 313, § 314 or § 315(1), (3) or (4), § 316b(1) or (3) or § 316c (1) to (3) or § 317(1),
3.   committing offences against the environment under § 330a(1) to (3),
4.   committing offences under the following provisions of the Weapons of War (Control) Act: §19 (1) to (3), § 20(1) or (2), § 20a(1) to (3), § 19 (2) No 2 or (3) No 2, § 20(1) or (2), or § 20a(1) to (3), in each case also in conjunction with § 21, or under § 22a(1) to (3) or
5.   committing offences under § 51(1) to (3) of the Weapons Act;

or by any person who participates in such a group as a member, if one of the offences stipulated in Nos 1 to 5 is intended to seriously intimidate the population, to unlawfully coerce a public authority or an international organisation through the use of force or the threat of the use of force, or to significantly impair or destroy the fundamental political, constitutional, economic or social structures of a state or an international organisation, and which, given the nature or consequences of such offences, may seriously damage a state or an international organisation.

(3)   If the aims or activities of the group are directed at threatening the commission of one of the offences listed in subsection (1) or (2) above, the penalty shall be imprisonment from six months to five years.

(4)   If the offender is one of the ringleaders or hintermen the penalty shall be imprisonment of not less than three years in cases under subsections (1) and (2) above, and imprisonment from one to ten years in cases under subsection (3) above.

(5)   Whosoever supports a group as described in subsections (1), (2) or (3) above shall be liable to imprisonment from six months to ten years in cases under subsections (1) and (2), and to imprisonment of not more than five years or a fine in cases under subsection (3). Whosoever recruits members or supporters for a group as described in subsection (1) or subsection (2) above shall be liable to imprisonment from six months to five years.

(6)   In the cases of accomplices whose guilt is of a minor nature and whose contribution is of minor significance, the court may, in cases under subsections (1), (2), (3) and (5) above, mitigate the sentence in its discretion (§ 49(2)).

(7)   § 129(6) shall apply mutatis mutandis.

(8) In addition to a sentence of imprisonment of not less than six months, the court may order the loss of the ability to hold public office, to vote and be elected in public elections (§ 45(2) and (5)).

(9) In cases under subsections (1), (2) and (4) above the court may make a supervision order (§ 68(1)).

§ 129b Criminal and terrorist organisations abroad; extended confiscation and deprivation

(1) § 129 and §129a shall apply to organisations abroad. If the offence relates to an organisation outside the member states of the European Union, this shall not apply unless the offence was committed by way of an activity exercised within the Federal Republic of Germany or if the offender or the victim is a German or is found within Germany. In cases which fall under the 2nd sentence above the offence shall only be prosecuted on authorisation by the Federal Ministry of Justice. Authorisation may be granted for an individual case or in general for the prosecution of future offences relating to a specific organisation. When deciding whether to give authorisation, the Federal Ministry of Justice shall take into account whether the aims of the organisation are directed against the fundamental values of a state order which respects human dignity or against the peaceful coexistence of nations and which appear reprehensible when weighing all the circumstances of the case.

(2) § 73d and § 74a shall apply to cases under § 129 and § 129a, in each case also in conjunction with subsection (1) above.

§ 130 Incitement to hatred

(1) Whosoever, in a manner capable of disturbing the public peace

1. incites hatred against segments of the population or calls for violent or arbitrary measures against them; or
2. assaults the human dignity of others by insulting, maliciously maligning, or defaming segments of the population,

shall be liable to imprisonment from three months to five years.

(2) Whosoever

1. with respect to written materials (§ 11(3)) which incite hatred against segments of the population or a national, racial or religious group, or one characterised by its ethnic customs, which call for violent or arbitrary measures against them, or which assault the human dignity of others by insulting, maliciously maligning or defaming segments of the population or a previously indicated group

   (a) disseminates such written materials;
   (b) publicly displays, posts, presents, or otherwise makes them accessible;

114

(c) offers, supplies or makes them accessible to a person under eighteen years; or

(d) produces, obtains, supplies, stocks, offers, announces, commends, undertakes to import or export them, in order to use them or copies obtained from them within the meaning of Nos (a) to (c) or facilitate such use by another; or

2. disseminates a presentation of the content indicated in No 1 above by radio, media services, or telecommunication services

shall be liable to imprisonment of not more than three years or a fine.

(3) Whosoever publicly or in a meeting approves of, denies or downplays an act committed under the rule of National Socialism of the kind indicated in § 6(1) of the Code of International Criminal Law, in a manner capable of disturbing the public peace shall be liable to imprisonment of not more than five years or a fine.

(4) Whosoever publicly or in a meeting disturbs the public peace in a manner that violates the dignity of the victims by approving of, glorifying, or justifying National Socialist rule of arbitrary force shall be liable to imprisonment of not more than three years or a fine.

(5) Subsection (2) above shall also apply to written materials (§ 11(3)) of a content such as is indicated in subsections (3) and (4) above.

(6) In cases under subsection (2) above, also in conjunction with subsection (5) above, and in cases of subsections (3) and (4) above, § 86(3) shall apply mutatis mutandis.

§ 130a Attempting to cause the commission of offences by means of publication

(1) Whosoever disseminates, publicly displays, posts, presents, or otherwise makes accessible written material (§ 11(3)) capable of serving as an instruction for an unlawful act named in § 126(1) and intended by its content to encourage or cause others to commit such an act, shall be liable to imprisonment of not more than three years or a fine.

(2) Whosoever

1. disseminates, publicly displays, posts, presents, or otherwise makes accessible written material (§ 11(3)) capable of serving as an instruction for an unlawful act named in § 126(1); or

2. gives instructions for an unlawful act named in § 126(1) publicly or in a meeting,

in order to encourage or cause others to commit such an act, shall incur the same penalty.

(3) § 86(3) shall apply mutatis mutandis.

§ 131 Dissemination of depictions of violence

(1) Whosoever

1. disseminates written materials (§ 11(3)), which describe cruel or otherwise inhuman acts of violence against humans or humanoid beings in a manner expressing glorification or which downplays such acts of violence or which represents the cruel or inhuman aspects of the event in a manner which violates human dignity;

2. publicly displays, posts, presents, or otherwise makes them accessible;

3. offers, supplies or makes them accessible to a person under eighteen years; or

4. produces, obtains, supplies, stocks, offers, announces, commends, undertakes to import or export them, in order to use them or copies obtained from them within the meaning of numbers 1 to 3 above or facilitate such use by another,

shall be liable to imprisonment of not more than one year or a fine.

(2) Whosoever disseminates a presentation with a content indicated in subsection (1) above by radio, media services, or telecommunication services shall incur the same penalty.

(3) Subsections (1) and (2) above shall not apply in cases of reporting about current or historical events.

(4) Subsection (1) No 3 above shall not apply if the person authorised to care for another person acts; this shall not apply if that person grossly neglects his duty of education by offering, giving, or making them accessible.

§ 132 Arrogation of public office

Whosoever unlawfully engages in the exercise of a public office or undertakes an act which may only be undertaken with the authority of a public office, shall be liable to imprisonment of not more than two years or a fine.

§ 132a Abuse of titles, professional classifications and symbols

(1) Whosoever, without authorisation

1. uses domestic or foreign titles of office or government service, academic degrees, honorific titles or public honours;

2. uses the professional designation physician, dentist, psychological psychotherapist, child or youth psychotherapist, psychotherapist, veterinarian, pharmacist, attorney, patent attorney, certified public accountant, sworn auditor, tax consultant or tax agent;

3. uses the title of publicly appointed expert;[7] or

---

[7] It is doubtful whether this provision protects the German titles under Nos 2 and 3 in their translations, because they are specified for the German context. The translation is therefore merely an aid to understanding the provision.

4. wears domestic or foreign uniforms, official dress or official insignia,

shall be liable to imprisonment of not more than one year or a fine.

(2) Academic degrees, titles, honours, uniforms, official dress or official insignia which are easy to confuse with those named in subsection (1) above shall be equal to those named in subsection (1).

(3) Subsections (1) and (2) above shall also apply to titles, honours, official dress and official insignia of churches and other religious associations under public law.

(4) Objects to which a crime under subsection (1) No 4 above relates, alone, or in conjunction with subsections (2) or (3) above, may be subject to a deprivation order.

§ 133 Destruction of materials under official safekeeping

(1) Whosoever destroys, damages or removes from official access documents or other chattels in official safekeeping or which have been officially placed in his or another's safekeeping, shall be liable to imprisonment of not more than two years or a fine.

(2) The same shall apply to documents or other chattels in the official safekeeping of a church or another religious association under public law or which have been officially placed by them in the safekeeping of the offender.

(3) Whosoever commits the offence in relation to an object which has been entrusted to or made accessible to him as a public official or a person entrusted with special public service functions shall be liable to imprisonment of not more than five years or a fine.

§ 134 Defacing official notices

Whosoever knowingly destroys, removes, disfigures, defaces or distorts the meaning of an official document that has been publicly displayed as an announcement shall be liable to imprisonment of not more than one year or a fine.

§ 135 *(repealed)*

§ 136 Destruction of objects under seizure or seal

(1) Whosoever destroys, damages or entirely or in part removes an object under lien or otherwise under official seizure, shall be liable to imprisonment of not more than one year or a fine.

(2) Whosoever damages, replaces or defaces an official seal applied in order to seize, officially seal or mark objects, or whosoever entirely or in part renders the attachment produced by the seal ineffective, shall incur the same penalty.

(3) The offence shall not be punishable under subsections (1) and (2) above if the lien, the seizure or the application of the seal was not executed by lawful

official act. This shall also apply if the offender mistakenly assumes that the official act was lawful.

(4)   § 113(4) shall apply mutatis mutandis.

§ 137 (repealed)

§ 138 Omission to bring planned offences to the attention of the authorities

(1)   Whosoever has credible information about the planning or the commission of the following offences:

    1.   preparation of a war of aggression (§ 80);
    2.   high treason under §§ 81 to 83(1);
    3.   treason or an endangerment of peace under §§ 94 to 96, § 97a or § 100;
    4.   counterfeiting money or securities under § 146, § 151, § 152 or counterfeiting debit cards and blank eurocheque forms under § 152b(1) to (3);
    5.   murder under specific aggravating circumstances (§ 211), murder (§ 212), genocide (§ 6 of the Code of International Criminal Law), a crime against humanity (§ 7 of the Code of International Criminal Law), or a war crime (§ 8, § 9, § 10, § 11 or § 12 of the Code of International Criminal Law);
    6.   an offence against personal liberty in cases under § 232(3), (4), or (5), § 233(3), each to the extent it involves a felony, § 234, § 234a, § 239a or § 239b;
    7.   robbery or blackmail using force or threat to life and limb (§§ 249 to 251 or § 255); or
    8.   offences creating a danger to the public under §§ 306 to 306c, § 307(1) to (3), § 308(1) to (4), § 309(1) to (5), § 310, § 313, § 314, § 315(3), § 315b(3), § 316a or § 316c

at a time when the commission or result can still be averted, and fails to report it in time to the public authorities or the person threatened, shall be liable to imprisonment of not more than five years or a fine.

(2)   Whosoever credibly learns of the planning or execution of a crime under § 129a, also in conjunction with § 129b(1), 1st and 2nd sentences, at a time when the commission can still be averted, and fails to report it promptly to the public authorities, shall incur the same penalty. § 129b(1) 3rd to 5th sentences shall apply mutatis mutandis.

(3)   Whosoever by gross negligence fails to make a report although he has credible information about the planning or the commission of an unlawful act, shall be liable to imprisonment of not more than one year or a fine.

§ 139 Exceptions to liability

(1)   If in cases under § 138 the offence has not been attempted the court may order a discharge.

(2) A clergyman shall not be obliged to report what has been confided to him in his capacity as a spiritual counsellor.

(3) Whosoever fails to report an offence, if the report would have had to be made against a relative, shall be exempt from liability if he made earnest efforts to dissuade him from committing the offence or to avert the result, unless it is a case of

1. murder (§ 211 or § 212);
2. genocide under § 6 No 1 of the Code of International Criminal Law, or a crime against humanity under § 7(1) of the Code of International Criminal Law, or a war crime under § 8(1) No 1 of the Code of International Criminal Law;
3. abduction for the purpose of blackmail (§ 239a(1)), hostage taking (§ 239b(1)) or an attack on air or maritime traffic (§ 316c(1)) by a terrorist organisation (§ 129a, also in conjunction with § 129b(1)).

Under the same conditions an attorney, defence counsel, physician, psychotherapist, or child or youth psychotherapist shall not be obliged to report what was confided to them in their professional capacity. The professional assistants of those persons named in the 2nd sentence above and those persons who work for them as part of their professional education shall not be obliged to report what they learn in their professional capacity.

(4) Whosoever averts the commission or the result of the offence other than by reporting shall be exempt from liability. If the commission or result of the offence does not take place regardless of the contribution of the person obliged to report his earnest efforts to avert the result shall suffice for exemption from liability.

§ 140 Rewarding and approving of offences

Whosoever

1. rewards or
2. publicly, in a meeting or through dissemination of written materials (§ 11(3)), and in a manner that is capable of disturbing the public peace, approves of

one of the unlawful acts named in § 138(1) Nos 1 to 4 and § 126(1), or an unlawful act pursuant to § 176(3), § 176a and § 176b, § 177 and § 178, or § 179(3), (5) and 6 after it has been committed or attempted shall be liable to imprisonment of not more than three years or a fine.

§ 141 (repealed)

§ 142 Leaving the scene of an accident without cause

(1) A party to a road traffic accident who leaves the scene of the accident before he

1. has facilitated, on behalf of the other parties to the accident and any persons suffering injury or damage, the determination of his identity, his vehicle and the nature of his involvement through his presence and a statement that he was involved in the accident; or
2. has waited for an appropriate period of time under the circumstances, during which no one was willing to make such determinations,

shall be liable to imprisonment of not more than three years or a fine.

(2) A party to an accident shall also be liable under subsection (1) above if he

1. after expiry of the waiting period (subsection (1) No 2 above); or
2. justifiably or excusably

left the scene of the accident but subsequently does not without undue delay make these determinations possible.

(3) A party to the accident satisfies the obligation to subsequently make the determinations possible if he informs the persons entitled to receive such information (subsection (1) No 1 above) or a nearby police station that he was involved in the accident, and if he states his address and whereabouts as well as the licence plate number and location of his vehicle, and makes it available for prompt examination for a reasonable period. This shall not apply if he intentionally obstructs the determinations by his conduct.

(4) The court shall mitigate the sentence (§ 49(1)) in cases under subsections (1) and (2) above or may order a discharge under these provisions if the party to the accident subsequently voluntarily makes the determinations possible (subsection (3) above) within twenty-four hours after an accident which did not take place in flowing traffic and which resulted in merely minor property damage.

(5) A party to an accident shall be deemed to be anyone whose conduct under the circumstances may have contributed to causing the accident.

§ 143 (repealed)

§ 144 (repealed)

§ 145 Abuse of emergency phones; tampering with means of accident prevention and first aid

(1) Whosoever intentionally or knowingly

1. abuses emergency calls or distress signals; or
2. pretends that assistance by other persons is required due to an accident or a common danger or emergency,

shall be liable to imprisonment of not more than one year or a fine.

(2) Whosoever intentionally or knowingly

1. removes, defaces or distorts the meaning of warning or prohibition signs which serve to prevent accidents or common danger; or
2. removes, alters or renders unusable protective equipment which serves to prevent accidents or common danger, or rescue equipment designed for rendering assistance during accidents or common danger,

shall be liable to imprisonment of not more than two years or a fine unless the act is punishable under § 303 or § 304.

§ 145a Violating the directions of a supervision order

Whosoever violates a particular direction as indicated in § 68b(1) during the operational period of a supervision order and thereby endangers the objective of the measure, shall be liable to imprisonment of not more than one year or a fine. The offence may only be prosecuted upon the request of the supervising authority (§ 68a).

§ 145b (repealed)

§ 145c Violation of a professional disqualification

Whosoever engages in a profession, branch of profession, trade or branch of trade for himself or another or allows another to engage in it for him although he or the other are subject to a professional disqualification order shall be liable to imprisonment of not more than one year or a fine.

§ 145d Misleading the authorities about the commission of an offence

(1) Whosoever intentionally and knowingly misleads a public authority or an agency competent to receive criminal complaints about the fact

1. that an unlawful act has been committed; or
2. that the commission of one of the unlawful acts under § 126(1) is imminent,

shall be liable to imprisonment of not more than three years or a fine unless the offence is punishable under § 164, § 258 or § 258a.

(2) Whosoever intentionally and knowingly attempts to mislead one of the authorities indicated in subsection (1) above about the participants

1. in an unlawful act; or
2. in an imminent unlawful act under § 126(1)

shall incur the same penalty.

CHAPTER EIGHT
COUNTERFEITING OF MONEY AND OFFICIAL STAMPS

§ 146 Counterfeiting money

(1) Whosoever

    1. counterfeits money with the intent that it be brought into circulation as genuine or that such bringing into circulation be facilitated, or alters money with such intent, so that it appears to be of a higher value;

    2. procures or offers for sale counterfeit money with such intent; or

    3. brings counterfeit money which he counterfeited, altered or procured under the provisions of Nos 1 or 2 above into circulation as genuine,

    shall be liable to imprisonment of not less than one year.

(2) If the offender acts on a commercial basis or as a member of a gang whose purpose is the continued counterfeiting of money the penalty shall be imprisonment of not less than two years.

(3) In less serious cases under subsection (1) above, the penalty shall be imprisonment from three months to five years, in less serious cases under subsection (2) above, imprisonment from one to ten years.

§ 147 Circulation of counterfeit money

(1) Whosoever brings counterfeit money into circulation other than in cases under § 146 shall be liable to imprisonment of not more than five years or a fine.

(2) The attempt shall be punishable.

§ 148 Counterfeiting official stamps

(1) Whosoever

    1. counterfeits official stamps with the intent that they be used or brought into circulation as genuine or that such use or bringing into circulation be facilitated, or alters official stamps with such intent, so that they appear to be of a higher value;

    2. procures counterfeit official stamps with such intent; or

    3. uses, offers for sale or brings into circulation counterfeit official stamps as genuine,

    shall be liable to imprisonment of not more than five years or a fine.

(2) Whosoever uses or brings into circulation as valid used official stamps from which the devaluation mark has been removed, shall be liable to imprisonment of not more than one year or a fine.

(3) The attempt shall be punishable.

§ 149 Preparatory acts

(1) Whosoever prepares to counterfeit money or stamps by producing, procuring for himself or another, offering for sale, storing or giving to another

1. plates, frames, type, blocks, negatives, stencils, computer programs or similar equipment which by its nature is suitable for the commission of the offence;
2. paper, which is identical or easy to confuse with the type of paper designated for the production of money or official stamps and especially protected against imitation; or
3. holograms or other elements affording protection against counterfeiting

shall be liable to imprisonment of not more than five years or a fine if he prepared to counterfeit money, otherwise with imprisonment of not more than two years or a fine.

(2) Whosoever voluntarily

1. gives up the commission of the offence prepared for and averts a danger caused by him that others continue to prepare the offence or commit it, or prevents the completion of the offence; and
2. destroys or renders unusable the means for counterfeiting, to the extent that they still exist and are useful for counterfeiting, or reports their existence to a public authority or surrenders them there,

shall not be liable under subsection (1) above.

(3) If the danger that others continue to prepare or commit the offence is averted, or the completion of the act prevented regardless of the contribution of the offender his voluntary and earnest efforts to achieve this aim shall suffice in lieu of subsection (2) No 1 above.

§ 150 Extended confiscation and deprivation

(1) In cases under § 146, §148(1) or the preparation to counterfeit money under § 149(1) and § 152a as well as § 152b, § 73d shall apply if the offender acts on a commercial basis or as the member of a gang whose purpose is the continued counterfeiting of money.

(2) If a crime under this chapter has been committed the counterfeit money, the counterfeit or devalued stamps and the means of counterfeiting listed in § 149 shall be subject to a deprivation order.

§ 151 Securities

The following securities shall be equivalent to money within the meaning of § 146, § 147, §149 and § 150 if they are especially protected against imitation by print and type of paper:

1. bearer and order bonds which are parts of an entire issue, if the payment of a specified sum of money is promised in the bonds;

2. shares of stock;
3. share certificates issued by capital investment companies;
4. interest, dividend and renewal coupons of the types of securities indicated in Nos 1 to 3 above as well as certificates of delivery of such securities;
5. traveller's cheques.

§ 152 Foreign money, stamps and securities

§§ 146 to 151 shall apply to money, stamps and securities of a foreign currency area.

§ 152a Counterfeiting of debit cards, etc, cheques, and promissory notes

(1) Whosoever for the purpose of deception in legal commerce or to facilitate such deception

   1. counterfeits or alters domestic or foreign payment cards, cheques or promissory notes; or
   2. procures for himself or another, offers for sale, gives to another or uses such counterfeit cards, cheques, or promissory notes

shall be liable to imprisonment of not more than five years or a fine.

(2) The attempt shall be punishable.
(3) If the offender acts on a commercial basis or as a member of a gang whose purpose is the continued commission of offences under subsection (1) above the penalty shall be imprisonment from six months to ten years.
(4) Payment cards within the meaning of subsection (1) above are cards

   1. which are provided by a credit or financial services institution, and
   2. which are specially protected against imitation through design or coding.

(5) § 149 to the extent that it refers to the counterfeiting of stamps and § 150(2) shall apply mutatis mutandis.

§ 152b Counterfeiting of credit cards, etc, and blank eurocheque forms

(1) Whosoever commits an offence listed in § 152a(1) with regard to guaranteed payment cards or blank eurocheque forms shall be liable to imprisonment from one to ten years.
(2) If the offender acts on a commercial basis or as the member of a gang whose purpose is the continued commission of offences under subsection (1) above the penalty shall be imprisonment of not less than two years.
(3) In less serious cases under subsection (1) above the penalty shall be imprisonment from three months to five years and in less serious cases under subsection (2) above imprisonment from one to ten years.

(4) Guaranteed payment cards within the meaning of subsection 1 above are credit cards, eurocheque cards, and other cards

    1. the use of which can oblige the issuer to make a guaranteed payment by money transfer; and

    2. which are especially protected against imitation through design or coding.

(5) § 149 to the extent that it refers to the counterfeiting of money and § 150(2) shall apply mutatis mutandis.

CHAPTER NINE
FALSE TESTIMONY AND PERJURY

§ 153 False testimony

Whosoever as a witness or expert gives false unsworn testimony before a court or other authority competent to examine witnesses and experts under oath shall be liable to imprisonment from three months to five years.

§ 154 Perjury

(1) Whosoever falsely takes an oath before a court or another authority competent to administer oaths, shall be liable to imprisonment of not less than one year.

(2) In less serious cases the penalty shall be imprisonment from six months to five years.

§ 155 Affirmations equivalent to oath

The following shall be equivalent to an oath:

    1. the affirmation in lieu of oath;

    2. any invocation of a previous oath or affirmation in lieu of oath.

§ 156 False sworn affidavits

Whosoever before a public authority competent to administer sworn affidavits, falsely makes such an affidavit or falsely testifies while referring to such an affidavit shall be liable to imprisonment of not more than three years or a fine.

§ 157 Duress

(1) If a witness or an expert has perjured himself or given false unsworn testimony, the court in its discretion may mitigate the sentence (§ 49(2)) or in the case of unsworn testimony order a discharge, if the offender told a lie in order to avert from a relative or himself a danger of being punished or subjected to a custodial measure of rehabilitation and incapacitation.

(2)   The court in its discretion may also mitigate the sentence (§ 49(2)) or order a discharge if a person not yet competent to take an oath has given false unsworn testimony.

§ 158 Correction of false testimony

(1)   The court in its discretion may mitigate the sentence (§ 49(2)) for perjury, false sworn affidavit or false unsworn testimony or order a discharge if the offender corrects his false testimony in time.
(2)   The correction is no longer in time if it can no longer be used in reaching the decision, if detriment to another has been caused by the offence, or if a complaint has already been laid against the offender or an investigation been initiated.
(3)   The correction may be made to the authority before whom the false testimony was given or by whom it is to be evaluated in the proceedings, to a court, a public prosecutor or a police authority.

§ 159 Attempt to abet false testimony

§ 30(1), § 31(1) No 1 shall apply mutatis mutandis to an attempt to abet false unsworn testimony (§ 153) and a false sworn affidavit (§ 156).

§ 160 Procuring false testimony

(1)   Whosoever procures another to take a false oath shall be liable to imprisonment of not more than two years or a fine; whosoever procures another to make a false sworn affidavit or give false unsworn testimony shall be liable to imprisonment of not more than six months or a fine of not more than one hundred and eighty daily units.
(2)   The attempt shall be punishable.

§§ 161 and 162 (repealed)

§ 163 Negligent offences

(1)   If a person commits one of the offences listed in §§ 154 to 156 negligently the penalty shall be imprisonment of not more than one year or a fine.
(2)   The offender shall be exempt from liability if he corrects his false testimony in time. The provisions of § 158(2) and (3) shall apply mutatis mutandis.

CHAPTER TEN
FALSE ACCUSATION

§ 164 False accusation

(1) Whosoever intentionally and knowingly and with the purpose that official proceedings or other official measures be brought or be continued against another before a public authority accuses another before a public authority or a public official competent to receive a criminal information or a military superior or publicly, of having committed an unlawful act or a violation of an official duty, shall be liable to imprisonment of not more than five years or a fine.

(2) Whosoever intentionally and knowingly and with the same purpose, makes any other assertion of fact about another before one of the authorities indicated in subsection (1) above or publicly which is capable of causing official proceedings or other official measures to be brought or continued against that person shall incur the same penalty.

§ 165 Publication of conviction

(1) If the offence under § 164 was committed publicly or through dissemination of written materials (§ 11(3)) and if a sentence was imposed the court shall order, upon application of the victim, that the conviction for false accusation be publicly announced upon request. If the victim dies the right to file the application passes to the relatives indicated in § 77(2). § 77(2) to (4) shall apply mutatis mutandis.

(2) § 200(2) shall apply mutatis mutandis with regard to the procedure for publication.

CHAPTER ELEVEN
OFFENCES RELATED TO RELIGION AND IDEOLOGY

§ 166 Defamation of religions, religious and ideological associations

(1) Whosoever publicly or through dissemination of written materials (§ 11(3)) defames the religion or ideology of others in a manner that is capable of disturbing the public peace, shall be liable to imprisonment of not more than three years or a fine.

(2) Whosoever publicly or through dissemination of written materials (§ 11(3)) defames a church or other religious or ideological association within Germany, or their institutions or customs in a manner that is capable of disturbing the public peace, shall incur the same penalty.

§ 167 Disturbing the exercise of religion

(1) Whosoever

  1. intentionally and inappropriately disturbs a religious service or an act of religious worship of a church or other religious association within Germany or
  2. commits defamatory mischief at a place dedicated to the religious worship of such a religious association

  shall be liable to imprisonment of not more than three years or a fine.

(2) The ceremonies of an ideological association within Germany shall be equivalent to religious worship.

§ 167a Disturbing a funeral

Whosoever intentionally or knowingly disturbs a funeral shall be liable to imprisonment of not more than three years or a fine.

§ 168 Desecration of graves etc

(1) Whosoever unlawfully takes away the body or parts of the body of a deceased person, a dead foetus or parts thereof or the ashes of a deceased person from the custody of the person entitled thereto or whosoever commits defamatory mischief on them, shall be liable to imprisonment of not more than three years or a fine.

(2) Whosoever destroys or damages the place where a body is laid in state, a burial site or a public memorial for the dead or whosoever commits defamatory mischief on them shall incur the same penalty.

(3) The attempt shall be punishable.

CHAPTER TWELVE
OFFENCES RELATED TO THE PERSONAL STATUS REGISTRY, MARRIAGE AND THE FAMILY

§ 169 Falsification of personal status

(1) Whosoever declares a child to be somebody else's or falsely gives or suppresses the personal status of another to a public authority responsible for the maintenance of personal status registers or the determination of personal status, shall be liable to imprisonment of not more than two years or a fine.

(2) The attempt shall be punishable.

§ 170 Non-payment of child support etc

(1) Whosoever evades a statutory maintenance obligation so that the necessities of the person entitled to maintenance are endangered or would be endangered without the assistance of others, shall be liable to imprisonment of not more than three years or a fine.

(2) Whosoever is obliged to provide maintenance to a pregnant woman and withholds this maintenance in an inappropriate manner and thereby causes a termination of the pregnancy, shall be liable to imprisonment of not more than five years or a fine.

§ 171 Violation of duties of care or education

Whosoever grossly neglects his duty to provide care or education for a person under the age of sixteen and thereby creates a danger that the person's physical or mental development could be seriously damaged, that the person will engage in crime or in prostitution, shall be liable to imprisonment of not more than three years or a fine.

§ 172 Bigamy

Whosoever contracts a marriage although he is already married, or whosoever contracts a marriage with a married person, shall be liable to imprisonment of not more than three years or a fine.

§ 173 Incest

(1) Whosoever performs an act of sexual intercourse with a consanguine descendant shall be liable to imprisonment of not more than three years or a fine.

(2) Whosoever performs an act of sexual intercourse with a consanguine relative in an ascending line shall be liable to imprisonment of not more than two years or a fine; this shall also apply if the relationship as a relative has ceased to exist. Consanguine siblings who perform an act of sexual intercourse with each other shall incur the same penalty.

(3) Descendants and siblings shall not be liable pursuant to this provision if they were not yet eighteen years of age at the time of the act.

CHAPTER THIRTEEN
OFFENCES AGAINST SEXUAL SELF-DETERMINATION

§ 174 Abuse of position of trust

(1) Whosoever engages in sexual activity

  1. with a person under sixteen years of age who is entrusted to him for upbringing, education or care;

2. with a person under eighteen years of age who is entrusted to him for upbringing, education or care or who is his subordinate within an employment or a work relationship, by abusing the dependence associated with the upbringing, educational, care, employment or work relationship; or
3. with his biological or adopted child not yet eighteen years of age,

or allows them to engage in sexual activities with himself, shall be liable to imprisonment from three months to five years.

(2) Whosoever, under the conditions of subsection (1) Nos 1 to 3 above

1. engages in sexual activity in the presence of the person; or
2. induces the person to engage in sexual activity in his presence,

in order to obtain sexual gratification for himself or the person shall be liable to imprisonment of not more than three years or a fine.

(3) The attempt shall be punishable.
(4) In cases under subsection (1) No 1 above, or subsection (2) above in conjunction with subsection (1) No 1, the court may order a discharge under this provision if taking into consideration the conduct of the person the harm of the offence is of a minor nature.

§ 174a Sexual abuse of prisoners, patients and institutionalised persons

(1) Whosoever engages in sexual activity with a prisoner or a person detained by order of a public authority, who is entrusted to him for upbringing, education, supervision or care, by abusing his position, or allows them to engage in sexual activity with himself shall be liable to imprisonment from three months to five years.
(2) Whosoever abuses a person who has been admitted to an institution for persons who are ill or in need of assistance and are entrusted to him for supervision or care, by engaging in sexual activity with the person by exploiting the person's illness or need of assistance, or allows them to engage in sexual activity with himself shall incur the same penalty.
(3) The attempt shall be punishable.

§ 174b Abuse of official position

(1) Whosoever in his capacity as a public official charged with participation in criminal proceedings or proceedings with the aim of imposing a custodial measure of rehabilitation and incapacitation or detention imposed by a public authority, by abusing the dependency caused by the proceedings, engages in sexual activity with the person against whom the proceedings are directed or allows them to engage in sexual activity with himself shall be liable to imprisonment from three months to five years.
(2) The attempt shall be punishable.

§ 174c Abuse of a relationship of counselling, treatment or care

(1) Whosoever engages in sexual activity with a person entrusted to him for counselling, treatment or care because of a mental illness or disability including an addiction, or because of a physical illness or disability, and abuses the counselling, treatment or care relationship, or allows the person to engage in sexual activity with himself shall be liable to imprisonment from three months to five years.

(2) Whosoever engages in sexual activity with a person entrusted to him for psychotherapeutic treatment by abusing the treatment relationship or allows them to engage in sexual activity with himself shall incur the same penalty.

(3) The attempt shall be punishable.

§ 175 (repealed)

§ 176 Child abuse

(1) Whosoever engages in sexual activity with a person under fourteen years of age (child) or allows the child to engage in sexual activity with himself shall be liable to imprisonment from six months to ten years.

(2) Whosoever induces a child to engage in sexual activity with a third person or to allow third persons to engage in sexual activity with the child shall incur the same penalty.

(3) In especially serious cases the penalty shall be imprisonment of not less than one year.

(4) Whosoever

    1. engages in sexual activity in the presence of a child;

    2. induces the child to engage in sexual activity on their own person;

    3. presents a child with written materials (§ 11(3)) to induce him to engage in sexual activity with or in the presence of the offender or a third person or allow the offender or a third person to engage in sexual activity with him; or

    4. presents a child with pornographic illustrations or images, audio recording media with pornographic content or pornographic speech,

shall be liable to imprisonment from three months to five years.

(5) Whosoever supplies or promises to supply a child for an offence under subsections (1) to (4) above or who agrees with another to commit such an offence shall be liable to imprisonment from three months to five years.

(6) The attempt shall be punishable; this shall not apply to offences under subsection (4) Nos 3 and 4 and subsection (5) above.

§ 176a Aggravated child abuse

(1) The sexual abuse of children under § 176(1) and (2) shall entail a sentence of imprisonment of not less than one year if the offender was convicted of such an offence by final judgment within the previous five years.

(2) The sexual abuse of children under § 176(1) and (2) shall entail a sentence of imprisonment of not less than two years if

   1. a person over eighteen years of age performs sexual intercourse or similar sexual acts with the child which include a penetration of the body, or allows them to be performed on himself by the child;
   2. the offence is committed jointly by more than one person; or
   3. the offender by the offence places the child in danger of serious injury or substantial impairment of his physical or emotional development.

(3) Whosoever under § 176(1) to (3), (4) Nos 1 or 2 or § 176(6) acts as a principal or secondary participant with the intent of making the act the object of a pornographic medium (§ 11(3)) which is to be disseminated pursuant to § 184b(1) to (3) shall be liable to imprisonment of not less than two years.

(4) In less serious cases under subsection (1) above the penalty shall be imprisonment from three months to five years, in less serious cases under subsection (2) above imprisonment from one to ten years.

(5) Whosoever under § 176(1) to (3) seriously physically abuses the child or places the child in danger of death shall be liable to imprisonment of not less than five years.

(6) Any period during which the offender was detained in an institution pursuant to an order of a public authority shall not be credited to the term indicated in subsection (1) above. An offence resulting in a conviction abroad shall be equivalent, under subsection (1) above, to an offence resulting in a domestic conviction if under German criminal law it would have been an offence under § 176(1) or (2).

§ 176b Child abuse causing death

If the offender in cases under § 176 and § 176a causes the death of the child at least by gross negligence the penalty shall be imprisonment for life or not less than ten years.

§ 177 Sexual assault by use of force or threats; rape

(1) Whosoever coerces another person

   1. by force;
   2. by threat of imminent danger to life or limb; or
   3. by exploiting a situation in which the victim is unprotected and at the mercy of the offender,

to suffer sexual acts by the offender or a third person on their own person or to engage actively in sexual activity with the offender or a third person, shall be liable to imprisonment of not less than one year.

(2) In especially serious cases the penalty shall be imprisonment of not less than two years. An especially serious case typically occurs if

    1. the offender performs sexual intercourse with the victim or performs similar sexual acts with the victim, or allows them to be performed on himself by the victim, especially if they degrade the victim or if they entail penetration of the body (rape); or

    2. the offence is committed jointly by more than one person.

(3) The penalty shall be imprisonment of not less than three years if the offender

    1. carries a weapon or another dangerous instrument;

    2. otherwise carries an instrument or other means for the purpose of preventing or overcoming the resistance of another person through force or threat of force; or

    3. by the offence places the victim in danger of serious injury.

(4) The penalty shall be imprisonment of not less than five years if

    1. the offender uses a weapon or another dangerous instrument during the commission of the offence; or if

    2. the offender

        (a) seriously physically abuses the victim during the offence; or

        (b) by the offence places the victim in danger of death.

(5) In less serious cases under subsection (1) above the penalty shall be imprisonment from six months to five years, in less serious cases under subsections (3) and (4) above imprisonment from one to ten years.

§ 178 Sexual assault by use of force or threat of force and rape causing death

If the offender through sexual assault or rape (§ 177) causes the death of the victim at least by gross negligence the penalty shall be imprisonment for life or not less than ten years.

§ 179 Abuse of persons who are incapable of resistance

(1) Whosoever abuses another person who is incapable of resistance

    1. because of a mental illness or disability including an addiction or because of a profound consciousness disorder; or

    2. is physically incapable,

and by exploiting the incapability to resist engages in sexual activity with the person or allows them actively to engage in sexual activity on his person shall be liable to imprisonment from six months to ten years.

(2)　Whosoever abuses a person incapable of resistance (subsection (1) above), by inducing the person, under exploitation of the incapability of resistance, to engage actively in sexual activity with a third person or to allow a third person to engage in sexual activity with them, shall incur the same penalty.

(3)　In especially serious cases the penalty shall be imprisonment of not less than one year.

(4)　The attempt shall be punishable.

(5)　The penalty shall be imprisonment of not less than two years if

    1.　the offender performs sexual intercourse or similar sexual acts with the victim which include penetration of the body, or allows them to be committed on himself by the victim;

    2.　the offence is committed jointly by more than one person; or

    3.　by the offence the offender places the victim in danger of serious injury or substantial impairment of his physical or emotional development.

(5)　In less serious cases under subsection (5) above the penalty shall be imprisonment from one to ten years.

(6)　§ 177(4) No 2 and § 178 shall apply mutatis mutandis.

§ 180 Causing minors to engage in sexual activity

(1)　Whosoever encourages a person under sixteen years of age to engage in sexual activity with or in the presence of a third person or whosoever encourages sexual acts of a third person on a person under sixteen years of age

    1.　by acting as an intermediary; or

    2.　by creating an opportunity,

shall be liable to imprisonment of not more than three years or a fine. The 1st sentence No 2 above shall not apply if the offender is the person responsible for the care of the minor unless the offender, if responsible for the care of the minor, grossly violates his duty of education.

(2)　Whosoever induces a person under eighteen years of age to engage in sexual activity with or in the presence of a third person or to suffer sexual acts by a third person for a financial reward, or whosoever encourages such acts by acting as an intermediary, shall be liable to imprisonment of not more than five years or a fine.

(3)　Whosoever induces a person under eighteen years of age who is entrusted to him for upbringing, education or care or who is his subordinate within an employment or a work relationship, by abusing the dependence associated with the upbringing, educational, care, employment or work relationship to engage in sexual activity with or in the presence of a third person or to suffer sexual acts by a third person shall be liable to imprisonment of not more than five years or a fine.

(4)　In cases under subsections (2) and (3) above the attempt shall be punishable.

§ 180a Exploitation of prostitutes

(1) Whosoever on a commercial basis maintains or manages an operation in which persons engage in prostitution and in which they are held in personal or financial dependency shall be liable to imprisonment of not more than three years or a fine.

(2) Whosoever

   1. provides a dwelling or on a commercial basis an abode or a residence to a person under eighteen years of age for the exercise of prostitution; or
   2. urges another person to whom he has furnished a dwelling for the exercise of prostitution to engage in prostitution or exploits the person in that respect,

shall incur the same penalty.

§ 180b and § 181 (repealed)

§ 181a Controlling prostitution

(1) Whosoever

   1. exploits another person who engages in prostitution; or
   2. for his own material benefit supervises another person's engagement in prostitution, determines the place, time, extent or other circumstances of the engagement in prostitution, or takes measures to prevent the person from giving up prostitution, and for that purpose maintains a general relationship with the person beyond a particular occasion

shall be liable to imprisonment from six months to five years.

(2) Whosoever impairs another person's personal or financial independence by promoting that person's engagement in prostitution, by procuring sexual relations on a commercial basis, and for that purpose maintains a general relationship with the person beyond a particular occasion shall be liable to imprisonment of not more than three years or a fine.

(3) Whosoever commits the offences under subsection (1) Nos 1 and 2 above or the promotion under subsection (2) above in relation to his spouse shall incur the penalty under subsections (1) and (2) above.

§ 181b Supervision order

In cases under §§ 174 to 174c, §§ 176 to 180, § 181a and § 182 the court may make a supervision order (§ 68(1)).

§ 181c Confiscatory expropriation and extended confiscation

§ 182 Abuse of juveniles

(1)   A person over eighteen years of age who abuses a person under sixteen years of age by

    1.   engaging in sexual activity with the person or causing the person to engage actively in sexual activity with him by taking advantage of an exploitative situation or for a financial reward or

    2.   by taking advantage of an exploitative situation inducing the person to engage in sexual activity with a third person or to suffer sexual acts committed on their own body by a third person,

shall be liable to imprisonment of not more than five years or a fine.

(2)   A person over twenty-one years of age who abuses a person under sixteen years of age by

    1.   engaging in sexual activity with the person or causing the person to engage actively in sexual activity with him or

    2.   inducing the person to engage in sexual activity with a third person or to suffer sexual acts committed on their own body by a third person,

and thereby exploits the victim's lack of capacity for sexual self-determination shall be liable to imprisonment of not more than three years or a fine.

(3)   In cases under subsection (2) above the offence may only be prosecuted upon request unless the prosecuting authority considers propio motu that prosecution is required out of special public interest.

(4)   In cases under subsections (1) and (2) above the court may order a discharge under these provisions if in consideration of the conduct of the person against whom the offence was committed the harm of the offence is of a minor nature.

§ 183 Exhibitionism

(1)   A man who annoys another person by an exhibitionist act shall be liable to imprisonment of not more than one year or a fine.

(2)   The offence shall only be prosecuted upon request unless the prosecuting authority considers propio motu that prosecution is required out of special public interest.

(3)   The court may suspend the sentence if there is reason to believe that the offender will only cease to commit exhibitionist acts after lengthy medical treatment.

(4)   Subsection (3) above shall also apply if a man or a woman is convicted because of an exhibitionist act

    1.   under another provision which imposes a maximum term of imprisonment of no more than one year; or

    2.   under § 174(2) No 1 or § 176(3) No 1.

§ 183a Causing a public disturbance

Whosoever in public engages in sexual activity and thereby intentionally or knowingly creates a disturbance shall be liable to imprisonment of not more than one year or a fine unless the act is punishable under § 183.

§ 184 Distribution of pornography

(1) Whosoever with regard to pornographic written materials (§ 11(3))

1. offers, gives or makes them accessible to a person under eighteen years of age;
2. displays, presents or otherwise makes them accessible at a place accessible to persons under eighteen years of age, or which can be viewed by them;
3. offers or gives them to another in retail trade outside the business premises, in kiosks or other sales areas which the customer usually does not enter, through a mail-order business or in commercial lending libraries or reading circles;
3a. offers or gives them to another by means of commercial rental or comparable commercial supply for use, except for shops which are not accessible to persons under eighteen years of age and which cannot be viewed by them;
4. undertakes to import them by means of a mail-order business;
5. publicly offers, announces, or commends them at a place accessible to persons under eighteen years of age or which can be viewed by them, or through dissemination of written materials outside business transactions through the usual trade outlets;
6. allows another to obtain them without having been requested to do so;
7. shows them at a public film showing for an entry fee intended entirely or predominantly for this showing;
8. produces, obtains, supplies, stocks, or undertakes to import them in order to use them or copies made from them within the meaning of Nos 1 to 7 above or to facilitate such use by another; or
9. undertakes to export them in order to disseminate them or copies made from them abroad in violation of foreign penal provisions or to make them publicly accessible or to facilitate such use,

shall be liable to imprisonment of not more than one year or a fine.
(2) Subsection (1) No 1 above shall not apply if the offender is the person in charge of the care of the person, unless that person grossly violates his duty of education by offering, giving, or making them available. Subsection (1) No 3a above shall not apply if the act takes place in business transactions with commercial borrowers.

§ 184a Distribution of pornography depicting violence or sodomy

Whosoever

1. disseminates;
2. publicly displays, presents, or otherwise makes accessible; or
3. produces, obtains, supplies, stocks, offers, announces, commends, or undertakes to import or export, in order to use them or copies made from them within the meaning of Nos 1 or 2 above or facilitates such use by another,

pornographic written materials (§ 11(3)) that have as their object acts of violence or sexual acts of persons with animals shall be liable to imprisonment of not more than three years or a fine.

§ 184b Distribution, acquisition and possession of child pornography

(1) Whosoever

1. disseminates;
2. publicly displays, presents, or otherwise makes accessible; or
3. produces, obtains, supplies, stocks, offers, announces, commends, or undertakes to import or export in order to use them or copies made from them within the meaning of Nos 1 or 2 above or facilitates such use by another

pornographic written materials (§ 11(3)) related to the sexual abuse of children (§§ 176 to 176b) (child pornography) shall be liable to imprisonment from three months to five years.

(2) Whosoever undertakes to obtain possession for another of child pornography reproducing an actual or realistic activity shall incur the same penalty.

(3) In cases under subsection (1) or subsection (2) above the penalty shall be imprisonment of six months to ten years if the offender acts on a commercial basis or as a member of a gang whose purpose is the continued commission of such offences and the child pornography reproduces an actual or realistic activity.

(4) Whosoever undertakes to obtain possession of child pornography reproducing an actual or realistic activity shall be liable to imprisonment of not more than two years or a fine. Whosoever possesses the written materials set forth in the 1st sentence shall incur the same penalty.

(5) Subsections (2) and (4) above shall not apply to acts that exclusively serve the fulfilment of lawful official or professional duties.

(6) In cases under subsection (3) above § 73d shall apply. Objects to which an offence under subsection (2) or (4) above relates shall be subject to a deprivation order. § 74a shall apply.

§ 184c Distribution of pornographic performances by broadcasting, media services or telecommunications services

Whosoever disseminates pornographic performances via broadcast, media services, or telecommunications services shall be liable pursuant to §§ 184 to 184b. In cases under § 184(1) the 1st sentence above shall not apply to dissemination via media services or telecommunications services if it is ensured by technical or other measures that the pornographic performance is not accessible to persons under eighteen years of age.

§ 184d Unlawful prostitution

Whosoever persistently contravenes a prohibition enacted by ordinance against engaging in prostitution in particular places at all or during particular times of the day, shall be liable to imprisonment of not more than six months or a fine of not more than one hundred and eighty daily units.

§ 184e Prostitution likely to corrupt juveniles

Whosoever engages in prostitution

1. in the vicinity of a school or other locality which is intended to be visited by persons under eighteen years of age; or
2. in a house in which persons under eighteen years of age live,

in a way which is likely to morally corrupt these persons, shall be liable to imprisonment of not more than one year or a fine.

§ 184f Definitions

Within the meaning of this law

1. sexual acts and activities shall only be those which are of some relevance in relation to the protected legal interest in question;
2. sexual acts and activities in the presence of another shall be those which are committed in the presence of another who observes them.

CHAPTER FOURTEEN
LIBEL AND SLANDER

§ 185 Insult

An insult shall be punished with imprisonment of not more than one year or a fine and, if the insult is committed by means of an assault, with imprisonment of not more than two years or a fine.

§ 186 Defamation

Whosoever asserts or disseminates a fact related to another person which may defame him or negatively affect public opinion about him, shall, unless this fact can be proven to be true, be liable to imprisonment of not more than one year or a fine and, if the offence was committed publicly or through the dissemination of written materials (§ 11(3)), to imprisonment of not more than two years or a fine.

§ 187 Intentional defamation

Whosoever intentionally and knowingly asserts or disseminates an untrue fact related to another person, which may defame him or negatively affect public opinion about him or endanger his creditworthiness shall be liable to imprisonment of not more than two years or a fine, and, if the act was committed publicly, in a meeting or through dissemination of written materials (§ 11(3)) to imprisonment of not more than five years or a fine.

§ 188 Defamation of persons in the political arena

(1) If an offence of defamation (§ 186) is committed publicly, in a meeting or through dissemination of written materials (§ 11(3)) against a person involved in the popular political life based on the position of that person in public life, and if the offence may make his public activities substantially more difficult the penalty shall be imprisonment from three months to five years.

(2) An intentional defamation (§ 187) under the same conditions shall entail imprisonment from six months to five years.

§ 189 Violating the memory of the dead

Whosoever defames the memory of a deceased person shall be liable to imprisonment of not more than two years or a fine.

§ 190 Proof of truth by criminal judgment

If the asserted or disseminated fact is an offence proof of the truth thereof shall be provided if a final conviction for the act has been entered against the person insulted. Proof of truth is excluded if the insulted person had been acquitted by final judgment before the assertion or dissemination.

§ 191 (repealed)

§ 192 Insult despite proof of truth

Proof of truth of the asserted or disseminated fact shall not exclude punishment under § 185 if the insult results from the form of the assertion or dissemination or the circumstances under which it was made.

§ 193 Fair comment; defence

Critical opinions about scientific, artistic or commercial achievements, utterances made in order to exercise or protect rights or to safeguard legitimate interests, as well as remonstrations and reprimands by superiors to their subordinates, official reports or judgments by a civil servant, and similar cases shall only entail liability to the extent that the existence of an insult results from the form of the utterance of the circumstances under which it was made.

§ 194 Request to prosecute

(1) An insult may only be prosecuted upon request. If the act was committed through dissemination of written materials (§ 11(3)) or making them publicly accessible in a meeting or through a presentation by broadcast a request is not required if the victim was persecuted as a member of a group under the National Socialist or another authoritarian regime, if this group is a part of the population and the insult is connected to this persecution. The offence may not be prosecuted ex officio if the victim objects. The objection may not be withdrawn. If the victim dies the right to file a request and the right to object shall pass to the relatives indicated in § 77(2).

(2) If the memory of a deceased person has been defamed the relatives indicated in § 77(2) are entitled to file a request. If the act was committed through dissemination of written materials (§ 11(3)) or making them publicly accessible in a meeting or through a presentation by broadcast a request is not required if the deceased lost his life under the National Socialist or another authoritarian regime and the insult is connected to this persecution. The offence may not be prosecuted ex officio if the person entitled to file the request objects. The objection may not be withdrawn.

(3) If the insult was committed against a public official, a person entrusted with special public service functions or a soldier of the Armed Forces while in the execution of his duties or in relation to his duties, it may be prosecuted upon the request of his superior. If the offence is directed against a public authority or other agency that performs duties of public administration it may be prosecuted upon the request of the head of the public authority or the head of the supervisory authority. This applies mutatis mutandis to public officials and public authorities of churches and other religious associations under public law.

(4) If the offence is directed against a legislative body of the Federation or a state or another political body within the Federal Republic of Germany it may be prosecuted only upon the authorisation of that body.

§§ 195 to 198 (repealed)

§ 199 Mutual insults

If an insult is immediately reciprocated the court may order a discharge for one or both of the offenders.

§ 200 Publication of the conviction

(1) If the insult was committed publicly or through dissemination of written materials (§ 11(3)) and if a penalty is imposed the court shall, upon application of the victim or a person otherwise entitled to file a request, order that the conviction be publicly announced upon request.

(2) The manner of publication shall be indicated in the judgment. If the insult was committed through publication in a newspaper or magazine the publication shall also be included in a newspaper or magazine, if possible in the same one which contained the insult; this shall apply mutatis mutandis if the insult was committed through publication by broadcast.

CHAPTER FIFTEEN
VIOLATION OF PRIVACY

§ 201 Violation of the privacy of the spoken word

(1) Whosoever unlawfully

1. makes an audio recording of the privately spoken words of another; or
2. uses, or makes a recording thus produced accessible to a third party,

shall be liable to imprisonment of not more than three years or a fine.

(2) Whosoever unlawfully

1. overhears with an eavesdropping device the privately spoken words of another not intended for his attention; or
2. publicly communicates, verbatim or the essential content of, the privately spoken words of another recorded pursuant to subsection (1) No 1 above or overheard pursuant to subsection (2) No 1 above.

shall incur the same penalty. The offence under the 1st sentence No 2 above, shall only entail liability if the public communication may interfere with the legitimate interests of another. It is not unlawful if the public communication was made for the purpose of safeguarding overriding public interests.

(3) Whosoever, as a public official or a person entrusted with special public service functions violates the privacy of the spoken word (subsections (1) and (2) above) shall be liable to imprisonment of not more than five years or a fine.

(4) The attempt shall be punishable.

(5) The audio recording media and eavesdropping devices which the principal or secondary participant used may be subject to a deprivation order. § 74a shall apply.

§ 201a Violation of intimate privacy by taking photographs

(1) Whosoever unlawfully creates or transmits pictures of another person located in a dwelling or a room especially protected from view and thereby violates their intimate privacy shall be liable to imprisonment of not more than one year or a fine.
(2) Whosoever uses or makes available to a third party a picture created by an offence under subsection (1) above shall incur the same penalty.
(3) Whosoever unlawfully and knowingly makes available to third parties a picture that was created with the consent of another person located in a dwelling or a room especially protected from view and thereby violates his intimate privacy shall be liable to imprisonment of not more than one year or a fine.
(4) The visual media and the visual recording devices or other technical means that the principal or secondary or participant used may be subject to a deprivation order. § 74a shall apply.

§ 202 Violation of the privacy of the written word

(1) Whosoever unlawfully

   1. opens a sealed letter or another sealed document not intended for him; or
   2. obtains knowledge of the content of such a document without opening the seal by using technical means,

   shall be liable to imprisonment of not more than one year or a fine unless the act is punishable under § 206.
(2) Whosoever unlawfully obtains knowledge of the contents of a document not intended for him and which was specially protected by means of a sealed container after he has opened the container shall incur the same penalty.
(3) An illustration shall be equivalent to a document within the meaning of subsections (1) and (2) above.

§ 202a Data espionage

(1) Whosoever unlawfully obtains data for himself or another that were not intended for him and were especially protected against unauthorised access, if he has circumvented the protection, shall be liable to imprisonment of not more than three years or a fine.
(2) Within the meaning of subsection (1) above data shall only be those stored or transmitted electronically or magnetically or otherwise in a manner not immediately perceivable.

§ 202b Phishing

Whosoever unlawfully intercepts data (§ 202a(2)) not intended for him, for himself or another by technical means from a non-public data processing facility or from the electromagnetic broadcast of a data processing facility, shall be liable to imprisonment of not more than two years or a fine, unless the offence incurs a more severe penalty under other provisions.

§ 202c Acts preparatory to data espionage and phishing

(1) Whosoever prepares the commission of an offence under § 202a or § 202b by producing, acquiring for himself or another, selling, supplying to another, disseminating or making otherwise accessible

    1. passwords or other security codes enabling access to data (§ 202a(2)), or
    2. software for the purpose of the commission of such an offence shall be liable to imprisonment of not more than one year or a fine.

(2) § 149(2) and (3) shall apply mutatis mutandis.

§ 203 Violation of private secrets

(1) Whosoever unlawfully discloses a secret of another, in particular, a secret which belongs to the sphere of personal privacy or a business or trade secret, which was confided to or otherwise made known to him in his capacity as a

    1. physician, dentist, veterinarian, pharmacist or member of another health-care profession which requires state-regulated education for engaging in the profession or to use the professional title;
    2. professional psychologist with a final scientific examination recognised by the State;
    3. attorney, patent attorney, notary, defence counsel in statutorily regulated proceedings, certified public accountant, sworn auditor, tax consultant, tax agent, or organ or member of an organ of a law, patent law, accounting, auditing or tax consulting firm in the form of a company;
    4. marriage, family, education or youth counsellor as well as addiction counsellor at a counselling agency which is recognised by a public authority or body, institution or foundation under public law;
    4a. member or agent of a counselling agency recognised under § 3 and § 8 of the Act on Pregnancies in Conflict Situations;
    5. a state-recognised social worker or state-recognised social education worker; or
    6. member of a private health, accident or life insurance company or a private medical or attorney invoicing service,

shall be liable to imprisonment of not more than one year or a fine.

(2) Whosoever unlawfully discloses a secret of another, in particular, a secret which belongs to the sphere of personal privacy or a business or trade secret, which was confided to or otherwise made known to him in his capacity as a

1. public official;
2. person entrusted with special public service functions;
3. person who exercises duties or powers under the law on staff employment representation;
4. member of an investigative committee working for a legislative body of the Federation or a state, another committee or council which is not itself part of the legislative body, or as an assistant for such a committee or council; or
5. publicly appointed expert who is formally obliged by law to conscientiously fulfil his duties,

shall incur the same penalty. Particular statements about personal or material relationships of another which have been collected for public administration purposes shall be deemed to be equivalent to a secret within the meaning of the 1st sentence above; the 1st sentence above shall not apply to the extent that such particular statements are made known to other public authorities or other agencies for public administration purposes unless the law forbids it.

(2a) Subsections (1) and (2) above shall apply mutatis mutandis when a data protection officer without authorisation discloses the secret of another within the meaning of these provisions, which was entrusted to or otherwise revealed to one of the persons named in subsections (1) or (2) above in their professional capacity and of which he has gained knowledge in the course of the fulfilment of his duties as data protection officer.

(3) Other members of a bar association shall be deemed to be equivalent to an attorney named in subsection (1) No 3 above. The persons named in subsection (1) and the 1st sentence above shall be equivalent to their professionally active assistants and those persons who work with them in training for the exercise of their profession. After the death of the person obliged to keep the secret, whosoever acquired the secret from the deceased or from his estate shall be equivalent to the persons named in subsection (1) and in the 1st and 2nd sentences above.

(4) Subsections (1) to (3) above shall also apply if the offender unlawfully discloses the secret of another person after the death of that person.

(5) If the offender acts for material gain or with the intent of enriching himself or another or of harming another the penalty shall be imprisonment of not more than two years or a fine.

§ 204 Exploitation of the secrets of another

(1) Whosoever unlawfully exploits the secret of another, in particular a business or trade secret, which he is obliged to keep secret pursuant to § 203, shall be liable to imprisonment of not more than two years or a fine.

(2)   § 203(4) shall apply mutatis mutandis.

§ 205 Request to prosecute

(1)   In cases under § 201(1) and (2) and §§ 201a to 204 the offence may only be prosecuted upon request.
(2)   If the victim dies the right to file a request shall pass to the relatives pursuant to § 77(2); this shall not apply to offences under § 202a or § 202b. If the secret does not relate to the sphere of the personal privacy of the victim the right to file a request for offences under § 203 and § 204 shall pass to the heirs. If the offender discloses or exploits the secret after the death of the person in cases under § 203 and § 204, the 1st and 2nd sentences above shall apply mutatis mutandis.

§ 206 Violation of the postal and telecommunications secret

(1)   Whosoever unlawfully discloses to another person facts which are subject to the postal or telecommunications secret and which became known to him as the owner or employee of an enterprise in the business of providing postal or telecommunications services, shall be liable to imprisonment of not more than five years or a fine.
(2)   Whosoever, as an owner or employee of an enterprise indicated in subsection (1) above unlawfully

    1.   opens a piece of sealed mail which has been entrusted to such an enterprise for delivery or gains knowledge of its content without breaking the seal by using technical means;
    2.   suppresses a piece of mail entrusted to such an enterprise for delivery; or
    3.   permits or encourages one of the offences indicated in subsection (1) or in Nos 1 or 2 above,

    shall incur the same penalty.
(3)   Subsections (1) and (2) above shall apply to persons who

    1.   perform tasks of supervision over an enterprise indicated in subsection (1) above;
    2.   are entrusted by such an enterprise or with its authorisation, to provide postal or telecommunications services; or
    3.   are entrusted with the establishment of facilities serving the operation of such an enterprise or with performing work thereon.

(4)   Whosoever unlawfully discloses to another person facts which became known to him as a public official outside the postal or telecommunications service on the basis of an authorised or unauthorised infringement of the postal or telecommunications secret shall be liable to imprisonment of not more than two years or a fine.
(5)   The immediate circumstances of the postal operations of particular persons as well as the content of pieces of mail are subject to the postal secret. The

146

content of telecommunications and their immediate circumstances, especially the fact whether someone has participated in or is participating in a telecommunications event, are subject to the telecommunications secret. The telecommunications secret also extends to the immediate circumstances of unsuccessful attempts to make a connection.

§§ 207 to 210 (repealed)

CHAPTER SIXTEEN
OFFENCES AGAINST LIFE

§ 211 Murder under specific aggravating circumstances[8]

(1) Whosoever commits murder under the conditions of this provision shall be liable to imprisonment for life.
(2) A murderer under this provision is any person who kills a person for pleasure, for sexual gratification, out of greed or otherwise base motives, by stealth or cruelly or by means that pose a danger to the public or in order to facilitate or to cover up another offence.

§ 212 Murder

(1) Whosoever kills a person without being a murderer under § 211 shall be convicted of murder and be liable to imprisonment of not less than five years.
(2) In especially serious cases the penalty shall be imprisonment for life.

§ 213 Murder under mitigating circumstances

If the murderer (under § 212) was provoked to rage by maltreatment inflicted on him or a relative, or was seriously insulted by the victim and immediately lost self-control and committed the offence, or in the event of an otherwise less serious case, the penalty shall be imprisonment from one to ten years.

§§ 214 and 215 (repealed)

---

[8] This translation is awkward but is due to the fact that German law knows of two forms of intentional killing. In German, they have different names, Mord (§ 211) and Totschlag (§ 212). The relationship between § 211 and § 212 is controversial. The courts view them as separate offences, whereas most academic commentary sees the one as a qualification of the other or vice versa. This translation therefore had to make a choice. It follows the predominant literature opinion that sees § 212 as the basic offence and § 211 as an aggravated form. This made a few additions to the text of both provisions necessary.

§ 216 Killing at the request of the victim; mercy killing

(1) If a person is induced to kill by the express and earnest request of the victim the penalty shall be imprisonment from six months to five years.
(2) The attempt shall be punishable.

§ 217 (repealed)

§ 218 Abortion

(1) Whosoever terminates a pregnancy shall be liable to imprisonment of not more than three years or a fine. Acts the effects of which occur before the conclusion of the nidation shall not be deemed to be an abortion within the meaning of this law.
(2) In especially serious cases the penalty shall be imprisonment from six months to five years. An especially serious case typically occurs if the offender

  1. acts against the will of the pregnant woman; or
  2. through gross negligence causes a risk of death or serious injury to the pregnant woman.

(3) If the act is committed by the pregnant woman the penalty shall be imprisonment of not more than one year or a fine.
(4) The attempt shall be punishable. The pregnant woman shall not be liable for attempt.

§ 218a Exception to liability for abortion

(1) The offence under § 218 shall not be deemed fulfilled if

  1. the pregnant woman requests the termination of the pregnancy and demonstrates to the physician by certificate pursuant to § 219(2) 2nd sentence that she obtained counselling at least three days before the operation;
  2. the termination of the pregnancy is performed by a physician; and
  3. not more than twelve weeks have elapsed since conception.

(2) The termination of pregnancy performed by a physician with the consent of the pregnant woman shall not be unlawful if, considering the present and future living conditions of the pregnant woman, the termination of the pregnancy is medically necessary to avert a danger to the life or the danger of grave injury to the physical or mental health of the pregnant woman and if the danger cannot reasonably be averted in another way from her point of view.
(3) The conditions of subsection (2) above shall also be deemed fulfilled with regard to a termination of pregnancy performed by a physician with the consent of the pregnant woman, if according to medical opinion an unlawful act has been committed against the pregnant woman under §§ 176 to 179, there

is strong reason to support the assumption that the pregnancy was caused by the act, and not more than twelve weeks have elapsed since conception.

(4) The pregnant woman shall not be liable under § 218 if the termination of pregnancy was performed by a physician after counselling (§ 219) and not more than twenty-two weeks have elapsed since conception. The court may order a discharge under § 218 if the pregnant woman was in exceptional distress at the time of the operation.

§ 218b Abortion without or under incorrect medical certification

(1) Whosoever terminates a pregnancy in cases under § 218a(2) or (3) without having received the written determination of a physician, who did not himself perform the termination of the pregnancy, as to whether the conditions of § 218a(2) or (3) were met shall be liable to imprisonment of not more than one year or a fine unless the offence is punishable under § 218. Whosoever as a physician intentionally and knowingly makes an incorrect determination as to the conditions of § 218a(2) or (3) for presentation under the 1st sentence above shall be liable to imprisonment of not more than two years or a fine unless the act is punishable under § 218. The pregnant woman shall not be liable under the 1st or 2nd sentences above.

(2) A physician must not make determinations pursuant to § 218a(2) or (3) if a competent agency has prohibited him from doing so because he has been convicted by final judgment for an unlawful act under subsection (1) or under § 218, § 219a or § 219b or for another unlawful act which he committed in connection with a termination of pregnancy. The competent agency may provisionally prohibit a physician from making determinations under § 218a(2) and (3) if an indictment has been admitted to trial based on a suspicion that he committed unlawful acts indicated in the 1st sentence above.

§ 218c Violation of medical duties in connection with an abortion

(1) Whosoever terminates a pregnancy

1. without having given the woman an opportunity to explain the reasons for her request for a termination of pregnancy;
2. without having given the pregnant woman medical advice about the significance of the operation, especially about the circumstances of the procedure, after-effects, risks, possible physical or mental consequences;
3. in cases under § 218a(1) and (3) without having previously convinced himself on the basis of a medical examination as to the state of the pregnancy; or
4. despite having counselled the woman with respect to § 218a (1) pursuant to § 219,

shall be liable to imprisonment of not more than one year or a fine unless the act is punishable under § 218.

(2)   The pregnant woman shall not be liable under subsection (1) above.

§ 219 Counselling of the pregnant woman in a situation of emergency or conflict

(1)   The counselling serves to protect unborn life. It should be guided by efforts to encourage the woman to continue the pregnancy and to open her to the prospects of a life with the child; it should help her to make a responsible and conscientious decision. The woman must thereby be aware that the unborn child has its own right to life with respect to her at every stage of the pregnancy and that a termination of pregnancy can therefore only be considered under the law in exceptional situations, when carrying the child to term would give rise to a burden for the woman which is so serious and extraordinary that it exceeds the reasonable limits of sacrifice. The counselling should, through advice and assistance, contribute to overcoming the conflict situation which exists in connection with the pregnancy and remedying an emergency situation. Further details shall be regulated by the Act on Pregnancies in Conflict Situations.

(2)   The counselling must take place pursuant to the Act on Pregnancies in Conflict Situations through a recognised pregnancy conflict counselling agency. After the conclusion of the counselling on the subject, the counselling agency must issue the pregnant woman with a certificate including the date of the last counselling session and the name of the pregnant woman in accordance with the Act on Pregnancies in Conflict Situations. The physician who performs the termination of pregnancy is excluded from being a counsellor.

§ 219a Advertising services for abortion

(1)   Whosoever publicly, in a meeting or through dissemination of written materials (§ 11(3)), for material gain or in a grossly inappropriate manner, offers, announces or commends

   1.   his own services for performing terminations of pregnancy or for supporting them, or the services of another; or
   2.   means, objects or procedures capable of terminating a pregnancy with reference to this capacity,

or makes declarations of such a nature shall be liable to imprisonment of not more than two years or a fine.

(2)   Subsection (1) No 1 above shall not apply when physicians or statutorily recognised counselling agencies provide information about which physicians, hospitals or institutions are prepared to perform a termination of pregnancy under the conditions of § 218a(1) to (3).

(3)   Subsection (1) No 2 above shall not apply if the offence was committed with respect to physicians or persons who are authorised to trade in the means or objects mentioned in subsection (1) No 2 or through a publication in professional medical or pharmaceutical journals.

§ 219b Distribution of substances for the purpose of abortion

(1) Whosoever with intent to encourage unlawful acts under § 218 distributes means or objects which are capable of terminating a pregnancy shall be liable to imprisonment of not more than two years or a fine.

(2) The secondary participation by a woman preparing the termination of her own pregnancy shall not be punishable under subsection (1) above.

(3) Means or objects to which the offence relates may be subject to a deprivation order.

§§ 220 and 220a (repealed)

§ 221 Abandonment

(1) Whosoever

1. places a person in a helpless situation; or
2. abandons a person in a helpless situation although he gives him shelter or is otherwise obliged to care for him,

and thereby exposes him to a danger of death or serious injury shall be liable to imprisonment from three months to five years.

(2) The penalty shall be imprisonment from one to ten years if the offender

1. commits the offence against his own child or a person entrusted to him for education or care; or
2. through the offence causes serious injury to the victim.

(3) If the offender causes the death of the victim the penalty shall be imprisonment of not less than three years.

(4) In less serious cases under subsection (2) above the penalty shall be imprisonment from six months to five years, in less serious cases under subsection (3) above imprisonment from one to ten years.

§ 222 Negligent manslaughter

Whosoever through negligence causes the death of a person shall be liable to imprisonment of not more than five years or a fine.

CHAPTER SEVENTEEN
OFFENCES AGAINST THE PERSON

§ 223 Causing bodily harm

(1) Whosoever physically assaults or damages the health of another person, shall be liable to imprisonment of not more than five years or a fine.

151

(2)   The attempt shall be punishable.

§ 224 Causing bodily harm by dangerous means

(1)   Whosoever causes bodily harm

    1.   by administering poison or other noxious substances;
    2.   by using a weapon or other dangerous instrument;
    3.   by acting by stealth;
    4.   by acting jointly with another; or
    5.   by methods that pose a danger to life,

shall be liable to imprisonment from six months to ten years, in less serious cases to imprisonment from three months to five years.

(2)   The attempt shall be punishable.

§ 225 Abuse of position of trust

(1)   Whosoever tortures or seriously abuses or by maliciously neglecting his duty of care for a person damages the health of a person under eighteen years of age or a person who is defenceless due to frailty or illness and who

    1.   is in his care or custody;
    2.   belongs to his household;
    3.   has been placed under his control by the person obliged to provide care; or
    4.   is subordinated to him within a relationship of employment,

shall be liable to imprisonment from six months to ten years.

(2)   The attempt shall be punishable.

(3)   The penalty shall be imprisonment of not less than one year if the offender places the person in danger of

    1.   death or serious injury; or
    2.   a substantial impairment of his physical or mental development.

(4)   In less serious cases under subsection (1) above the penalty shall be imprisonment from three months to five years, in less serious cases under subsection (3) above imprisonment from six months to five years.

§ 226 Causing grievous bodily harm

(1)   If the injury results in the victim

    1.   losing his sight in one eye or in both eyes, his hearing, his speech or his ability to procreate;
    2.   losing or losing permanently the ability to use an important member;
    3.   being permanently and seriously disfigured or contracting a lingering illness, becoming paralysed, mentally ill or disabled,

the penalty shall be imprisonment from one to ten years.

(2) If the offender intentionally or knowingly causes one of the results indicated in subsection (1) above the penalty shall be imprisonment of not less than three years.

(3) In less serious cases under subsection (1) above the penalty shall be imprisonment from six months to five years, in less serious cases under subsection (2) above imprisonment from one to ten years.

§ 227 Infliction of bodily harm causing death

(1) If the offender causes the death of the victim through the infliction of bodily harm (§§ 223 to 226) the penalty shall be imprisonment of not less than three years.

(2) In less serious cases the penalty shall be imprisonment from one to ten years.

§ 228 Consent

Whosoever causes bodily harm with the consent of the victim shall be deemed to act lawfully unless the act violates public policy, the consent notwithstanding.

§ 229 Causing bodily harm by negligence

Whosoever by negligence causes bodily harm to another shall be liable to imprisonment of not more than three years or a fine.

§ 230 Request to prosecute

(1) Causing bodily harm intentionally under § 223 and negligently under § 229 may only be prosecuted upon request unless the prosecuting authority considers propio motu that prosecution is required because of special public interest. If the victim dies the right to file a request in cases of intentional bodily harm shall pass to the relatives pursuant to § 77(2).

(2) If the act has been committed against a public official, a person entrusted with special public service functions, or a soldier of the Armed Forces during the discharge of their duties or in relation to their duties it may also be prosecuted upon the request of their superiors. The same shall apply to public officials of churches and other religious associations under public law.

§ 231 Taking part in a brawl

(1) Whosoever takes part in a brawl or an attack committed against one person by more than one person shall be liable for this participation to imprisonment of not more than three years or a fine if the death of a person or grievous bodily harm (§ 226) is caused by the brawl or the attack.

(2) Whosoever took part in the brawl or the attack without being to blame for it shall not be liable under subsection (1) above.

CHAPTER EIGHTEEN
OFFENCES AGAINST PERSONAL FREEDOM

§ 232 Human trafficking for the purpose of sexual exploitation

(1) Whosoever exploits another person's predicament or helplessness arising from being in a foreign country in order to induce them to engage in or continue to engage in prostitution, to engage in exploitative sexual activity with or in the presence of the offender or a third person or to suffer sexual acts on his own person by the offender or a third person shall be liable to imprisonment from six months to ten years. Whosoever induces a person under twenty-one years of age to engage in or continue to engage in prostitution or any of the sexual activity mentioned in the 1st sentence above shall incur the same penalty.

(2) The attempt shall be punishable.

(3) The penalty shall be imprisonment from one to ten years if

1. the victim is a child (§ 176(1));
2. the offender through the act seriously physically abuses the victim or places the victim in danger of death; or
3. the offender commits the offence on a commercial basis or as a member of a gang whose purpose is the continued commission of such offences.

(4) The penalty under subsection (3) above shall be imposed on any person who

1. induces another person by force, threat of serious harm or by deception to engage in or continue to engage in prostitution or any of the sexual activity mentioned in subsection (1) 1st sentence above or
2. gains physical control of another person by force, threat of serious harm or deception to induce them to engage in or continue to engage in prostitution or any of the sexual activity mentioned in subsection (1) 1st sentence above.

(5) In less serious cases under subsection (1) above the penalty shall be imprisonment from three months to five years, in less serious cases under subsections (3) and (4) above imprisonment from six months to five years.

§ 233 Human trafficking for the purpose of work exploitation

(1) Whosoever exploits another person's predicament or helplessness arising from being in a foreign country to subject them to slavery, servitude or bonded labour, or makes him work for him or a third person under working conditions that are in clear discrepancy to those of other workers performing the same or a similar activity, shall be liable to imprisonment from six months to ten years. Whosoever subjects a person under twenty-one years of age to slavery, servitude or bonded labour or makes him work as mentioned in the 1st sentence above shall incur the same penalty.

(2)   The attempt shall be punishable.

(3)   § 232(3) to (5) shall apply mutatis mutandis.

§ 233a Assisting in human trafficking

(1)   Whosoever assists in human trafficking under § 232 or § 233 by recruiting, transporting, referring, harbouring or sheltering another person shall be liable to imprisonment from three months to five years.

(2)   The penalty shall be imprisonment from six months to ten years if

    1.   the victim is a child (§ 176(1));

    2.   the offender through the act seriously physically abuses the victim or places the victim in danger of death; or

    3.   the offender commits the offence on a commercial basis or as a member of a gang whose purpose is the continued commission of such offences.

(3)   The attempt shall be punishable.

§ 233b Supervision order, extended confiscation

(1)   In cases under §§ 232 to 233a the court may make a supervision order (§ 68(1)).

(2)   § 73d shall apply in cases under §§ 232 to 233a if the offender acts on a commercial basis or as a member of a gang whose purpose is the continued commission of such offences.

§ 234 Abduction for the purpose of abandonment or facilitating service in foreign military or para-military forces

(1)   Whosoever gains physical control of another person by force, threat of serious harm, or deception in order to abandon them in a helpless situation or to introduce them into military or para-military service abroad shall be liable to imprisonment from one to ten years.

(2)   In less serious cases the penalty shall be imprisonment from six months to five years.

§ 234a Causing a danger of political persecution through use of force, threats or deception

(1)   Whosoever by deception, threat or force transports another into a territory outside the Federal Republic of Germany or causes him to go abroad, or prevents him from returning from abroad and thereby exposes him to the danger of being persecuted for political reasons and, in violation of the principles of the rule of law, of suffering harm to life and limb through violence or arbitrary measures, of being deprived of his freedom or of being seriously prejudiced in his professional or financial circumstances shall be liable to imprisonment of not less than one year.

(2) In less serious cases the penalty shall be imprisonment from three months to five years.

(3) Whosoever prepares the commission of such an offence shall be liable to imprisonment of not more than five years or a fine.

§ 235 Abduction of minors from the care of their parents etc

(1) Whosoever removes from the custody of one or both of his parents or his guardian[9] or denies them access to

    1. a person under eighteen years of age by force, threat of serious harm or deception; or
    2. a child, without being a relative,

shall be liable to imprisonment of not more than five years or a fine.

(2) Whosoever

    1. removes a child from the custody of one or both of his parents or his guardian in order to take him abroad; or
    2. denies access to him abroad after having removed him there or the child having gone there,

shall incur the same penalty.

(3) In cases under subsection (1) No 2 and subsection (2) No 1 above the attempt shall be punishable.

(4) The penalty shall be imprisonment from one to ten years if the offender

    1. by the offence places the victim in danger of death or serious injury or of a substantial impairment of his physical or mental development; or
    2. commits the offence for material gain or with the intent of enriching himself or a third person.

(5) If by the offence the offender causes the death of the victim the penalty shall be imprisonment of not less than three years.

(6) In less serious cases under subsection (4) above the penalty shall be imprisonment from six months to five years, in less serious cases under subsection (5) above imprisonment from one to ten years.

(7) The abduction may only be prosecuted upon request in cases under subsections (1) to (3) above unless the prosecuting authority considers propio motu that prosecution is required because of special public interest.

---

[9] The German text uses two words which have both been translated as 'guardian', namely 'Vormund' under §§ 1773 ff of the Civil Code, and 'Pfleger' under §§ 1671, 1680 and 1909 ff of the Civil Code. The difference lies in the ambit of the powers of the guardian, with the Vormund having the wider powers.

§ 236 Child trafficking

(1) Whosoever in gross neglect of his duties of care and education leaves his child, ward or foster child under eighteen years of age with another for an indefinite period for material gain or with the intent of enriching himself or a third person shall be liable to imprisonment of not more than five years or a fine. Whosoever in cases under the 1st sentence above takes the child, ward or foster child into his home for an indefinite period and awards compensation for it shall incur the same penalty.

(2) Whosoever unlawfully

1. procures the adoption of a person under eighteen years of age; or
2. engages in procurement activity with the aim of a third person taking a person under eighteen years of age into his home for an indefinite period,

and acts for consideration or with the intent of enriching himself or a third person shall be liable to imprisonment of not more than three years or a fine. If the offender in cases under the 1st sentence above causes the procured person to be brought into Germany or abroad the penalty shall be imprisonment of not more than five years or a fine.

(3) The attempt shall be punishable.

(4) The penalty shall be imprisonment from six months to ten years if the offender

1. seeks profit or acts on a commercial basis or as a member of a gang whose purpose is the continued commission of child trafficking or
2. by the act places the child or the procured person in danger of a substantial impairment of his physical or mental development.

(5) The court may in its discretion mitigate the sentence (§ 49(2)) for accomplices in cases under subsections (1) and (3) above and for secondary participants in cases under subsections (2) and (3) above, or order a discharge under subsections (1) to (3), if their guilt, taking into consideration the physical or mental welfare of the child or the procured person, is of a minor nature.

§ 237 *(repealed)*

§ 238 Stalking

(1) Whosoever unlawfully stalks a person by

1. seeking his proximity,
2. trying to establish contact with him by means of telecommunications or other means of communication or through third persons,
3. abusing his personal data for the purpose of ordering goods or services for him or causing third persons to make contact with him,

4. threatening him or a person close to him with loss of life or limb, damage to health or deprivation of freedom, or

5. committing similar acts

and thereby seriously infringes his lifestyle shall be liable to imprisonment of not more than three years or a fine.

(2) The penalty shall be three months to five years if the offender places the victim, a relative of or another person close to the victim in danger of death or serious injury.

(3) If the offender causes the death of the victim, a relative of or another person close to the victim the penalty shall be imprisonment from one to ten years.

(4) Cases under subsection (1) above may only be prosecuted upon request unless the prosecuting authority considers propio motu that prosecution is required because of special public interest.

§ 239 Unlawful imprisonment

(1) Whosoever imprisons a person or otherwise deprives him of his freedom shall be liable to imprisonment of not more than five years or a fine.

(2) The attempt shall be punishable.

(3) The penalty shall be imprisonment from one to ten years if the offender

1. deprives the victim of his freedom for more than a week; or

2. by the offence or an act committed during the offence causes serious injury to the victim.

(4) If by the offence or an act committed during the offence the offender causes the death of the victim the penalty shall be imprisonment of not less than three years.

(5) In less serious cases under subsection (3) above the penalty shall be imprisonment from six months to five years, in less serious cases under subsection (4) above imprisonment from one to ten years.

§ 239a Abduction for the purpose of blackmail

(1) Whosoever abducts or gains physical control of a person in order to exploit, for the purpose of blackmail (§ 253), the victim's concern for his own welfare or the concern of a third person for the welfare of the victim, and whosoever for the purpose of blackmail exploits a person's situation thus caused by him shall be liable to imprisonment of not less than five years.

(2) In less serious cases the penalty shall be imprisonment of not less than one year.

(3) If by the offence the offender at least through gross negligence causes the death of the victim the penalty shall be imprisonment for life or not less than ten years.

(4) The court may mitigate the sentence pursuant to § 49(1) if the offender allows the victim to return to his normal surroundings and waives the

desired outcome. If this occurs regardless of the contribution of the offender his earnest efforts to achieve that result shall suffice.

§ 239b Taking hostages

(1) Whosoever abducts or gains physical control of a person in order to cause him or a third person, by threatening death or grievous bodily harm (§ 226) to the victim or the deprivation of his freedom for more than a week, to commit, suffer or omit an act, or whosoever for purposes of such coercion exploits a person's situation thus caused by him shall be liable to imprisonment of not less than five years.

(2) § 239a(2) to (4) shall apply mutatis mutandis.

§ 239c Supervision order

In cases under § 239a and § 239b the court may make a supervision order (§ 68(1)).

§ 240 Using threats or force to cause a person to do, suffer or omit an act

(1) Whosoever unlawfully with force or threat of serious harm causes a person to commit, suffer or omit an act shall be liable to imprisonment of not more than three years or a fine.

(2) The act shall be unlawful if the use of force or the threat of harm is deemed inappropriate for the purpose of achieving the desired outcome.

(3) The attempt shall be punishable.

(4) In especially serious cases the penalty shall be imprisonment from six months to five years. An especially serious case typically occurs if the offender

    1. causes another person to engage in sexual activity or to enter into marriage;

    2. causes a pregnant woman to terminate the pregnancy; or

    3. abuses his powers or position as a public official.

§ 241 Threatening the commission of a felony

(1) Whosoever threatens a person with the commission of a felony against him or a person close to him shall be liable to imprisonment of not more than one year or a fine.

(2) Whosoever intentionally and knowingly pretends to another person that the commission of a felony against him or a person close to him is imminent shall incur the same penalty.

§ 241a Causing the danger of political persecution by informing on a person

(1) Whosoever through a criminal complaint or by informing on a person exposes him to the danger of being persecuted for political reasons and, in

violation of the principles of the rule of law, to suffering harm to life and limb through violence or arbitrary measures, to be deprived of his freedom or to be seriously prejudiced in his professional or financial circumstances shall be liable to imprisonment of not more than five years or a fine.

(2) Whosoever provides information about another or transmits such information and thereby exposes him to the danger of political persecution indicated in subsection (1) above shall incur the same penalty.

(3) The attempt shall be punishable.

(4) If an untrue assertion is made in the complaint, when informing on the person or in the information against another or if the offence is committed with the intent of procuring the results indicated in subsection (1) above or if the case is otherwise especially serious the penalty shall be imprisonment from one to ten years.

CHAPTER NINETEEN
THEFT AND UNLAWFUL APPROPRIATION

§ 242 Theft

(1) Whosoever takes chattels belonging to another away from another with the intention of unlawfully appropriating them for himself or a third person shall be liable to imprisonment of not more than five years or a fine.

(2) The attempt shall be punishable.

§ 243 Aggravated theft

(1) In especially serious cases of theft the penalty shall be imprisonment from three months to ten years. An especially serious case typically occurs if the offender

1. for the purpose of the commission of the offence breaks into or enters a building, official or business premises or another enclosed space or intrudes by using a false key or other tool not typically used for gaining access or hides in the room;

2. steals property which is especially protected by a sealed container or other protective equipment;

3. steals on a commercial basis;

4. steals property which is dedicated to religious worship or used for religious veneration from a church or other building or space used for the practice of religion;

5. steals property of significance for science, art or history or for technical development which is located in a generally accessible collection or is publicly exhibited;

6. steals by exploiting the helplessness of another person, an accident or a common danger; or
7. steals a firearm for the acquisition of which a licence is required under the Weapons Act, a machine gun, a submachine gun, a fully or semi-automatic rifle or a military weapon containing an explosive within the meaning of the Weapons of War (Control) Act or an explosive.

(2) In cases under subsection (1) 2nd sentence Nos 1 to 6 above an especially serious case shall be excluded if the property is of minor value.

§ 244 Carrying weapons; acting as a member of a gang; burglary of private homes

(1) Whosoever

1. commits a theft during which he or another accomplice

    (a) carries a weapon or another dangerous instrument;
    (b) otherwise carries an instrument or means in order to prevent or overcome the resistance of another person by force or threat of force;

2. steals as a member of a gang whose purpose is the continued commission of robbery or theft under participation of another member of the gang; or
3. commits a theft for the commission of which he breaks into or enters a dwelling or intrudes by using a false key or other tool not typically used for gaining access or hides in the dwelling

shall be liable to imprisonment from six months to ten years.
(2) The attempt shall be punishable.
(3) In cases under subsection (1) No 2 above, § 43a and § 73d shall apply.

§ 244a Aggravated gang theft

(1) Whosoever commits theft under the conditions listed in § 243 (1) 2nd sentence or in cases under § 244(1) Nos 1 or 3 as a member of a gang whose purpose is the continued commission of robbery or theft under participation of another member of the gang shall be liable to imprisonment from one to ten years.
(2) In less serious cases the penalty shall be imprisonment from six months to five years.
(3) § 43a and § 73d shall apply.

§ 245 Supervision order

In cases under §§ 242 to 244a the court may make a supervision order (§ 68(1)).

§ 246 Unlawful appropriation

(1) Whosoever unlawfully appropriates chattels belonging to another for himself or a third person shall be liable to imprisonment of not more than three years or a fine unless the offence is subject to a more severe penalty under other provisions.
(2) If in cases under subsection (1) above the property was entrusted to the offender the penalty shall be imprisonment of not more than five years or a fine.
(3) The attempt shall be punishable.

§ 247 Theft from relatives or persons living in the same home

If a relative, the guardian or the carer of the offender is the victim of the theft or if the victim lives in the same household as the offender the offence may only be prosecuted upon request.

§ 248 (repealed)

§ 248a Theft and unlawful appropriation of objects of minor value

Theft and unlawful appropriation of property of minor value may only be prosecuted upon request in cases under § 242 and § 246, unless the prosecuting authority considers propio motu that prosecution is required because of special public interest.

§ 248b Unlawful taking of a motor-vehicle or bicycle

(1) Whosoever uses a motor-vehicle or a bicycle against the will of the person authorised to use it shall be liable to imprisonment of not more than three years or a fine unless the act is subject to a more severe penalty under other provisions.
(2) The attempt shall be punishable.
(3) The offence may only be prosecuted upon request.
(4) Motor-vehicles within the meaning of this provision are vehicles which are driven by machine power; this applies to terrestrial motor-vehicles only to the extent that they are not rail-bound vehicles.

§ 248c Theft of electrical energy

(1) Whosoever taps the electrical energy of another from an electrical facility or installation by means of a conductor which is not intended for the regular withdrawal of energy from the facility or installation, shall, if the offence was committed with the intent of appropriating the electrical energy for himself or a third person, be liable to imprisonment of not more than five years or a fine.

(2) The attempt shall be punishable.

(3) § 247 and § 248a shall apply mutatis mutandis.

(4) If the offence under subsection (1) above is committed with the intent of unlawfully inflicting damage on another the penalty shall be imprisonment of not more than two years or a fine. The offence may only be prosecuted upon request.

CHAPTER TWENTY
ROBBERY AND BLACKMAIL

§ 249 Robbery

(1) Whosoever, by force against a person or threats of imminent danger to life or limb, takes chattels belonging to another from another with the intent of appropriating the property for himself or a third person, shall be liable to imprisonment of not less than one year.

(2) In less serious cases the penalty shall be imprisonment from six months to five years.

§ 250 Aggravated robbery

(1) The penalty shall be imprisonment of not less than three years if

  1. the offender or another accomplice to the robbery

      (a) carries a weapon or other dangerous instrument;
      (b) otherwise carries an instrument or means in order to prevent or overcome the resistance of another person by force or threat force;
      (c) by the act places another person in danger of serious injury; or

  2. the offender commits the robbery as a member of a gang whose purpose is the continued commission of robbery or theft under participation of another member of the gang.

(2) The penalty shall be imprisonment of not less than five years if the offender or another accomplice to the robbery

  1. uses a weapon or other dangerous instrument during the commission of the offence;
  2. carries a weapon in cases under subsection (1) No 2 above; or
  3. during or by the offence

      (a) seriously physically abuses another person; or
      (b) places another person in danger of death.

(3) In less serious cases under subsections (1) and (2) above the penalty shall be imprisonment from one to ten years.

§ 251 Robbery causing death

If by the robbery (§ 249 and § 250) the offender at least by gross negligence causes the death of another person the penalty shall be imprisonment for life or not less than ten years.

§ 252 Theft and use of force to retain stolen goods

Whosoever when caught in the act during the commission of a theft uses force against a person or threats of imminent danger to life and limb in order to retain possession of the stolen property shall be liable to the same penalty as a robber.

§ 253 Blackmail

(1) Whosoever unlawfully with force or threat of serious harm causes a person to commit, suffer or omit an act and thereby causes damage to the assets of that person or of another in order to enrich himself or a third person unlawfully shall be liable to imprisonment of not more than five years or a fine.

(2) The act shall be unlawful if the use of force or the threat of harm is deemed inappropriate to the purpose of achieving the desired outcome.

(3) The attempt shall be punishable.

(4) In especially serious cases the penalty shall be imprisonment of not less than one year. An especially serious case typically occurs if the offender acts on a commercial basis or as a member of a gang whose purpose is the continued commission of blackmail.

§ 254 *(repealed)*

§ 255 Blackmail and use of force or threats against life or limb

If the blackmail is committed by using force against a person or threats of imminent danger to life or limb the offender shall be liable to the same penalty as a robber.

§ 256 Supervision order, confiscatory expropriation order and extended confiscation

(1) In cases under §§ 249 to 255 the court may make a supervision order (§ 68(1)).

(2) In cases under § 253 and § 255, § 43a and § 73d shall apply if the offender acts as a member of a gang whose purpose is the continued commission of such offences. § 73d shall also apply if the offender acts on a commercial basis.

CHAPTER TWENTY-ONE
ASSISTANCE AFTER THE FACT AND HANDLING STOLEN GOODS

§ 257 Assistance after the fact

(1) Whosoever renders assistance to another who has committed an unlawful act, with the intent of securing for him the benefits of that act, shall be liable to imprisonment of not more than five years or a fine.
(2) The penalty must not be more severe than that for the act.
(3) Whosoever is liable as an accomplice to the act shall not be liable for assistance after the fact. This shall not apply to a person who abets another person who did not take part in the act to provide assistance after the fact.
(4) An offence of assistance after the fact may only be prosecuted upon request, authorisation or a request by the foreign state if the offender could only be prosecuted upon request, authorisation or a request by the foreign state if he had been a principal or secondary participant to the act. § 248 shall apply mutatis mutandis.

§ 258 Assistance in avoiding prosecution or punishment

(1) Whosoever intentionally or knowingly obstructs in whole or in part the punishment of another in accordance with the criminal law because of an unlawful act or his being subjected to a measure (§ 11(1) No 8) shall be liable to imprisonment of not more than five years or a fine.
(2) Whosoever intentionally or knowingly obstructs in whole or in part the enforcement of a sentence or measure imposed on another shall incur the same penalty.
(3) The penalty must not be more severe than that for the act.
(4) The attempt shall be punishable.
(5) Whosoever by the offence simultaneously intends to avoid, in whole or in part, his own punishment or being subjected to a measure or that a sentence or measure imposed on him be enforced shall not be liable under this provision.
(6) Whosoever commits the offence for the benefit of a relative shall be exempt from liability.

§ 258a Assistance given in official capacity

(1) If the offender under § 258(1) is a public official involved in the criminal proceedings or the proceedings for measure (§ 11(1) No 8), or in cases under § 258(2) is a public official involved in the enforcement of the sentence or measure the penalty shall be imprisonment from six months to five years, in less serious cases imprisonment of not more than three years or a fine.
(2) The attempt shall be punishable.

(3)   § 258(3) and (6) shall not apply.

§ 259   Handling stolen goods

(1)   Whosoever in order to enrich himself or a third person, buys, otherwise procures for himself or a third person, disposes of, or assists in disposing of property that another has stolen or otherwise acquired by an unlawful act directed against the property of another shall be liable to imprisonment of not more than five years or a fine.

(2)   § 247 and § 248a shall apply mutatis mutandis.

(3)   The attempt shall be punishable.

§ 260   Handling on a commercial basis or as a member of a gang

(1)   Whosoever handles stolen goods

     1.   on a commercial basis; or
     2.   as a member of a gang whose purpose is the continued commission of robbery, theft or handling stolen goods

     shall be liable to imprisonment from six months to ten years.

(2)   The attempt shall be punishable.

(3)   In cases under subsection (1) No 2 above, § 43a and §73d shall apply. § 73d shall also apply in cases under subsection (1) No 1 above.

§ 260a   Commercial handling as a member of a gang

(1)   Whosoever on a commercial basis handles stolen goods as a member of a gang, whose purpose is the continued commission of robbery, theft or handling stolen goods shall be liable to imprisonment from one to ten years.

(2)   In less serious cases the penalty shall be imprisonment from six months to five years.

(3)   § 43a and §73d shall apply.

§ 261   Money laundering; hiding unlawfully obtained financial benefits

(1)   Whosoever hides an object which is a proceed of an unlawful act listed in the 2nd sentence below, conceals its origin or obstructs or endangers the investigation of its origin, its being found, its confiscation, its deprivation or its being officially secured shall be liable to imprisonment from three months to five years. Unlawful acts within the meaning of the 1st sentence shall be

     1.   felonies;
     2.   misdemeanours under

         (a)   § 332(1), also in conjunction with subsection (3), and § 334;
         (b)   § 29(1) 1st sentence No 1 of the Drugs Act and § 29(1) No 1 of the Drug Precursors (Control) Act;

3. misdemeanours under § 373 and under § 374(2) of the Fiscal Code, and also in conjunction with § 12(1) of the Common Market Organisations and Direct Payments (Implementation) Act;
4. misdemeanours

    (a) under § 152a, § 181a, § 232(1) and (2), § 233(1) and (2), § 233a, § 242, § 246, § 253, § 259, §§ 263 to 264, § 266, § 267, § 269, § 284, § 326(1), (2) and (4), and § 328(1), (2) and (4);
    (b) under § 96 of the Residence Act and § 84 of the Asylum Procedure Act and § 370 of the Fiscal Code

    which were committed on a commercial basis or by a member of a gang whose purpose is the continued commission of such offences; and
5. misdemeanours under § 129 and § 129a(3) and (5), all of which also in conjunction with § 129b(1), as well as misdemeanours committed by a member of a criminal or terrorist organisation (§ 129 and § 129a, all of which also in conjunction with § 129b(1)).

The 1st sentence shall apply in cases of tax evasion committed on a commercial basis or as a gang under § 370 of the Fiscal Code, to expenditure saved by virtue of the tax evasion, of unlawfully acquired tax repayments and allowances, and in cases under the 2nd sentence no 3 the 1st sentence shall also apply to an object in relation to which fiscal charges have been evaded.

(2) Whosoever

1. procures an object indicated in subsection (1) above for himself or a third person; or
2. keeps an object indicated in subsection (1) above in his custody or uses it for himself or a third person if he knew the origin of the object at the time of obtaining possession of it

shall incur the same penalty.

(3) The attempt shall be punishable.
(4) In especially serious cases the penalty shall be imprisonment from six months to ten years. An especially serious case typically occurs if the offender acts on a commercial basis or as a member of a gang whose purpose is the continued commission of money laundering.
(5) Whosoever, in cases under subsections (1) or (2) above is, through gross negligence, unaware of the fact that the object is a proceed from an unlawful act named in subsection (1) above shall be liable to imprisonment of not more than two years or a fine.
(6) The act shall not be punishable under subsection (2) above if a third person previously acquired the object without having thereby committed an offence.
(7) Objects to which the offence relates may be subject to a deprivation order. § 74a shall apply. § 43a and § 73d shall apply if the offender acts as a

member of a gang whose purpose is the continued commission of money laundering. § 73d shall also apply if the offender acts on a commercial basis.

(8)   Objects which are proceeds from an offence listed in subsection (1) above committed abroad shall be equivalent to the objects indicated in subsections (1), (2) and (5) above if the offence is also punishable at the place of its commission.

(9)   Whosoever

1.   voluntarily reports the offence to the competent public authority or voluntarily causes such a report to be made, unless the act had already been discovered in whole or in part at the time and the offender knew this or could reasonably have known and

2.   in cases under subsections (1) or (2) above under the conditions named in No 1 above causes the object to which the offence relates to be officially secured

shall not be liable under subsections (1) to (5) above.

Whosoever is liable because of his participation in the antecedent act shall not be liable under subsections (1) to (5) above, either.

(10) The court in its discretion may mitigate the sentence (§ 49(2)) in cases under subsections (1) to (5) above or order a discharge under these provisions if the offender through voluntary disclosure of his knowledge has substantially contributed to the discovery of the offence beyond his own contribution thereto, or of an unlawful act of another named in subsection (1) above.

§ 262 Supervision order

In cases under §§ 259 to 261 the court may make a supervision order (§ 68(1)).

CHAPTER TWENTY-TWO
FRAUD AND EMBEZZLEMENT

§ 263 Fraud

(1)   Whosoever with the intent of obtaining for himself or a third person an unlawful material benefit damages the property of another by causing or maintaining an error by pretending false facts or by distorting or suppressing true facts shall be liable to imprisonment of not more than five years or a fine.

(2)   The attempt shall be punishable.

(3)   In especially serious cases the penalty shall be imprisonment from six months to ten years. An especially serious case typically occurs if the offender

1.   acts on a commercial basis or as a member of a gang whose purpose is the continued commission of forgery or fraud;

2. causes a major financial loss of or acts with the intent of placing a large number of persons in danger of financial loss by the continued commission of offences of fraud;

3. places another person in financial hardship;

4. abuses his powers or his position as a public official; or

5. pretends that an insured event has happened after he or another have for this purpose set fire to an object of significant value or destroyed it, in whole or in part, through setting fire to it or caused the sinking or beaching of a ship.

(4) § 243(2), § 247 and § 248a shall apply mutatis mutandis.

(5) Whosoever on a commercial basis commits fraud as a member of a gang, whose purpose is the continued commission of offences under §§ 263 to 264 or §§ 267 to 269 shall be liable to imprisonment from one to ten years, in less serious cases to imprisonment from six months to five years.

(6) The court may make a supervision order (§ 68(1)).

(7) § 43a and 73d shall apply if the offender acts as a member of a gang whose purpose is the continued commission of offences under §§ 263 to 264 or §§ 267 to 269. § 73d shall also apply if the offender acts on a commercial basis.

§ 263a Computer fraud

(1) Whosoever with the intent of obtaining for himself or a third person an unlawful material benefit damages the property of another by influencing the result of a data processing operation through incorrect configuration of a program, use of incorrect or incomplete data, unauthorised use of data or other unauthorised influence on the course of the processing shall be liable to imprisonment of not more than five years or a fine.

(2) § 263(2) to (7) shall apply mutatis mutandis.

(3) Whosoever prepares an offence under subsection (1) above by writing computer programs the purpose of which is to commit such an act, or procures them for himself or another, offers them for sale, or holds or supplies them to another shall be liable to imprisonment of not more than three years or a fine.

(4) In cases under subsection (3) above § 149(2) and (3) shall apply mutatis mutandis.

§ 264 Subsidy fraud

(1) Whosoever

1. makes incorrect or incomplete statements about facts relevant for granting a subsidy to himself or another that are advantageous for himself or the other, to a public authority competent to approve a subsidy or to another agency or person which is involved in the subsidy procedure (subsidy giver);

169

2. uses an object or monetary benefit the use of which is restricted by law or by the subsidy giver in relation to a subsidy contrary to that restriction;
3. withholds, contrary to the law relating to grants of subsidies, information about facts relevant to the subsidy from the subsidy giver; or
4. uses a certificate of subsidy entitlement or about facts relevant to a subsidy, which was acquired through incorrect or incomplete statements in subsidy proceedings,

shall be liable to imprisonment of not more than five years or a fine.

(2) In especially serious cases the penalty shall be imprisonment from six months to ten years. An especially serious case typically occurs if the offender

1. acquires, out of gross self-seeking or by using counterfeit or falsified documentation, an unjustified large subsidy for himself or another;
2. abuses his powers or his position as a public official; or
3. uses the assistance of a public official who abuses his powers or his position.

(3) § 263(5) shall apply mutatis mutandis.

(4) Whosoever acts in gross negligence in cases under subsection (1) Nos 1 to 3 above shall be liable to imprisonment of not more than three years or a fine.

(5) Whosoever voluntarily prevents the granting of a subsidy on the basis of the offence shall not be liable pursuant to subsections (1) and (4) above. If the subsidy is not granted regardless of the contribution of the offender he shall be exempt from liability if he voluntarily and earnestly makes efforts to prevent the subsidy from being granted.

(6) In addition to a sentence of imprisonment of at least one year for an offence under subsections (1) to (3) above the court may order the loss of the ability to hold public office, to vote and be elected in public elections (§ 45(2) and (5)). Objects to which the offence relates may be subject to a deprivation order; § 74a shall apply.

(7) A subsidy for the purposes of this provision shall mean

1. a benefit from public funds under Federal or state law for businesses or enterprises, which at least in part

   (a) is granted without market-related consideration; and
   (b) is intended for the promotion of the economy;

2. a benefit from public funds under the law of the European Communities which is granted at least in part without market-related consideration.

A public enterprise shall also be deemed to be a business or enterprise within the meaning of the 1st sentence No 1 above.

(8) Facts shall be relevant to a subsidy within the meaning of subsection (1) above

1. if they are designated as being relevant to a subsidy by law or by the subsidy giver on the basis of a law; or
2. if the approval, grant, reclaiming, renewal or continuation or a subsidy depends on them for reasons of law.

§ 264a Capital investment fraud

(1) Whosoever in connection with

1. the sale of securities, subscription rights or shares intended to grant participation in the yield of an enterprise; or
2. an offer to increase the capital investment in such shares,

makes incorrect favourable statements or keeps unfavourable facts secret in prospectuses or in representations or surveys about the net assets to a considerable number of persons in relation to circumstances relevant to the decision about acquisition or increase, shall be liable to imprisonment of not more than three years or a fine.

(2) Subsection (1) above shall apply mutatis mutandis if the act is related to shares in assets which an enterprise administers in its own name but for the account of a third party.

(3) Whosoever voluntarily prevents the benefit contingent upon the acquisition or the increase from accruing shall not be liable pursuant to subsections (1) and (2) above. If the benefit does not accrue regardless of the contribution of the offender he shall be exempt from liability if he voluntarily and earnestly makes efforts to prevent the benefit from accruing.

§ 265 Insurance fraud

(1) Whosoever damages, destroys, impairs the usefulness of, disposes of or supplies to another an object which is insured against destruction, damage, impairment of use, loss or theft in order to obtain for himself or a third party a payment from the insurance shall be liable to imprisonment of not more than three years or a fine unless the offence is punishable under § 263.

(2) The attempt shall be punishable.

§ 265a Obtaining services by deception

(1) Whosoever obtains the service of a machine or a telecommunications network serving public purposes or uses a means of transportation or obtains entrance to an event or institution by deception with the intent of not paying for them shall be liable to imprisonment of not more than one year or a fine unless the act is punishable under other provisions with a more severe penalty.

(2) The attempt shall be punishable.

(3) § 247 and § 248a shall apply mutatis mutandis.

§ 265b Obtaining credit by deception

(1) Whosoever, in connection with an application for or for a continuance of credit or modification of the terms of credit for a business or enterprise or for a fictitious business or enterprise

   1. (a) submits incorrect or incomplete documentation, in particular, calculations of balance, profit and loss, summaries of assets and liabilities or appraisal reports; or
       (b) makes incorrect or incomplete written statements,

       about financial circumstances that are favourable to the credit applicant and relevant to the decision on such an application, to a business or enterprise; or

   2. does not inform a business or enterprise in the submission about any deterioration in the financial circumstances represented in the documentation or statements that are relevant to the decision on such an application,

   shall be liable to imprisonment of not more than three years or a fine.

(2) Whosoever voluntarily prevents the creditor from providing the credit applied for shall not be liable pursuant to subsection (1) above. If the credit is not provided regardless of the contribution of the offender he shall be exempt from liability if he voluntarily and earnestly makes efforts to prevent the credit from being provided.

(3) Within the meaning of subsection (1) above

   1. businesses and enterprises shall be those which require by their nature and size, but regardless of their purpose, a properly organised operation applying the appropriate commercial customs, rules and standards;

   2. credits shall be money loans of all kinds, acceptance credits, the acquisition for payment or the deferment of monetary claims, the discounting of promissory notes and cheques and the assumption of sureties, guarantees and other warranties.

§ 266 Embezzlement and abuse of trust

(1) Whosoever abuses the power accorded him by statute, by commission of a public authority or legal transaction to dispose of assets of another or to make binding agreements for another, or violates his duty to safeguard the property interests of another incumbent upon him by reason of statute, commission of a public authority, legal transaction or fiduciary relationship, and thereby causes damage to the person, whose property interests he was responsible for, shall be liable to imprisonment of not more than five years or a fine.

(2) § 243(2), § 247, § 248a and § 263(3) shall apply mutatis mutandis.

§ 266a Non-payment and misuse of wages and salaries

(1) Whosoever, as an employer, withholds contributions of an employee to the social security system including employment promotion, regardless of whether wages or salaries are actually being paid, shall be liable to imprisonment of not more than five years or a fine.

(2) Whosoever as an employer

1. makes incorrect or incomplete statements regarding facts relevant to the social insurance system to the agency responsible for collecting contributions, or
2. contrary to his duty withholds from the agency responsible for collecting contributions information about facts relevant to the social insurance system,

and thereby withholds the contributions to be paid by the employer for social insurance including employment promotion, regardless of whether salary or wages are being paid, shall incur the same penalty.

(3) Whosoever as an employer otherwise withholds parts of wages or salaries which he is under a duty to pay to another on behalf of the employee but does not pay them to the other and fails to inform the employee about the failure to make the payment no later than the due date or without undue delay thereafter shall be liable to imprisonment of not more than five years or a fine. The 1st sentence above shall not apply to those parts of the wage or salary which are deducted as income tax on wages and salaries.

(4) In especially serious cases under subsections (1) and (2) above the penalty shall be imprisonment from six months to ten years. An especially serious case typically occurs if the offender

1. withholds, out of gross self-seeking, contributions of a large amount;
2. by using counterfeit or falsified documentation continually withholds contributions; or
3. exploits the assistance of a public official who abuses his powers or his position.

(5) A person who hires persons who work or conduct a trade at home or who are equal to them within the meaning of the Work at Home Act, as well as the intermediary[10] shall be equivalent to an employer.

(6) In cases under subsections (1) and (2) above the court may order a discharge pursuant to this provision if the employer no later than the due date or without undue delay thereafter

1. informs the collecting agency in writing of the amount of the withheld contributions; and

---

[10] The German word for this intermediary is 'Zwischenmeister' under § 12(4) of Book IV of the Social Code which denotes a person who assigns work given to him to persons working at home. There is no appropriate translation for the word.

2. explains why payment on time is not possible although he has made earnest efforts to do so.

If the conditions of the 1st sentence above are met and the contributions are subsequently paid within the appropriate period determined by the collecting agency the offender shall not be liable. In cases under subsection (3) above, the 1st and 2nd sentences above shall apply mutatis mutandis.

§ 266b Misuse of cheque and credit cards

(1) Whosoever abuses the possibility accorded him through delivery of a cheque or credit card of obliging the issuer to make a payment and thereby causes damage to the issuer shall be liable to imprisonment of not more than three years or a fine.
(2) § 248a shall apply mutatis mutandis.

CHAPTER TWENTY-THREE
FORGERY

§ 267 Forgery

(1) Whosoever for the purpose of deception in legal commerce produces a counterfeit document, falsifies a genuine document or uses a counterfeit or a falsified document, shall be liable to imprisonment of not more than five years or a fine.
(2) The attempt shall be punishable.
(3) In especially serious cases the penalty shall be imprisonment from six months to ten years. An especially serious case typically occurs if the offender

    1. acts on a commercial basis or as a member of a gang whose purpose is the continued commission of fraud or forgery;
    2. causes major financial loss;
    3. substantially endangers the security of legal commerce through a large number of counterfeit or falsified documents; or
    4. abuses his powers or his position as a public official.

(4) Whosoever commits forgery on a commercial basis as a member of a gang whose purpose is the continued commission of offences under §§ 263 to 264 or §§ 267 to 269 shall be liable to imprisonment from one to ten years, in less serious cases to imprisonment from six months to five years.

§ 268 Forgery of technical records

(1) Whosoever for the purpose of deception in legal commerce

1. produces a counterfeit technical record or falsifies a technical record or
2. uses a counterfeit or falsified technical record

shall be liable to imprisonment of not more than five years or a fine.

(2) A technical record shall mean a presentation of data, measurements or calculations, conditions or sequences of events, which, in whole or in part, is produced automatically by a technical device, allows the object of the record to be recognised either generally or by informed persons and is intended as proof of a legally relevant fact, regardless of whether this was already the purpose of the presentation when it was produced or only later.

(3) It shall be equivalent to the production of a counterfeit technical record if the offender influences the result of the record by interfering with the recording process.

(4) The attempt shall be punishable.

(5) § 267(3) and (4) shall apply mutatis mutandis.

§ 269 Forgery of data intended to provide proof

(1) Whosoever for the purposes of deception in legal commerce stores or modifies data intended to provide proof in such a way that a counterfeit or falsified document would be created upon their retrieval, or uses data stored or modified in such a manner, shall be liable to imprisonment of not more than five years or a fine.

(2) The attempt shall be punishable.

(3) § 267(3) and (4) shall apply mutatis mutandis.

§ 270 Meaning of deception in the context of data processing

Falsely influencing data processing operations in legal commerce shall be equivalent to deception in legal commerce.

§ 271 Causing wrong entries to be made in public records

(1) Whosoever causes declarations, negotiations or facts which are of relevance for rights or legal relationships to be recorded or stored in public documents, books, data storage media or registers as having been made or having occurred, when they either were not made or did not occur, or were made or occurred differently or were made by a person lacking a professed quality or by a different person, shall be liable to imprisonment of not more than three years or a fine.

(2) Whosoever for the purpose of deception in legal commerce uses a false certification or stored data of the type indicated in subsection (1) above shall incur the same penalty.

(3) If the offender acts for material gain or with the intent of enriching himself or a third person or of harming another person the penalty shall be imprisonment from three months to five years.

(4) The attempt shall be punishable.

§ 272 (repealed)

§ 273 Tampering with official identity documents

(1) Whosoever for the purpose of deception in legal commerce

    1. removes, renders unrecognisable, covers up or suppresses an entry in an official identity document or removes a single page from an official identity document or

    2. uses an official identity document altered in such a way,

shall be liable to imprisonment of not more than three years or a fine unless the offence is punishable under § 267 or § 274.

(2) The attempt shall be punishable.

§ 274 Suppression of documents; changing a border mark

(1) Whosoever

    1. destroys, damages or suppresses a document or a technical record which does not belong to him or not exclusively to him with the intent of causing damage to another;

    2. deletes, suppresses, renders unusable or alters legally relevant data (§ 202a(2)), which are not or not exclusively at his disposal, with the intent of causing damage to another; or

    3. takes away, destroys, renders unrecognisable, moves or falsely places a border stone or another sign intended as a designation of a border or water level with the intent of causing damage to another,

shall be liable to imprisonment of not more than five years or a fine.

(2) The attempt shall be punishable.

§ 275 Preparatory acts to tampering with official identity documents

(1) Whosoever prepares for counterfeiting of official identity documents by producing, procuring for himself or another, offering for sale, storing, supplying to another, or undertaking to import or export

    1. plates, frames, type, blocks, negatives, stencils or similar equipment which by its nature is suited to the commission of the offence or

    2. paper, which is identical to the type of paper or can be easily confused with paper which is used in the production of official identity documents and is especially protected against imitation or

    3. blank forms for official identity documents,

shall be liable to imprisonment of not more than two years or a fine.

(2) If the offender acts on a commercial basis or as a member of a gang whose purpose is the continued commission of offences under subsection (1) above the penalty shall be imprisonment from three months to five years.

(3)   § 149(2) and (3) shall apply mutatis mutandis.

§ 276 Acquisition of false official identity documents

(1)   Whosoever

    1.   undertakes to import or export; or,
    2.   with the intent of using it to facilitate a deception in legal commerce, procures for himself or another, stores or supplies to another

    a counterfeit or falsified official identity document or an official identity document which contains a false certification of the type indicated in § 271 and § 348 shall be liable to imprisonment of not more than two years or a fine.
(2)   If the offender acts on a commercial basis or as a member of a gang, whose purpose is the continued commission of offences under subsection (1) above the penalty shall be imprisonment from three months to five years.

§ 276a Papers relating to rights of residence; vehicle papers

§ 275 and § 276 shall also apply for residence status documents, in particular residence permits and documents certifying a temporary stay of deportation, as well as vehicle papers, in particular vehicle registration and vehicle ownership certificates.

§ 277 Forgery of health certificates

Whosoever using the title of physician or of another registered medical practitioner without having the right to do so, or illegitimately using the name of such persons, issues a certificate relating to his own state of health or that of another, or falsifies a genuine certificate of that type, and makes use of it in order to deceive public authorities or insurance companies shall be liable to imprisonment of not more than one year or a fine.

§ 278 Issuing incorrect health certificates

Physicians and other registered medical practitioners who intentionally and knowingly issue an incorrect certificate relating to the state of health of a person for use with a public authority or insurance company shall be liable to imprisonment of not more than two years or a fine.

§ 279 Using incorrect health certificates

Whosoever, in order to deceive a public authority or an insurance company about his own state of health or that of another, makes use of a certificate of the type indicated in § 277 and § 278, shall be liable to imprisonment of not more than one year or a fine.

§ 280　(repealed)

§ 281　Misuse of identity documents

(1) Whosoever for the purpose of deception in legal commerce uses an identity document which was issued to another, or whosoever for the purpose of deception in legal commerce supplies to another an identity document that was not issued to that person, shall be liable to imprisonment of not more than one year or a fine. The attempt shall be punishable.

(2) Certificates and other documents which are used as identity documents in commerce shall be equivalent to identity documents.

§ 282　Confiscatory expropriation order, extended confiscation and deprivation orders

(1) In cases under §§ 267 to 269, § 275 and § 276, § 43a and § 73d shall apply if the offender acts as a member of a gang whose purpose is the continued commission of such offences. § 73d shall also apply if the offender acts on a commercial basis.

(2) Objects, to which an offence under § 267, § 268, § 271(2) and (3), § 273 or § 276, the latter also in conjunction with § 276a, or under § 269, relates may be subject to a deprivation order. In cases under § 275, also in conjunction with § 276a, the means of falsification indicated therein shall be subject to a deprivation order.

CHAPTER TWENTY-FOUR
OFFENCES IN THE STATE OF INSOLVENCY

§ 283　Bankruptcy

(1) Whosoever due to his liabilities exceeding his assets or current or impending inability to pay his debts

　　1. disposes of or hides, or, in a manner contrary to regular business standards, destroys, damages or renders unusable parts of his assets, which in the case of institution of insolvency proceedings would belong to the available assets;

　　2. in a manner contrary to regular business standards enters into losing or speculative ventures or futures trading in goods or securities or consumes excessive sums or becomes indebted through uneconomical expenditures, gambling or wagering;

　　3. procures goods or securities on credit and sells or otherwise distributes them or things produced from these goods substantially under their value in a manner contrary to regular business standards;

4. pretends the existence of another's rights or recognises fictitious rights;
5. fails to keep books of account which he is statutorily obliged to keep, or keeps or modifies them in such a manner that a survey of his net assets is made more difficult;
6. disposes of, hides, destroys or damages books of account or other documentation, which a merchant is obliged by commercial law to keep, before expiry of the archiving periods which exist for those obliged to keep books, and thereby makes a survey of his net assets more difficult;
7. contrary to commercial law

    (a) draws up balance sheets in such a manner that a survey of his net assets is made more difficult; or
    (b) fails to draw up a balance sheet of his assets or the inventory in the prescribed time; or

8. in another manner which grossly violates regular business standards diminishes his net assets or hides or conceals the actual circumstances of his business,

shall be liable to imprisonment of not more than five years or a fine.

(2) Whosoever causes his liabilities to exceed his assets or the inability to pay by one of the acts indicated in subsection (1) above shall incur the same penalty.

(3) The attempt shall be punishable.

(4) Whosoever in cases

1. under subsection (1) above negligently fails to be aware of the excess of liabilities or the impending or current inability to pay or
2. under subsection (2) above causes the excess of liabilities or inability to pay by gross negligence

shall be liable to imprisonment of not more than two years or a fine.

(5) Whosoever in cases

1. under subsection (2) Nos 2, 5 or 7 above acts negligently and at least negligently fails to be aware of the excess of liabilities or the impending or current inability to pay; or
2. under subsection (2) in conjunction with subsection (1) Nos 2, 5 or 7 above acts negligently and at least by gross negligence causes the excess of liabilities or inability to pay,

shall be liable to imprisonment of not more than two years or a fine.

(6) The offence shall only entail liability if the offender has suspended payments or if insolvency proceedings have been instituted in relation to his assets or the application to institute proceedings has been rejected due to lack of available assets.

§ 283a Aggravated bankruptcy

In especially serious cases under § 283(1) to (3) the offender shall be liable to imprisonment from six months to ten years. An especially serious case typically occurs if the offender

1. acts out of profit-seeking; or
2. knowingly places many persons in danger of losing their assets that were entrusted to him, or in financial hardship.

§ 283b Violation of book-keeping duties

(1) Whosoever

1. fails to keep books of account which he is statutorily obliged to keep, or keeps or modifies them in such a manner that a survey of his net assets is made more difficult;
2. disposes of, hides, destroys or damages books of account or other documentation, which a merchant is obliged by commercial law to keep, before expiry of the archiving periods which exist for those obliged to keep books, and thereby makes a survey of his net assets more difficult;
3. contrary to commercial law

    (a) draws up balance sheets in such a manner that a survey of his net assets is made more difficult; or
    (b) fails to draw up a balance sheet of his assets or the inventory in the prescribed time

    shall be liable to imprisonment of not more than two years or a fine.

(2) Whosoever acts negligently in cases under subsection (1) Nos 1 or 3 above shall be liable to imprisonment of not more than one year or a fine.
(3) § 283(6) shall apply mutatis mutandis.

§ 283c Extending unlawful benefits to creditors

(1) Whosoever with knowledge of his own inability to pay grants a creditor a security or satisfaction to which he is not entitled at all or not in such a manner or at the time, and thereby intentionally or knowingly accords him preferential treatment over the other creditors shall be liable to imprisonment of not more than two years or a fine.
(2) The attempt shall be punishable.
(3) § 283(6) shall apply mutatis mutandis.

§ 283d Extending unlawful benefits to debtors

(1) Whosoever

1. with knowledge of another's impending inability to pay; or

2. after the suspension of payments, in an insolvency proceeding or in a proceeding about the institution of insolvency proceedings of another,

with his consent or on his behalf disposes of or hides, or, in a manner contrary to regular business standards, destroys, damages or renders unusable parts of the other's assets, which in the case of institution of insolvency proceedings would belong to the available assets, shall be liable to imprisonment of not more than five years or a fine.

(2) The attempt shall be punishable.

(3) In especially serious cases the penalty shall be imprisonment from six months to ten years. An especially serious case typically occurs if the offender

1. acts out of profit-seeking; or
2. knowingly places many persons in danger of losing their assets that were entrusted to him, or in financial hardship.

(4) The offence shall only entail liability if the other person has suspended payments or if insolvency proceedings have been instituted in relation to his assets or the application to institute proceedings has been rejected due to lack of available assets.

CHAPTER TWENTY-FIVE
CRIMINAL SELF-SEEKING

§ 284 Organising unlawful gaming

(1) Whosoever without the permission of a public authority publicly organises or operates a game of chance or makes equipment for it available shall be liable to imprisonment of not more than two years or a fine.

(2) Games of chance in clubs or private societies in which games of chance are regularly organised shall be deemed to be publicly organised.

(3) Whosoever in cases under subsection (1) above acts

1. on a commercial basis; or
2. as a member of a gang whose purpose is the continued commission of such offences,

shall be liable to imprisonment from three months to five years.

(4) Whosoever advertises a public game of chance (subsections (1) and (2) above), shall be liable to imprisonment of not more than one year or a fine.

§ 285 Participation in unlawful gaming

Whosoever participates in a public game of chance (§ 284) shall be liable to imprisonment of not more than six months or a fine of not more than one hundred and eighty daily units.

§ 286 Confiscatory expropriation order, extended confiscation and deprivation orders

(1) In cases under § 284(3) No 2, § 43a and § 73d shall apply. § 73d shall also apply in cases under § 284(3) No 1.

(2) In cases under § 284 and § 285 the gambling equipment and the money found on the gaming table or in the bank shall be subject to a deprivation order if they belong to the principal or secondary participant at the time of the decision. Otherwise the objects may be subject to a deprivation order; § 74a shall apply.

§ 287 Organising an unlawful lottery etc

(1) Whosoever without permission of a public authority organises public lotteries or raffles of chattels or immovable property, in particular by offering to conclude gambling contracts for a public lottery or raffle, or accepts offers directed toward the conclusion of such gambling contracts shall be liable to imprisonment of not more than two years or a fine.

(2) Whosoever advertises public lotteries or raffles (subsection (1) above) shall be liable to imprisonment of not more than one year or a fine.

§ 288 Avoiding enforcement of judgments

(1) Whosoever, at the time of an impending enforcement of a judgment and with the intent of obstructing satisfaction of the creditor sells or disposes of parts of his assets shall be liable to imprisonment of not more than two years or a fine.

(2) The offence may only be prosecuted upon request.

§ 289 Taking of pawns

(1) Whosoever with unlawful intent takes away his own chattel or that of another for the benefit of its owner, from the usufructuary, pawnee or another person entitled to use or to retain the chattel shall be liable to imprisonment of not more than three years or a fine.

(2) The attempt shall be punishable.

(3) The offence may only be prosecuted upon request.

§ 290 Unlawful use of pawns

Public pawnbrokers who make unauthorised use of the chattels which they have taken as a pawn shall be liable to imprisonment of not more than one year or a fine.

§ 291 Usury

(1) Whosoever exploits the predicament, lack of experience, lack of judgment or substantial weakness of will of another by allowing material benefits to be promised or granted to himself or a third person

1. for the rent of living space or additional services connected therewith;
2. for the granting of credit;
3. for any other service; or
4. for the procurement of one of the previously indicated services,

which are in striking disproportion to the value of the service or its procurement, shall be liable to imprisonment of not more than three years or a fine. If more than one person contribute as providers of benefits, procurers or in other ways, and if the result is thereby a striking disproportion between the sum of the material benefits and the value of the services the 1st sentence above shall apply to each of the persons who exploits the predicament or other weakness of the other for himself or a third person in order to obtain excessive material benefits.

(2) In especially serious cases the penalty shall be imprisonment from six months to ten years. An especially serious case typically occurs if the offender

1. by the offence places the other in financial hardship;
2. commits the offence on a commercial basis;
3. accepts promissory notes representing usurious material benefits.

§ 292 Poaching

(1) Whosoever in violation of another's hunting rights or rights granted by a hunting licence

1. hunts, catches, kills or appropriates game for himself or a third person; or
2. appropriates for himself or a third person, damages or destroys an object which is subject to the hunting laws,

shall be liable to imprisonment of not more than three years or a fine.

(2) In especially serious cases the penalty shall be imprisonment from three months to five years. An especially serious case typically occurs if the act is committed

1. on a commercial basis or regularly;
2. during night-time, in close season, by the use of snares or in any manner that is not good hunting practice; or
3. jointly by several persons armed with firearms.

§ 293 Taking or destroying fish

Whosoever, in violation of another's fishing rights or rights granted by a fishing licence

1. fishes; or
2. appropriates for himself or a third person, damages or destroys an object which is subject to the fishing laws,

shall be liable to imprisonment of not more than two years or a fine.

§ 294 Request to prosecute

In cases under § 292(1) and § 293 the offence may only be prosecuted upon request of the victim if it was committed by a relative or at a place where the offender was permitted to engage in hunting or fishing to a limited extent.

§ 295 Deprivation order

Hunting and fishing equipment, dogs and other animals that the principal or secondary participant had with them or used during the commission of the offence may be subject to a deprivation order. § 74a shall apply.

§ 296 (repealed)

§ 297 Causing a danger of being impounded to ships, motor-vehicles and aircraft by taking prohibited goods on board etc

(1) Whosoever without the knowledge of the owner or the captain of the ship, or as captain without the knowledge of the owner, brings or takes property on board a German ship, the transport of which causes

1. the danger of seizure or deprivation of the ship or its cargo; or
2. the danger of criminal liability for the owner or the captain of the ship,

shall be liable to imprisonment of not more than two years or a fine.

(2) Whosoever as owner of a ship, without the knowledge of the ship's captain, brings or takes property on board a German ship, the transport of which causes the danger of criminal liability for the captain, shall incur the same penalty.

(3) Subsection (1) No 1 above shall also apply to foreign ships which have taken on their cargo in whole or in part in Germany.

(4) Subsections (1) to (3) above shall apply mutatis mutandis if goods are brought or taken on board motor-vehicles or aircraft. The registered user and the driver or pilot of the motor-vehicle or the aircraft shall be equivalent to the owner and the captain of a ship.

CHAPTER TWENTY-SIX
RESTRICTIVE PRACTICES OFFENCES

§ 298 Restricting competition through agreements in the context of public bids

(1) Whosoever upon an invitation to tender in relation to goods or commercial services makes an offer based on an unlawful agreement whose purpose is to cause the organiser to accept a particular offer shall be liable to imprisonment of not more than five years or a fine.

(2)   The private award of a contract after previous participation in a competition shall be equivalent to an invitation to tender within the meaning of subsection (1) above.

(3)   Whosoever voluntarily prevents the organiser from accepting the offer or from providing his service shall not be liable under subsection (1), also in conjunction with subsection (2) above. If the offer is not accepted or the service of the organiser not provided regardless of the contribution of the offender he shall be exempt from liability if he voluntarily and earnestly makes efforts to prevent the acceptance of the offer or the provision of the service.

§ 299 Taking and giving bribes in commercial practice

(1)   Whosoever as an employee or agent of a business, demands, allows himself to be promised or accepts a benefit for himself or another in a business transaction as consideration for according an unfair preference to another in the competitive purchase of goods or commercial services shall be liable to imprisonment of not more than three years or a fine.

(2)   Whosoever for competitive purposes offers, promises or grants an employee or agent of a business a benefit for himself or for a third person in a business transaction as consideration for such employee's or agent's according him or another an unfair preference in the purchase of goods or commercial services shall incur the same penalty.

(3)   Subsections (1) and (2) above shall also apply to acts in competition abroad.

§ 300 Aggravated cases of taking and giving bribes in commercial practice

In especially serious cases an offender under § 299 shall be liable to imprisonment from three months to five years. An especially serious case typically occurs if

1.   the offence relates to a major benefit or
2.   the offender acts on a commercial basis or as a member of a gang whose purpose is the continued commission of such offences.

§ 301 Request to prosecute

(1)   The offence of taking and giving bribes in commercial practice under § 299 may only be prosecuted upon request unless the prosecuting authority considers propio motu that prosecution is required because of special public interest.

(2)   The right to file the request under subsection (1) above belongs, in addition to the victim, to all of the business persons, associations and chambers indicated in § 8(3) Nos 1, 2, and 4 of the Restrictive Practices Act.

§ 302 Confiscatory expropriation order and extended confiscation

(1) In cases under § 299(1), § 73d shall apply if the offender acts on a commercial basis or as a member of a gang whose purpose is the continued commission of such offences.

(2) In cases under § 299(2), § 43a and § 73d shall apply, if the offender acts as a member of a gang whose purpose is the continued commission of such offences. § 73d shall also apply if the offender acts on a commercial basis.

CHAPTER TWENTY-SEVEN
CRIMINAL DAMAGE

§ 303 Criminal damage

(1) Whosoever unlawfully damages or destroys an object belonging to another shall be liable to imprisonment of not more than two years or a fine.

(2) Whosoever unlawfully alters the appearance of an object belonging to another substantially and permanently shall incur the same penalty.

(3) The attempt shall be punishable.

§ 303a Data tampering

(1) Whosoever unlawfully deletes, suppresses, renders unusable or alters data (§ 202a (2)) shall be liable to imprisonment of not more than two years or a fine.

(2) The attempt shall be punishable.

§ 303b Computer sabotage

(1) Whosoever interferes with data processing operations which are of substantial importance to another by

　　1. committing an offence under §303a(1); or
　　2. entering or transmitting data (§ 202a(2)) with the intention of causing damage to another; or
　　3. destroying, damaging, rendering unusable, removing or altering a data processing system or a data carrier,

shall be liable to imprisonment of not more than five years or a fine.

(2) If the data processing operation is of substantial importance for another's business, enterprise or a public authority, the penalty shall be imprisonment of not more than five years or a fine.

(3) The attempt shall be punishable.

(4) In especially serious cases under subsection (2) above the penalty shall be imprisonment from six months to ten years. An especially serious case typically occurs if the offender

1. causes major financial loss,
2. acts on a commercial basis or as a member of a gang whose purpose is the continued commission of computer sabotage, or
3. through the offence jeopardises the population's supply with vital goods or services or the national security of the Federal Republic of Germany.

(5) § 202c shall apply mutatis mutandis to acts preparatory to an offence under subsection (1) above.

§ 303c Request to prosecute

In cases under §§ 303 to 303b the offence may only be prosecuted upon request, unless the prosecuting authority considers propio motu that prosecution is required because of special public interest.

§ 304 Damage to objects of public interest

(1) Whosoever unlawfully damages or destroys objects of veneration of a religious association existing within Germany or property dedicated to religious worship, or tombstones, public monuments, natural monuments, objects of art, science or craft which are kept in public collections or publicly exhibited, or objects which serve a public need or add to the ambience of public paths, squares or parks, shall be liable to imprisonment of not more than three years or a fine.
(2) Whosoever unlawfully alters the appearance of an object listed under subsection (1) above substantially and permanently shall incur the same penalty
(3) The attempt shall be punishable.

§ 305 Destruction of buildings etc

(1) Whosoever unlawfully destroys, in whole or in part, a building, ship, bridge, dam, a constructed road, a railroad or another edifice belonging to another shall be liable to imprisonment of not more than five years or a fine.
(2) The attempt shall be punishable.

§ 305a Destruction of important means of production etc

(1) Whosoever unlawfully destroys, in whole or in part:

1. technical means of production belonging to another and of significant value, which is of substantial importance for the construction of a facility or an enterprise within the meaning of § 316b(1) Nos 1 or 2 or which serves the operation or the waste disposal of such facility or enterprise; or
2. a motor-vehicle of the police or the Armed Forces,

shall be liable to imprisonment of not more than five years or a fine.
(2) The attempt shall be punishable.

CHAPTER TWENTY-EIGHT
OFFENCES CAUSING A COMMON DANGER

§ 306 Arson

(1)   Whosoever sets fire to or by setting fire to them destroys in whole or in part

1.   buildings or huts;
2.   plants or technical facilities, in particular machines;
3.   warehouses or stored goods;
4.   motor-vehicles, rail vehicles, aircraft or watercraft;
5.   forests, heaths or moors;
6.   agricultural, nutrition or forestry facilities or products

belonging to another shall be liable to imprisonment from one to ten years.

(2)   In less serious cases the penalty shall be imprisonment from six months to five years.

§ 306a Aggravated arson

(1)   Whosoever sets fire to or by setting fire to them destroys, in whole or in part

1.   a building, ship, hut or other premises which serves as a dwelling for people;
2.   a church or another building serving the practice of religion;
3.   premises which from time to time serve as a residence for people at a time during which people usually reside there,

shall be liable to imprisonment of not less than one year.

(2)   Whosoever sets fire to an object listed in § 306(1) Nos 1 to 6 or destroys it in whole or in part by setting fire to it and thereby places another person in danger of injury shall incur the same penalty.

(3)   In less serious cases under subsections (1) and (2) above the penalty shall be imprisonment from six months to five years.

§ 306b Additionally aggravated arson

(1)   Whosoever through an offence of arson under § 306 or § 306a causes serious injury to another person or injury to a large number of people shall be liable to imprisonment of not less than two years.

(2)   The penalty shall be imprisonment of not less than five years if the offender in cases under § 306a

1.   through the offence places another person in danger of death;
2.   acts with the intent of facilitating or covering up another offence; or
3.   prevents the fire from being extinguished or makes extinguishing the fire more difficult.

§ 306c Arson causing death

If the offender through an offence of arson under §§ 306 to 306b at least by gross negligence causes the death of another person the penalty shall be imprisonment for life or not less than ten years.

§ 306d Arson by negligence

(1) Whosoever acts negligently in cases under § 306(1) or § 306a(1) or negligently causes the danger in cases under § 306a(2) shall be liable to imprisonment of not more than five years.

(2) Whosoever acts negligently in cases under § 306a(2) and negligently causes the danger shall be liable to imprisonment of not more than three years or a fine.

§ 306e Preventing completion of the offence

(1) The court in its discretion may mitigate the sentence (§ 49(2)) in cases under § 306, § 306a and § 306b or order a discharge pursuant to those provisions if the offender voluntarily extinguishes the fire before substantial damage occurs.

(2) Whosoever voluntarily extinguishes the fire before substantial damage occurs shall not be liable under § 306d.

(3) If the fire is extinguished regardless of the contribution of the offender before substantial damage occurs his voluntary and earnest efforts to extinguish it shall suffice.

§ 306f Causing the danger of fire

(1) Whosoever, by smoking, by an open fire or light, by throwing away burning or smouldering objects or otherwise causes the danger that

1. businesses or facilities that are easily inflammable;
2. agricultural or nutrition facilities and businesses in which their products are stored;
3. forests, heaths or moors; or
4. cultivated fields or easily inflammable agricultural produce stored in fields,

will catch fire shall be liable to imprisonment of not more than three years or a fine.

(2) Whosoever causes the danger that objects indicated in subsection (1) Nos 1 to 4 above will catch fire and thereby endangers the life or limb of another person or property of significant value belonging to another shall incur the same penalty.

(3) Whosoever acts negligently in cases under subsection (1) above or causes the danger negligently in cases under subsection (2) above shall be liable to imprisonment of not more than one year or a fine.

§ 307 Causing a nuclear explosion

(1) Whosoever undertakes to cause an explosion by the release of nuclear energy and thereby endangers the life or limb of another person or property of significant value belonging to another shall be liable to imprisonment of not less than five years.

(2) Whosoever causes an explosion by the release of nuclear energy and thereby negligently endangers the life or limb of another person or property of significant value belonging to another shall be liable to imprisonment from one to ten years.

(3) If by the offence the offender at least by gross negligence causes the death of another person the penalty shall

   1. in cases under subsection (1) above be imprisonment for life or not less than ten years;
   2. in cases under subsection (2) above be imprisonment of not less than five years.

(4) Whosoever acts negligently in cases under subsection (2) above and negligently causes the danger shall be liable to imprisonment of not more than three years or a fine.

§ 308 Causing an explosion

(1) Whosoever causes an explosion other than by the release of nuclear energy, in particular by the use of explosives, and thereby endangers the life or limb of another person or property of significant value belonging to another shall be liable to imprisonment of not less than one year.

(2) If by the offence the offender causes serious injury to another person or injury to a large number of people the penalty shall be imprisonment of not less than two years.

(3) If by the offence the offender at least by gross negligence causes the death of another person the penalty shall be imprisonment for life or not less than ten years.

(4) In less serious cases under subsection (1) above the penalty shall be imprisonment from six months to five years, in less serious cases under subsection (2) above imprisonment from one to ten years.

(5) Whosoever negligently causes the danger in cases under subsection (1) above shall be liable to imprisonment of not more than five years or a fine.

(6) Whosoever acts negligently in cases under subsection (1) above and negligently causes the danger shall be liable to imprisonment of not more than three years or a fine.

§ 309 Misuse of ionising radiation

(1)   Whosoever, with the intent of damaging the health of another person under-takes to expose him to ionising radiation capable of damaging his health shall be liable to imprisonment from one to ten years.

(2)   If the offender undertakes to expose a vast number of persons to such radia-tion the penalty shall be imprisonment of not less than five years.

(3)   If by the offence the offender causes serious injury to another person in cases under subsection (1) above or injury to a large number of people the penalty shall be imprisonment of not less than two years.

(4)   If by the offence the offender at least by gross negligence causes the death of another person the penalty shall be imprisonment for life or not less than ten years.

(5)   In less serious cases under subsection (1) above the penalty shall be impris-onment from six months to five years, in less serious cases under subsection (3) above imprisonment from one to ten years.

(6)   Whosoever with the intent

   1.   of impairing the usefulness of property of significant value belonging to another,

   2.   of permanently altering the qualities of a body of water, the air or the soil in a negative manner, or

   3.   of damaging animals or plants of a significant value belonging to another, exposes the property, the body of water, the air, the soil, the animals or the plants to ionising radiation capable of causing such impairments, alterations or damage, shall be liable to imprisonment of not more than five years or a fine. The attempt shall be punishable.

§ 310 Acts preparatory to causing an explosion or radiation offence

(1)   Whosoever, in preparation of

   1.   a particular offence within the meaning of § 307(1) or § 309(2); or

   2.   an offence under § 308(1) which is to be committed by using explosives,

   3.   an offence under § 309(1) or

   4.   an offence under § 309(6)

produces, procures for himself or another, stores or supplies to another nuclear fuel, other radioactive materials, explosives or any equipment required for the commission of the offence shall, in cases under No 1 above be liable to imprisonment from one to ten years, in cases under Nos 2 and 3 above to imprisonment from six months to five years, and in cases under No 4 above to imprisonment of not more than three years or a fine.

(2)   In less serious cases under subsection (1) No 1 above the penalty shall be imprisonment from six months to five years.

(3)   In cases under subsection (1) Nos 3 and 4 above the attempt shall be punishable.

§ 311 Releasing ionising radiation

(1) Whosoever in violation of duties under administrative law (§ 330d Nos 4 and 5)

    1. releases ionising radiation; or
    2. causes incidents of nuclear fission

capable of harming the life or limb of another person or damaging property of significant value belonging to another shall be liable to imprisonment of not more than five years or a fine.

(2) The attempt shall be punishable.

(3) Whosoever negligently

    1. in operating a facility, especially a plant, commits an offence within the meaning of subsection (1) above in a manner capable of causing damage outside the area belonging to the facility; or
    2. in other cases under subsection (1) above acts in gross violation of duties under administrative law

shall be liable to imprisonment of not more than two years or a fine.

§ 312 Construction of a defective nuclear facility

(1) Whosoever constructs or delivers a defective nuclear facility (§ 330d No 2) or objects which are intended for the construction or operation of such a facility, and thereby causes a danger for the life or limb of another person or for property of significant value belonging to another arising from the effects of an incident of nuclear fission or radiation from radioactive materials shall be liable to imprisonment from three months to five years.

(2) The attempt shall be punishable.

(3) If by the offence the offender causes serious injury to another person or injury to a large number of people the penalty shall be imprisonment from one to ten years.

(4) If by the offence the offender causes the death of another person the penalty shall be imprisonment of not less than three years

(5) In less serious cases under subsection (3) above the penalty shall be imprisonment from six months to five years, in less serious cases under subsection (4) above imprisonment from one to ten years.

(6) Whosoever in cases under subsection (1) above

    1. negligently causes the danger; or
    2. acts grossly negligently and negligently causes the danger

shall be liable to imprisonment of not more than three years or a fine.

§ 313 Causing flooding

(1) Whosoever causes a flood and thereby endangers the life or limb of another person or property of significant value belonging to another shall be liable to imprisonment from one to ten years.

(2) § 308(2) to (6) shall apply mutatis mutandis.

§ 314 Causing a common danger by poisoning

(1) Whosoever poisons or releases noxious substances into

    1. water in contained springs, wells, pipes or drinking water storage facilities; or

    2. objects intended for public sale or use,

or sells, offers for sale or otherwise distributes poisoned objects or those into which noxious substances have been released within the meaning of No 2 above shall be liable to imprisonment from one to ten years.

(2) § 308(2) to (4) shall apply mutatis mutandis.

§ 314a Preventing completion of the offence

(1) The court in its discretion may mitigate the sentence (§ 49(2)) in cases under § 307(2) and § 309(2) if the offender voluntarily gives up the further commission of the offence or otherwise averts the danger.

(2) The court in its discretion may mitigate the sentence (§ 49(2)) under the following provisions or order a discharge pursuant to these provisions if the offender:

    1. in cases under § 309(1) or § 314(1) voluntarily gives up the further commission of the offence or otherwise averts the danger; or

    2. in cases under

        (a) § 307(2);
        (b) § 308(1) and (5);
        (c) § 309(6);
        (d) § 311(1);
        (e) § 312(1) and (6) No 1;
        (f) § 313, also in conjunction with § 308(5),

voluntarily averts the danger before substantial damage occurs.

(3) Whosoever

    1. in cases under

        (a) § 307(4);
        (b) § 308(6);
        (c) § 311(3);

(d) § 312(6) No 2;

(e) § 313(2) in conjunction with § 308(6),

voluntarily averts the danger before substantial damage occurs or

2.   in cases under § 310 voluntarily gives up the further commission of the offence or otherwise averts the danger

shall not be liable under the preceding provisions.

(4)   If the danger is averted regardless of the contribution of the offender his voluntary and earnest efforts to avert it shall suffice.

§ 315 Dangerous disruption of rail, ship and air traffic

(1)   Whosoever interferes with the safety of traffic by rail, suspension rail, ship or air by

1.   destroying, damaging or removing facilities or means of transport;
2.   setting up obstacles;
3.   giving false signs or signals; or
4.   undertaking a similar act of intervention of equal dangerousness

and thereby endangers the life or limb of another person or property of significant value belonging to another shall be liable to imprisonment from six months to ten years.

(2)   The attempt shall be punishable.

(3)   The penalty shall be imprisonment of not less than one year if the offender

1.   acts with the intent of

(a) causing an accident;

(b) facilitating or covering up another offence; or

2.   by the offence causes serious injury to another person or injury to a large number of people.

(4)   In less serious cases under subsection (1) above the penalty shall be imprisonment from three months to five years, in less serious cases under subsection (3) above imprisonment from six months to five years.

(5)   Whosoever negligently causes the danger in cases under subsection (1) above shall be liable to imprisonment of not more than five years or a fine.

(6)   Whosoever acts negligently in cases under subsection (1) above and negligently causes the danger shall be liable to imprisonment of not more than two years or a fine.

§ 315a Endangering rail, ship and air traffic

(1)   Whosoever

1.   is in control of a rail or suspension vehicle, a ship or an aircraft although due to the consumption of alcoholic beverages or other intoxicants or

due to mental or physical defects he is not in a condition to control the vehicle safely; or

2. being in control of such a vehicle or otherwise as a person responsible for safety by a gross breach of his duties violates legal provisions relating to the safety of rail, suspension rail, ship or air traffic

and thereby endangers the life or limb of another person or property of significant value belonging to another shall be liable to imprisonment of not more than five years or a fine.

(2) In cases under subsection (1) No 1 above the attempt shall be punishable.

(3) Whosoever in cases under subsection (1) above

1. negligently causes the danger; or
2. acts negligently and negligently causes the danger

shall be liable to imprisonment of not more than two years or a fine.

§ 315b Dangerous disruption of road traffic

(1) Whosoever interferes with the safety of road traffic by

1. destroying, damaging or removing facilities or vehicles;
2. setting up obstacles; or
3. undertaking a similar act of interference of equal dangerousness,

and thereby endangers the life or limb of another person or property of significant value belonging to another shall be liable to imprisonment of not more than five years or a fine.

(2) The attempt shall be punishable.

(3) If the offender acts under the conditions of § 315(3) the penalty shall be imprisonment from one to ten years, in less serious cases imprisonment from six months to five years.

(4) Whosoever negligently causes the danger in cases under subsection (1) above shall be liable to imprisonment of not more than three years or a fine.

(5) Whosoever acts negligently in cases under subsection (1) above and negligently causes the danger shall be liable to imprisonment of not more than two years or a fine.

§ 315c Endangering road traffic

(1) Whosoever in road traffic

1. drives a vehicle, although

   (a) due to consumption of alcoholic beverages or other intoxicants; or
   (b) due to mental or physical defects,

he is not in a condition to drive the vehicle safely; or

2. in gross violation of traffic regulations and carelessly

    (a) does not observe the right of way;
    (b) overtakes improperly or drives improperly in the process of overtaking;
    (c) improperly drives near pedestrian crossings;
    (d) drives too fast in places with poor visibility, at road crossings or junctions or railroad crossings;
    (e) fails to keep to the right-hand side of the road in places with poor visibility;
    (f) turns, drives backwards or contrary to the direction of traffic or attempts to do so on a highway or motorway; or
    (g) fails to make vehicles which have stopped or broken down recognisable at a sufficient distance although it is required for the safety of traffic

and thereby endangers the life or limb of another person or property of significant value belonging to another shall be liable to imprisonment of not more than five years or a fine.

(2) In cases under subsection (1) No 1 above the attempt shall be punishable.

(3) Whosoever in cases under subsection (1) above

    1. negligently causes the danger; or
    2. acts negligently and negligently causes the danger,

shall be liable to imprisonment of not more than two years or a fine.

§ 315d Rail traffic on roads

To the extent that rail transport participates in road traffic only the provisions for the protection of road traffic (§ 315b and § 315c) shall apply.

§ 316 Driving while under the influence of drink or drugs

(1) Whosoever drives a vehicle in traffic (§§ 315 to 315d) although due to consumption of alcoholic beverages or other intoxicants he is not in a condition to drive the vehicle safely shall be liable to imprisonment of not more than one year or a fine unless the offence is punishable under § 315a or § 315c.

(2) Whosoever commits the offence negligently shall also be liable under subsection (1) above.

§ 316a Attacking a driver for the purpose of committing a robbery

(1) Whosoever for the purposes of committing a robbery (§§ 249 or 250), theft with use of force (§ 252) or blackmail with use of force (§ 255) commits an attack against the life or limb or the freedom of decision of the driver of a motor-vehicle or a passenger and thereby exploits the particular conditions of road traffic shall be liable to imprisonment of not less than five years.

(2) In less serious cases the penalty shall be imprisonment from one to ten years.

(3) If by the offence the offender at least by gross negligence causes the death of another person the penalty shall be imprisonment for life or not less than ten years.

§ 316b Disruption of public services

(1) Whosoever prevents or interferes with the operation of

  1. enterprises or facilities which serve the public provision of postal services or public transport;
  2. a facility which serves the public provision of water, light, heat or power or an enterprise which serves the vital needs of the population; or
  3. an installation or a facility serving public order and safety

by destroying, damaging, removing, altering or rendering unusable an object used in its operation or taps electrical power intended for its operation shall be liable to imprisonment of not more than five years or a fine.

(2) The attempt shall be punishable.

(3) In especially serious cases the penalty shall be imprisonment from six months to ten years. An especially serious case typically occurs if by the offence the offender disrupts the provision of vital goods to the population, in particular water, light, heat or power.

§ 316c Attacks on air and maritime traffic

(1) Whosoever

  1. uses force or attacks the freedom of decision of a person or engages in other conduct in order to gain control of, or influence the navigation of

    (a) an aircraft employed in civil air traffic which is in flight; or
    (b) a ship employed in civil maritime traffic; or

  2. uses firearms or undertakes to cause an explosion or a fire, in order to destroy or damage such an aircraft or ship or any cargo on board

shall be liable to imprisonment of not less than five years. An aircraft which has already been boarded by members of the crew or passengers or the loading of the cargo of which has already begun or which has not yet been deboarded by members of the crew or passengers or the unloading of the cargo of which has not been completed shall be equivalent to an aircraft in flight.

(2) In less serious cases the penalty shall be imprisonment from one to ten years.

(3) If by the act the offender at least by gross negligence causes the death of another person the penalty shall be imprisonment for life or not less than ten years.

(4)   Whosoever in preparation of an offence under subsection (1) above produces, procures for himself or another, stores or supplies to another firearms, explosives or other materials designed to cause an explosion or a fire shall be liable to imprisonment from six months to five years.

§ 317 Disruption of telecommunications facilities

(1)   Whosoever prevents or endangers the operation of a telecommunications facility which serves public purposes by destroying, damaging, removing, altering or rendering unusable an object which serves its operation, or taps electrical power intended for its operation shall be liable to imprisonment of not more than five years or a fine.
(2)   The attempt shall be punishable.
(3)   Whosoever commits the offence negligently shall be liable to imprisonment of not more than one year or a fine.

§ 318 Causing damage to important facilities

(1)   Whosoever damages or destroys water pipes, sluices, weirs, dikes, dams or other water works, or bridges, ferries, roads or bulwarks or equipment used in mining operations for water control, ventilation or for transporting employees in and out, and thereby endangers the life or limb of another person shall be liable to imprisonment from three months to five years.
(2)   The attempt shall be punishable.
(3)   If by the offence the offender causes serious injury to another person or injury to a large number of people the penalty shall be imprisonment from one to ten years.
(4)   If by the offence the offender causes the death of another person the penalty shall be imprisonment of not less than three years.
(5)   In less serious cases under subsection (3) above the penalty shall be imprisonment from six months to five years, in less serious cases under subsection (4) above imprisonment from one to ten years.
(6)   Whosoever in cases under subsection (1) above

1.   negligently causes the danger; or
2.   acts negligently and negligently causes the danger

shall be liable to imprisonment of not more than three years or a fine.

§ 319 Causing danger during construction works

(1)   Whosoever in the planning, management or execution of the construction or the demolition of a structure violates generally accepted engineering standards and thereby endangers the life or limb of another person shall be liable to imprisonment of not more than five years or a fine.
(2)   Whosoever in engaging in a profession or trade violates generally accepted engineering standards in the planning, management or execution of a

project to install technical fixtures in a structure or to modify installed fix-tures of this nature and thereby endangers the life or limb of another person shall incur the same penalty.

(3)   Whosoever causes the danger negligently, shall be liable to imprisonment of not more than three years or a fine.

(4)   Whosoever in cases under subsections (1) and (2) above acts negligently and causes the danger negligently shall be liable to imprisonment of not more than two years or a fine.

§ 320 Preventing completion of the offence

(1)   The court in its discretion may mitigate the sentence (§ 49(2)) in cases under § 316c(1) if the offender voluntarily gives up the further commission of the offence or otherwise averts the result.

(2)   The court in its discretion may mitigate the sentence (§ 49(2)) under the following provisions or order a discharge under these provisions if the offender in cases under

1.   § 315(1), (3), No 1 or (5);
2.   § 315b(1), (3), or (4), (3) in conjunction with § 315(3) No 1;
3.   § 318(1) or (6) No 1;
4.   § 319(1) to (3),

voluntarily averts the danger before substantial damage occurs.

(3)   Whosoever

1.   in cases under

(a) § 315(6);
(b) § 315b(5);
(c) § 318 (6) No 2;
(d) § 319(4)

voluntarily averts the danger before substantial damage occurs; or
2.   in cases under § 316c(4) voluntarily gives up the further commission of the offence or otherwise averts the danger

shall not be liable under the preceding provisions.

(4)   If the danger or the result is averted regardless of the contribution of the offender before substantial damage occurs his voluntary and earnest efforts to avert them shall suffice.

§ 321 Supervision order

In cases under §§ 306 to 306c, § 307(1) to (3), § 308(1) to (3), § 309(1) to (4), § 310(1) and § 316c(1) No 2 the court may make a supervision order (§ 68(1)).

§ 322 Deprivation order

If an offence under §§ 306 to 306c, §§307 to 314 or § 316c has been committed

1. objects that were generated by the act or used or intended for use in its commission or preparation; and
2. objects, to which an offence under §§ 310 to 312, § 314 or § 316c relates

may be subject to a deprivation order.

§ 323 *(repealed)*

§ 323a Committing offences in a senselessly drunken state

(1) Whosoever intentionally or negligently puts himself into a drunken state by consuming alcoholic beverages or other intoxicants shall be liable to imprisonment of not more than five years or a fine if he commits an unlawful act while in this state and may not be punished because of it because he was insane due to the intoxication or if this cannot be excluded.

(2) The penalty must not be more severe than the penalty provided for the offence which was committed while he was in the drunken state.

(3) The offence may only be prosecuted upon request, authorisation or upon request by a foreign state if the act committed in the drunken state may only be prosecuted upon complaint, authorisation or upon request by a foreign state.

§ 323b Endangering the treatment of addicts

Whosoever knowingly without the permission of the director of the institution or his agent, procures for or supplies alcoholic beverages or other intoxicants to another who has been placed in an institution for withdrawal treatment on the basis of an order of a public authority or without his consent or encourages him to consume such substances shall be liable to imprisonment of not more than one year or a fine.

§ 323c Omission to effect an easy rescue

Whosoever does not render assistance during accidents or a common danger or emergency although it is necessary and can be expected of him under the circumstances, particularly if it is possible without substantial danger to himself and without violation of other important duties shall be liable to imprisonment of not more than one year or a fine.

CHAPTER TWENTY-NINE
OFFENCES AGAINST THE ENVIRONMENT

§ 324 Water pollution

(1) Whosoever unlawfully pollutes a body of water or otherwise alters its qualities in a negative manner shall be liable to imprisonment of not more than five years or a fine.

(2) The attempt shall be punishable.

(3) If the offender acts negligently the penalty shall be imprisonment of not more than three years or a fine.

§ 324a Soil pollution

(1) Whosoever, in violation of duties under administrative law introduces, allows substances to penetrate or releases substances into the soil and thereby pollutes it or otherwise alters it negatively

    1. in a manner that is capable of harming the health of another, animals, plants, other property of significant value or a body of water; or

    2. to a significant extent

shall be liable to imprisonment of not more than five years or a fine.

(2) The attempt shall be punishable.

(3) If the offender acts negligently the penalty shall be imprisonment of not more than three years or a fine.

§ 325 Air pollution

(1) Whosoever, in the operation of a facility, especially a plant or machine, in violation of duties under administrative law, causes alterations of the air which are capable of harming the health of another, animals, plants or other property of significant value outside the area belonging to the facility shall be liable to imprisonment of not more than five years or a fine. The attempt shall be punishable.

(2) Whosoever, in the operation of a facility, especially a plant or machine, in gross violation of duties under administrative law, releases harmful substances in significant amounts into the air outside the grounds of the facility shall be liable to imprisonment of not more than five years or a fine.

(3) If the offender acts negligently the penalty shall be imprisonment of not more than three years or a fine.

(4) Harmful substances within the meaning of subsection (2) above are substances which are capable of

    1. harming the health of another, animals, plants or other property of significant value; or

2.   polluting or otherwise negatively and permanently altering a body of water, the air or the soil.

(5)   Subsections (1) to (3) above shall not apply to motor-vehicles, rail vehicles, aircraft or watercraft.

§ 325a Causing noise, vibrations and non-ionising radiation

(1)   Whosoever, in the operation of a facility, especially a plant or machine, in violation of duties under administrative law, causes noise which is capable of harming the health of another outside the area belonging to the facility, shall be liable to imprisonment of not more than three years or a fine.

(2)   Whosoever, in the operation of a facility, especially a plant or machine, in violation of duties under administrative law which serve to protect against noise, vibrations or non-ionising radiation, endangers the health of another, animals not his own or property of significant value belonging to another shall be liable to imprisonment of not more than five years or a fine.

(3)   If the offender acts negligently the penalty

1.   in cases under subsection (1) above shall be imprisonment of not more than two years or a fine;

2.   in cases under subsection (2) above shall be imprisonment of not more than three years or a fine.

(4)   Subsections (1) to (3) above shall not apply to motor-vehicles, rail vehicles, aircraft or watercraft.

§ 326 Unlawful disposal of dangerous waste

(1)   Whosoever unlawfully, outside the facility authorised therefor or in substantial deviation from the proscribed or authorised procedure, treats, stores, dumps, discharges or otherwise disposes of waste which

1.   contains or can generate poisons or carriers of diseases which are dangerous to the public and are communicable to persons or animals;

2.   is carcinogenic in humans, harmful to the foetus or can cause alterations in the genetic make-up;

3.   is prone to explode, spontaneously combustible, or of more than merely minor radioactive quality; or

4.   because of its nature, composition or quantity is capable of:

(a)   polluting or otherwise negatively and permanently altering a body of water, the air or the soil or

(b)   endangering an existing population of animals or plants

shall be liable to imprisonment of not more than five years or a fine.

(2)   Whosoever contrary to a prohibition or without the required permit moves waste within the meaning of subsection (1) above into, out of or through the Federal Republic of Germany shall incur the same penalty.

(3) Whosoever in violation of duties under administrative law fails to deliver radioactive waste shall be liable to imprisonment of not more than three years or a fine.

(4) In cases under subsections (1) and (2) above the attempt shall be punishable.

(5) If the offender acts negligently the penalty

  1. in cases under subsections (1) and (2) above shall be imprisonment of not more than three years or a fine;
  2. in cases under subsection (3) above shall be imprisonment of not more than one year or a fine.

(6) The offence shall not be punishable if harmful effects on the environment, especially on persons, bodies of water, the air, the soil, useful animals or useful plants, are obviously excluded due to the small quantity of waste.

§ 327 Unlawful operation of facilities

(1) Whosoever without the required permit or contrary to an enforceable prohibition

  1. operates a nuclear facility, possesses an operational or decommissioned nuclear facility or in whole or in part dismantles such a facility or substantially modifies its operation; or
  2. substantially modifies a plant in which nuclear fuels are used or its location

  shall be liable to imprisonment of not more than five years or a fine.

(2) Whosoever operates

  1. a facility which requires a permit or any other facility within the meaning of the Federal Emission Control Act the operation of which has been prohibited in order to prevent danger;
  2. a pipeline facility for the transportation of water-endangering substances within the meaning of the Water Resources Act which requires a permit or is subject to a duty to report; or
  3. a waste disposal facility within the meaning of the Recycling and Waste Act,

  without the permit or planning approval required by the respective statute or contrary to an enforceable prohibition based on the respective statute shall be liable to imprisonment of not more than three years or a fine.

(3) If the offender acts negligently the penalty

  1. in cases under subsection (1) above shall be imprisonment of not more than three years or a fine;
  2. in cases under subsection (2) above shall be imprisonment of not more than two years or a fine.

§ 328 Unlawful handling of radioactive substances, dangerous substances and goods

(1)   Whosoever keeps, transports, treats, processes or otherwise uses, imports or exports

1.   nuclear fuels without the required permit or contrary to an enforceable prohibition; or
2.   other radioactive substances which because of their nature, composition or quantity are capable of causing the death of or serious injury to another by ionising radiation, without the required permit or contrary to an enforceable prohibition and in gross violation of his duties

shall be liable to imprisonment of not more than five years or a fine.

(2)   Whosoever

1.   fails promptly to deliver nuclear fuels which he is obliged to deliver on the basis of the Peaceful Use of Nuclear Energy Act;
2.   delivers nuclear fuels or substances indicated in subsection (1) No 2 above to unauthorised persons or procures their distribution to unauthorised persons;
3.   causes a nuclear explosion; or
4.   encourages another to commit an act as indicated in No 3 above or supports such an act,

shall incur the same penalty.

(3)   Whosoever in gross violation of duties under administrative law

1.   in the operation of a facility, especially a plant or technical installation, stores, treats, processes, or otherwise uses radioactive substances or dangerous substances within the meaning of the Dangerous Substances (Protection) Act; or
2.   transports, forwards, packs, unpacks, loads or unloads, receives or supplies to another dangerous goods,

and thereby endangers the health of another, animals not his own or property of significant value belonging to another shall be liable to imprisonment of not more than five years or a fine.

(4)   The attempt shall be punishable.
(5)   If the offender acts negligently the penalty shall be imprisonment of not more than three years or a fine.
(6)   Subsections (4) and (5) above shall not apply to acts under subsection (2) No 4 above.

§ 329 Endangering protected areas

(1)   Whosoever contrary to an ordinance enacted on the basis of the Federal Emission Control Act relating to an area which requires special protection

against harmful environmental effects of air pollution or noise or in which a great increase in harmful environmental effects can be expected during periods of thermal inversion, operates facilities within the area shall be liable to imprisonment of not more than three years or a fine. Whosoever operates facilities in such an area contrary to an enforceable order, which was issued on the basis of an ordinance indicated in the 1st sentence above shall incur the same penalty. The 1st and 2nd sentences above shall not apply to motor-vehicles, rail vehicles, aircraft or watercraft.

(2)　Whosoever contrary to an ordinance or an enforceable prohibition enacted to protect a water or mineral spring conservation area

　　1.　operates in-plant facilities dealing with water-endangering substances;
　　2.　operates pipeline facilities to transport water-endangering substances or transports such substances; or
　　3.　mines gravel, sand, clay or other solid substances within the framework of a commercial operation,

shall be liable to imprisonment of not more than three years or a fine. A facility of a public enterprise is also an in-plant facility within the meaning of the 1st sentence.

(3)　Whosoever contrary to an ordinance or an enforceable prohibition enacted to protect a nature conservation area, an area provisionally set aside as a nature conservation area, or a national park

　　1.　mines or extracts mineral resources or other soil components;
　　2.　makes excavations or creates mounds;
　　3.　creates, alters or removes bodies of water;
　　4.　drains moors, swamps, marshes or other wetlands;
　　5.　clears woodland;
　　6.　kills, catches, hunts, or in whole or in part destroys or removes the eggs of, animals of an especially protected species within the meaning of the Federal Nature Conservation Act;
　　7.　damages or removes plants of a specially protected species within the meaning of the Federal Nature Conservation Act; or
　　8.　erects a building,

and thereby interferes not merely insubstantially with the respective protected interest shall be liable to imprisonment of not more than five years or a fine.

(4)　If the offender acts negligently the penalty

　　1.　in cases under subsections (1) and (2) above shall be imprisonment of not more than two years or a fine;
　　2.　in cases under subsection (3) above shall be imprisonment of not more than three years or a fine.

§ 330 Aggravated cases of environmental offences

(1)   In especially serious cases of an intentional offence under §§ 324 to 329 the penalty shall be imprisonment from six months to ten years. An especially serious case typically occurs if the offender

    1.   damages a body of water, the soil or a conservation area within the meaning of § 329(3) in such a manner that the damage cannot be eliminated or only at extraordinary expense or after a lengthy period of time;

    2.   endangers the public water supply;

    3.   permanently damages an existing population of animals or plants of species under threat of extinction;

    4.   acts out of profit-seeking.

(2)   Whosoever by an intentional offence under §§ 324 to 329

    1.   places another person in danger of death or serious injury or a large number of people in danger of injury; or

    2.   causes the death of another person,

    shall in cases under No 1 above be liable to imprisonment from one to ten years, in cases under No 2 above to imprisonment of not less than three years unless the act is punishable under § 330a(1) to (3).

(3)   In less serious cases under subsection (2) No 1 above the penalty shall be imprisonment from six months to five years, in less serious cases under subsection (2) No 2 above imprisonment from one to ten years.

§ 330a Causing a severe danger by releasing poison

(1)   Whosoever diffuses or releases substances which contain or can generate poisons and thereby causes the danger of death or serious injury to another person or the danger of injury to a large number of people shall be liable to imprisonment from one to ten years.

(2)   If by the offence the offender causes the death of another person the penalty shall be imprisonment of not less than three years.

(3)   In less serious cases under subsection (1) above the penalty shall be imprisonment from six months to five years, in less serious cases under subsection (2) above imprisonment from one to ten years.

(4)   Whosoever causes the danger negligently in cases under subsection (1) above shall be liable to imprisonment of not more than five years or a fine.

(5)   Whosoever acts grossly negligently in cases under subsection (1) above and negligently causes the danger shall be liable to imprisonment of not more than three years or a fine.

§ 330b Preventing completion of the offence

(1)   The court in cases under § 325a(2), § 326(1) to (3), § 328(1) to (3) and § 330a(1), (3) and (4) may in its discretion mitigate the sentence (§ 49(2)) or

order a discharge under these provisions if the offender voluntarily averts the danger or eliminates the condition he caused before substantial damage occurs. Under the same conditions the offender shall not be liable under § 325a(3) No 2, § 326(5), § 328(5) and § 330a(5).

(2) If the danger is averted or the unlawfully caused condition eliminated regardless of the contribution of the offender his voluntary and earnest efforts to avert or eliminate them shall suffice.

§ 330c Deprivation order

If an offence under § 326, § 327(1) or (2), § 328, § 329(1), (2) or (3), the latter also in conjunction with (4) has been committed,

1. objects, which were generated by the offence or used or intended for use in its commission or preparation; and
2. objects, to which the offence relates

may be subject to a deprivation order. § 74a shall apply.

§ 330d Definitions

Within the meaning of this chapter

1. a body of water shall be surface water, ground water and the sea;
2. a nuclear facility shall be a facility for the production or treatment or processing or fission of nuclear fuels or for the enrichment of irradiated nuclear fuels;
3. dangerous goods shall be goods within the meaning of the Transportation of Dangerous Goods Act or an ordinance based thereon and within the meaning of the provisions relating to the international transportation of dangerous goods in the respective territories of their application;
4. a duty under administrative law shall be a duty which arises from

    (a) a legal provision;
    (b) a judicial decision;
    (c) an enforceable administrative act;
    (d) an enforceable condition to an administrative act; or
    (e) a contract under public law to the extent that the duty could also have been imposed by an administrative act

    and which serves to protect against dangers or harmful effects on the environment, especially on persons, animals or plants, bodies of water, the air or the soil;
5. an act without a permit, planning approval or other permission shall be also an act on the basis of a permit, planning approval or other permission which was secured by threats, bribery or collusion or obtained by deception through incorrect or incomplete statements.

CHAPTER THIRTY
OFFENCES COMMITTED IN PUBLIC OFFICE

§ 331 Taking bribes

(1) A public official or a person entrusted with special public service functions who demands, allows himself to be promised or accepts a benefit for himself or for a third person for the discharge of an official duty shall be liable to imprisonment of not more than three years or a fine.

(2) A judge or arbitrator who demands, allows himself to be promised or accepts a benefit for himself or a third person in return for the fact that he performed or will in the future perform a judicial act shall be liable to imprisonment of not more than five years or a fine. The attempt shall be punishable.

(3) The offence shall not be punishable under subsection (1) above if the offender allows himself to be promised or accepts a benefit which he did not demand and the competent public authority, within the scope of its powers, either previously authorises the acceptance or the offender promptly makes a report to it and it authorises the acceptance.

§ 332 Taking bribes meant as an incentive to violating one's official duties

(1) A public official or person entrusted with special public service functions who demands, allows himself to be promised or accepts a benefit for himself or for a third person in return for the fact that he performed or will in the future perform an official act and thereby violated or will violate his official duties shall be liable to imprisonment from six months to five years. In less serious cases the penalty shall be imprisonment of not more than three years or a fine. The attempt shall be punishable.

(2) A judge or an arbitrator, who demands, allows himself to be promised or accepts a benefit for himself or for a third person in return for the fact that he performed or will in the future perform a judicial act and thereby violated or will violate his judicial duties shall be liable to imprisonment from one to ten years. In less serious cases the penalty shall be imprisonment from six months to five years.

(3) If the offender demands, allows himself to be promised or accepts a benefit in return for a future act, subsections (1) and (2) above shall apply even if he has merely indicated to the other his willingness to

   1. violate his duties by the act; or
   2. to the extent the act is within his discretion, to allow himself to be influenced by the benefit in the exercise of his discretion.

§ 333 Giving bribes

(1) Whosoever offers, promises or grants a benefit to a public official, a person entrusted with special public service functions or a soldier in the Armed Forces for that person or a third person for the discharge of a duty shall be liable to imprisonment of not more than three years or a fine.

(2) Whosoever offers promises or grants a benefit to a judge or an arbitrator for that person or a third person in return for the fact that he performed or will in the future perform a judicial act shall be liable to imprisonment of not more than five years or a fine.

(3) The offence shall not be punishable under subsection (1) above if the competent public authority, within the scope of its powers, either previously authorises the acceptance of the benefit by the recipient or authorises it upon prompt report by the recipient.

§ 334 Giving bribes as an incentive to the recipient's violating his official duties

(1) Whosoever offers, promises or grants a benefit to a public official, a person entrusted with special public service functions or a soldier of the Armed Forces for that person or a third person in return for the fact that he performed or will in the future perform an official act and thereby violated or will violate his official duties shall be liable to imprisonment from three months to five years. In less serious cases the penalty shall be imprisonment of not more than two years or a fine.

(2) Whosoever offers, promises or grants a benefit to a judge or an arbitrator for that person or a third person, in return for the fact that he

  1. performed a judicial act and thereby violated his judicial duties; or
  2. will in the future perform a judicial act and will thereby violate his judicial duties,

shall be liable in cases under No 1 above to imprisonment from three months to five years, in cases under No 2 above to imprisonment from six months to five years. The attempt shall be punishable.

(3) If the offender offers, promises or grants the benefit in return for a future act, then subsections (1) and (2) above shall apply even if he merely attempts to induce the other to

  1. violate his duties by the act; or
  2. to the extent the act is within his discretion, to allow himself to be influenced by the benefit in the exercise of his discretion.

§ 335 Aggravated cases

(1) In especially serious cases

  1. of an offence under

(a) § 332(1) 1st sentence, also in conjunction with (3); and

(b) § 334(1) 1st sentence and (2), each also in conjunction with (3),

the penalty shall be imprisonment from one to ten years and

2. of an offence under § 332(2), also in conjunction with (3), the penalty shall be imprisonment of not less than two years.

(2) An especially serious case within the meaning of subsection (1) above typically occurs when

1. the offence relates to a major benefit;
2. the offender continuously accepts benefits demanded in return for the fact that he will perform an official act in the future; or
3. the offender acts on a commercial basis or as a member of a gang whose purpose is the continued commission of such offences.

§ 336 Omission of an official act

The omission to act shall be equivalent to the performance of an official act or a judicial act within the meaning of §§ 331 to 335.

§ 337 Arbitration fees

The fees of an arbitrator shall only be a benefit within the meaning of §§ 331 to 335 if the arbitrator demands them, allows them to be promised him or accepts them from one party unbeknown to the other or if one party offers, promises or grants them to him unbeknown to the other.

§ 338 Confiscatory expropriation order and extended confiscation

(1) In cases under § 332, also in conjunction with § 336 and § 337, § 73d shall apply if the offender acts on a commercial basis or as a member of a gang whose purpose is the continued commission of such offences.

(2) In cases under § 334, also in conjunction with § 336 and § 337, § 43a and § 73d shall apply if the offender acts as a member of a gang whose purpose is the continued commission of such offences. § 73d shall also apply if the offender acts on a commercial basis.

§ 339 Perverting the course of justice

A judge, another public official or an arbitrator who in conducting or deciding a legal matter perverts the course of justice for the benefit or to the detriment of a party shall be liable to imprisonment from one to five years.

§ 340 Causing bodily harm while exercising a public office

(1) A public official who in the exercise of his duties causes bodily harm or allows it to be caused shall be liable to imprisonment from three months to five

years. In less serious cases the penalty shall be imprisonment of not more than five years or a fine.

(2) The attempt shall be punishable.

(3) §§ 224 to 229 shall apply mutatis mutandis to offences under subsection (1) 1st sentence above.

§§ 341 and 342 (repealed)

§ 343 Forcing someone to make a statement

(1) Whosoever as a public official involved in

  1. a criminal proceeding, a proceeding for the purpose of detention by a public authority;
  2. a proceeding to impose a summary fine;[11] or
  3. a disciplinary proceeding, disciplinary court or professional disciplinary court proceeding

physically abuses another, otherwise uses force against him, threatens him with force or abuses him mentally in order to force him to testify to or declare something in the proceeding or to fail to do so shall be liable to imprisonment from one to ten years.

(2) In less serious cases the penalty shall be imprisonment from six months to five years.

§ 344 Intentionally or knowingly prosecuting innocent persons

(1) Whosoever as a public official involved in a criminal proceeding other than a proceeding to order a non-custodial measure (§ 11(1) No 8) intentionally or knowingly criminally prosecutes an innocent person or someone who otherwise may not by law be criminally prosecuted or makes efforts to bring about such a prosecution shall be liable to imprisonment from one to ten years, in less serious cases to imprisonment from three months to five years. The 1st sentence above shall apply mutatis mutandis to a public official involved in a proceeding for the purpose of detention by a public authority.

(2) Whosoever as a public official involved in a proceeding to order a non-custodial measure (§ 11(1) No 8) intentionally or knowingly criminally prosecutes someone who may not by law be prosecuted or makes efforts to bring about such a prosecution shall be liable to imprisonment from three months to five years. The 1st sentence above shall apply mutatis mutandis to a public official involved in

---

[11] Meaning a non-criminal penalty for summary offences under the Ordnungswidrigkeitengesetz (OWiG) and similar laws.

1. a proceeding to impose a summary fine; or
2. a disciplinary proceeding, disciplinary court or professional disciplinary court proceeding.

The attempt shall be punishable.

§ 345 Enforcing penal sanctions against innocent persons

(1) Whosoever as a public official involved in the enforcement of a sentence of imprisonment, a custodial measure of rehabilitation and incapacitation or detention by a public authority enforces such a sentence, measure or detention although it may not by law be enforced shall be liable to imprisonment from one to ten years, in less serious cases to imprisonment from three months to five years.

(2) If the offender acts grossly negligently the penalty shall be imprisonment of not more than one year or a fine.

(3) Whosoever as a public official involved in the enforcement of a sentence or a measure (§ 11(1) No 8) other than in cases under subsection (1) above enforces a sentence or measure although it may not by law be enforced shall be liable to imprisonment from three months to five years. Whosoever as a public official involved in the enforcement of

1. juvenile detention;
2. a summary fine or ancillary order under the law on summary offences;
3. a fine or detention for disobedience of a judicial order; or
4. a disciplinary proceeding, disciplinary court or professional disciplinary court proceeding,

enforces such a sanction although it may not by law be enforced shall incur the same penalty. The attempt shall be punishable.

§§ 346 and 347 (repealed)

§ 348 Making false entries in public records

(1) A public official authorised to record public documents within his competence who falsely records a legally relevant fact or falsely registers or enters it into public registers, books or data storage media, shall be liable to imprisonment of not more than five years or a fine.

(2) The attempt shall be punishable.

§§ 349 to 351 (repealed)

§ 352 Demanding excessive fees

(1) If a public official, attorney or other person rendering legal assistance who charges fees or other compensation for the discharge of official functions,

charges fees or compensation which he knows are not due to him at all or only to a lesser amount shall be liable to imprisonment of not more than one year or a fine.

(2)   The attempt shall be punishable.

§ 353 Levying excessive taxes; granting reduced benefits

(1)   If a public official charged with collecting taxes, fees or other fiscal charges for a public treasury collects fiscal charges which he knows are not due at all or only to a lesser amount and in whole or in part does not deposit the unlawfully collected amount in the treasury shall be liable to imprisonment from three months to five years.

(2)   Whosoever as a public official in the course of official disbursements of money or in kind unlawfully withholds amounts from the recipient and charges the account as if the disbursements had been paid in full, shall incur the same penalty.

§ 353a Abuse of trust in the Foreign Service

(1)   Whosoever while representing the Federal Republic of Germany to a foreign government, a community of states or an intergovernmental institution, contravenes an official instruction or with the intent of misleading the Federal Government files untrue reports of a factual nature shall be liable to imprisonment of not more than five years or a fine.

(2)   The offence may only be prosecuted upon authorisation by the Federal Government.

§ 353b Breach of official secrets and special duties of confidentiality

(1)   Whosoever unlawfully discloses a secret which has been confided or become known to him in his capacity as

1.   a public official;
2.   a person entrusted with special public service functions; or
3.   a person who exercises duties or powers under the laws on staff representation

and thereby causes a danger to important public interests, shall be liable to imprisonment of not more than five years or a fine. If by the offence the offender has negligently caused a danger to important public interests he shall be liable to imprisonment of not more than one year or a fine.

(2)   Whosoever other than in cases under subsection (1) above unlawfully allows an object or information to come to the attention of another or makes it publicly known

1.   which he is obliged to keep secret on the basis of a resolution of a legislative body of the Federation or a state or one of their committees; or

2. which he has been formally put under an obligation to keep secret by another official agency under notice of criminal liability for a violation of the duty of secrecy,

and thereby causes a danger to important public interests shall be liable to imprisonment of not more than three years or a fine.

(3) The attempt shall be punishable.

(4) The offence may only be prosecuted upon authorisation. The authorisation shall be granted

1. by the president of the legislative body

   (a) in cases under subsection (1) above if the secret became known to the offender during his service in or for a legislative body of the Federation or a state;

   (b) in cases under subsection (2) No 1 above;

2. by the highest Federal public authority:

   (a) in cases under subsection (1) above if the secret became known to the offender during his service in or for a public authority or in another official agency of the Federation or for such an agency;

   (b) in cases under subsection (2) No 2 above if the offender was under put under obligation by an official agency of the Federation;

3. by the highest state public authority in all other cases under subsections (1) and (2) No 2 above.

§ 353c (repealed)

§ 353d Unlawful disclosure of facts sub judice

Whosoever

1. publicly makes a communication contrary to a statutory prohibition about a judicial hearing from which the public was excluded or about the content of an official document which concerns the matter;

2. unlawfully and contrary to a duty of silence imposed by the court on the basis of a statute discloses facts which came to his attention in a non-public judicial hearing or through an official document which concerns the matter; or

3. publicly communicates verbatim essential parts or all of the indictment or other official documents of a criminal proceeding, a proceeding to impose a summary fine or a disciplinary proceeding before they have been addressed in a public hearing or before the proceeding has been concluded

shall be liable to imprisonment of not more than one year or a fine.

§ 354 *(repealed)*

§ 355 Violation of the tax secret

(1) Whosoever unlawfully discloses or uses

    1. circumstances of another which became known to him as a public official

        (a) in an administrative proceeding or a judicial proceeding in tax matters;

        (b) in a criminal proceeding because of a tax offence or in a proceeding to impose a summary fine because of a summary tax offence;

        (c) on another occasion through a communication by a revenue authority or through the statutorily prescribed submission of a tax-assessment notice or a certificate concerning the findings made at the time of taxation; or

    2. the business or trade secret of another that became known to him as a public official in one of the proceedings listed under No 1 above

shall be liable to imprisonment of not more than two years or a fine.

(2) The following shall be equivalent to a public official within the meaning of subsection (1) above:

    1. persons entrusted with special public service functions;

    2. officially consulted experts; and

    3. those who hold offices in churches and other religious associations under public law.

(3) The offence may only be prosecuted upon request of the official superior or the victim. In the case of offences by officially consulted experts the head of the public authority whose proceeding has been affected shall be entitled to file a request apart from the victim.

§ 356 Violating the attorney-client relationship

(1) An attorney or other person rendering legal assistance who in relation to matters confided to him in this capacity in the same legal matter serves both parties with counsel and assistance in breach of his duty shall be liable to imprisonment from three months to five years.

(2) If the offender acts in collusion with the opposing party to the detriment of his client the penalty shall be imprisonment from one year to five years.

§ 357 Incitement of a subordinate to the commission of offences

(1) A superior who incites or undertakes to incite a subordinate to commit an unlawful act in public office or allows such an unlawful act of his subordinate to occur shall incur the penalty provided for this unlawful act.

(2) The same rule shall be applied to a public official to whom supervision or control over the official business of another public official has been transferred to the extent that the unlawful act committed by the supervised public official concerns the business subject to the supervision or control.

§ 358 Ancillary measures

In addition to a sentence of imprisonment of at least six months for an offence under § 332, § 335, § 339, § 340, § 343, § 344, § 345(1) and (3), § 348, §§ 352 to 353b(1), § 355 and § 357 the court may deprive the person of the capacity to hold public office (§ 45(2)).